WHAT OTHERS ARE SAYING ABOUT *THE UNDERDOG EDGE*

No matter what you do or who you do it with, you need to influence others to get the results you're looking for. How do you do it when it seems like the other side holds all the cards? In this powerful book, Amy Showalter shows you how. The big surprise? Less can be more. Based on her years of experience and savvy, Amy explains why and how being the underdog can be a plus. We're all underdogs sometime. Amy's book is a must read if you want to use that status to get results.

> — *Scott Eblin, author, The Next Level: What Insiders Know About Executive Success*

As a veteran lobbyist, I know that Amy has the pulse of what really matters when it comes to effective engagement in the legislative process. Her years of research with professional lobbyists, powerful interest groups and some of the most effective grassroots advocates in the nation gives her exclusive insights into what really works when influencing up. It's required reading for anyone who needs to get powerful people on their side.

> — *James Clarke, CAE , Senior Vice President, Public Policy American Society of Association Executives*

Senior Vice President, Public Policy American Society of Association Executives As one who has written the book on guerilla marketing tactics, I identify with the principles in this book. I recommend it for anyone who needs to influence up the food chain.

> — *Mitch Meyerson, Founder of Guerrilla Marketing Coaching and author of 9 business/personal development books*

i

THE UNDERDOG EDGE

*How Ordinary People
Change the Minds of the Powerful*

EDGE

...and Live to Tell About It

AMY SHOWALTER

Morgan James Publishing • NEW YORK

THE UNDERDOG EDGE

ISBN: 978-1-60037-998-7 (Paperback)
      978-1-61448-020-4 (eBook)
Library of Congress Control Number: 2011927218

Published by:
MORGAN JAMES PUBLISHING
1225 Franklin Ave Ste 32
Garden City, NY 11530-1693
Toll Free 800-485-4943
www.MorganJamesPublishing.com

Cover/Interior Design by:
Rachel Lopez
rachel@r2cdesign.com

For Patricia Ann Showalter, the champion of underdogs everywhere

ACKNOWLEDGMENTS

I thank my teachers—my clients, their grassroots advocates, and my friends.

I am grateful to everyone who connected me with the inspiring individuals featured in this book; they are true talent scouts.

I also thank those who took the time to advise, counsel, cajole, and embolden me on this journey. Special thanks to the brilliant and nice Mark Levy, the encouraging Sam Horn, the clever Ann Gallagher, the cashmere chainsaw Nora Rubinoff, the tenacious Mary O'Doherty, the super smart Dr. Kelton Rhoads, the ultra-competent Barbara McNichol, the strategic Sue Pechilio Polis, the effervescent Ellen Shuman, the never-miss-a-deadline team of Francine Wright and Jackie Harris, the bright and earnest Larry Robertson, the generous Kelly Benedetti, the steel magnolia Susan Goodman, and The Fabulous Randy.

To all of the inspiring, influential underdogs in this book—you truly are the "ethereal fluid that flows from the stars." Thank you for energizing me.

To the elected officials who told me your stories, you have illuminated what it takes for citizens to succeed in civic life. Thank you!

To the business executives who shared your insights, thank you for showing that anyone can effect change, even in large organizations.

I also thank the following friends and colleagues who made this project possible through their insights and feedback:

Lydia Bennett	Dave Gardner	Sharon Smith
Jenny Boese	Julia Hurst	Vickie Sullivan
Bruce Carroll	Carolyn Husten	Connie Tipton
David Clark	Micah Intermill	Chris Vest
Jim Clarke	Christopher Kemm	Betsy Vetter
Travis Doster	Brian Pallasch	Peter Weichlein
Sally Estvanic	Al Ribeiro	Lena West
Brad Fitch	Lori Robertson	
Leann Fox	Brad Smith	

And thanks to these venues that inspired my thought, clarity, and gave comfort:

Grand Teton National Park
The Bunnery - Jackson Hole
Servatii Pastry Shop and Deli - Cincinnati

CONTENTS

INTRODUCTION

Think of a problem you're trying to solve. Maybe you want to get raises for your team members or abate traffic congestion in a new housing development next door. Perhaps you have a dispute with the IRS. Maybe you are the CEO who needs a legislator to vote for a bill that enables your company to expand into new markets. And you want a law changed to increase penalties for those who abuse animals. Maybe you want that "plum" job.

In these situations, no matter what your title or reputation, you're not involved in an equal partnership. You're the underdog. If you're the team leader, you're the underdog to your boss. If you're the neighborhood association leader, you're the underdog to the zoning board. If you're the taxpayer, you're the underdog to the IRS. If you're the CEO, you're the underdog to the elected official. If you're the interview candidate, you're the underdog to the potential employer.

As an underdog, you have no power or advantage. You hold none of the "cards" while the person you want to persuade holds all of them. And because you're the underdog, influencing the top dog in extreme situations *requires different tactics* than in typical influence situations. It calls for *extreme* influence.

Influencing others when you're an underdog isn't a type of blunt force trauma. Rather, when done well, it retains the goodwill of the top dog. After all, one of the definitions of influence is to produce an effect "without apparent exertion of force." It's also defined as an "ethereal fluid that flows from the stars." Doesn't that evoke a sense of beauty, purity, and calm as if the stars are guiding your decision-making without any coercion?

Can the underdogs you'll read about in this book be considered "stars" who've learned to guide behavior without force to champion their causes? I believe they are—and you're about to understand why.

In my business, I show "ordinary" people in big and small organizations—underdogs—how to get powerful people on their side of an issue. These underdogs learn to confidently go into tough situations and persuade top dogs to change their minds. In my 25+ years working with such organizations as Southwest Airlines, the American Heart Association, and the National Association of REALTORS, I've seen people with few external trappings of power master *extreme* influence encounters. These "everyday" people have learned to flourish in difficult situations, and you can, too.

Through interviews, literature reviews, and survey research with thousands of underdogs, I've been fortunate to observe and study their exploits (a positive term where I come from). I've discovered a pattern to their behaviors that works both inside and outside of the political arena. On the flip side, I've also studied powerful people who changed their minds encountering effective underdog persuaders. They've taught me what factors of underdog behavior have worked to influence them.

Conversely, I've seen competent, articulate people quickly and irrevocably lose their persuasion skills when speaking to someone more powerful than them. It's uncanny how smart people can instantly become tongue-tied. I've seen it with C-level executives, nonprofit board chairpersons, top sales professionals, physicians of every specialty group, and on and on.

Why do some people in extreme influence situations succeed and others do not? What common patterns of behaviors work for them? My findings show that their success doesn't come from "yaktivists," those who make noise without having anything to show for it. Rather, it's from following specific behaviors of those who have learned to change the minds of top dogs in big ways.

Some of their behaviors might seem obvious, like being aware of the values of the big dog before asking for anything, or building a team to demonstrate broader support for a cause. I have found nuances to their behaviors that may seem counterintuitive, yet they still work.

One of them, for instance, is using vivid communications tactics. Whether it's through an event or conversation, these tactics require "close to home" proximity. That means using face-to-face communications to persuade rather than relying on remote communication tactics.

Today, it's assumed that the prime way for the disempowered to gain power is through social media tactics such as Facebook, Twitter, and LinkedIn. As effective as these tools can be, I learned that 100 percent of the underdogs who changed the minds of those they wanted to influence engaged in "vivid communications"— that is, face-to-face interaction—to make their cases. And they did it not once but numerous times.

Successful underdogs also keep their passion in check. Everyone parades the "be passionate" mantra as the key to getting what you want in life. However, every powerful person I interviewed whose mind had been changed by an underdog told me that those who were overly passionate doomed their own missions. Why? Because an appeal fueled by passion creates an aura of unpredictability, which makes it hard for a top dog to work with that person. Yes, there are modifiers around when and why influence works, but being passionate isn't the panacea. As Patrice Dell, one of the underdog influencers featured in this book, reminded me, "Don't waste your passion on your influence target. Save it to motivate your troops."

Successful underdogs also have what I call "underdog street cred" that commands respect. Just being the "little guy" with few resources doesn't entitle someone to underdog status. (If that were true, every underdog would rule, right?) However, how the underdog's circumstances are conveyed is important—that is, the top dog must understand *under what circumstances someone is viewed as a true underdog and thus worthy of assistance.* After all, it's human nature for people to legitimately help the "little guy" so they can feel better about themselves.

Winning underdogs also demonstrate "grit." They not only do this by the amount of time they invest pursuing their goals but by the intrepid manner in which they stalk their goal. Here's an example of an underdog who used all of these tactics—

vivid communications, street cred, and grit—to help get a law changed so a local Habitat for Humanity Blitz Build project could get funded.

* * *

I had met Dewey Reynolds while speaking to a state association in Virginia. On the back of his card he had written a mini-novel listing issues he was involved in, complete with names and dates of each key persuasion encounter. Obviously, Dewey had something to say about influencing others—and I wanted to hear it.

When I called Dewey, he told me he'd been a member of the Virginia Association of REALTORS (VAR) for several years. Instead of wildly handing out money to every elected official who asks, its Political Action Committee (PAC) requires candidates to interview with its trustees to find out if they meet the criteria that aligns with the association's philosophy. Dewey served as a PAC trustee and helped interview then-Virginia gubernatorial candidate George Allen. The trustees did not, however, endorse candidate George Allen; Dewey and his fellow PAC trustees chose his opponent instead.

A few months later at an event just before the election, Dewey talked to George Allen face to face. According to Dewey, Allen had a mean way of letting people know when he wasn't happy. Allen immediately recognized Dewey as a PAC trustee and told him he'd "ram that decision down their throats when I take office."

Dewey was floored at Allen's extreme response, thinking, "Surely this politician understands that failure to win endorsements is part of running for office." George Allen went on to become governor of Virginia and, some time later, won election to the U.S. Senate.

Underdogs behave differently than most people. After that rebuke, Dewey could have deemed it unwise to ask Senator Allen for *anything*. He might have assumed Senator Allen would never grant him an audience, let alone say, "yes" to his request. But here's what happened in Dewey's words.

"I'm active with Habitat for Humanity in Central Virginia. We do what's called Blitz Build and get subcontractors, volunteers, homebuyers, and others to quickly build a large number of homes—45 of them within a month. Our Blitz Build program needs infrastructure, which means we have to go through Housing and Urban Development's (HUD) regulations to get infrastructure grants.

"But the way HUD has interpreted the regs, Habitat homebuyers wouldn't have time to complete the required number of 'sweat equity' hours in this Blitz Build project. As a result, the infrastructure grants wouldn't be available where funds were needed most. We needed the regulations changed to allow subcontractors and volunteers access to those funds, or we wouldn't be able to build those forty-five homes in a month. Because a change like this requires congressional action, an elected official has to introduce legislation that would be voted on by Congress."

Dewey was assigned to get support from key Virginia legislators, one of whom was Senator George Allen. So Dewey hatched a plan. After learning that Senator Allen would participate in a Habitat for Humanity homebuilding event, he decided to show up there. Unfazed by his previous unpleasant exchange with Senator Allen, he explained the dilemma and asked directly for the senator's help.

As Dewey recalled, "Senator Allen kept nailing nails, and I kept talking. He said he understood the issue and graciously told me to let him know the best timing, that he would make it happen." The result? Senator Allen and Representative Eric Cantor facilitated passage of legislation that allowed HUD funds to be used for the Blitz Build project.

Dewey's experience aligns with that of each and every one of the underdogs featured in this book. They use vivid communications; they have street cred; they display grit; and they intrepidly go after what they want. As Dewey said, "It's always helpful to meet face to face but it's absolutely necessary when talking with someone who's opposed to your point of view. Plus, you can't take the objections of your opponents personally."

I thought I would be teaching underdogs on how to champion their causes. In actuality, I was in *their* classroom leaning forward and taking notes from lots of people like Dewey Reynolds. What inspiring teachers they have been. And now I'm sharing their secrets with you so you can get what you want in extreme influence situations…and be the guiding stars that change minds.

CHAPTER 1

The Upside of Under:
Why Underdogs Have Power

"Think and act like an underdog."

> — *From Google's Core Values Statement posted in Google's German offices*

"What was compelling was that they were the ordinary people, not the medical experts."

> — *Montana Lt. Governor John Bohlinger*

"…the little guy no one has ever heard of before, the guy who is with his truck, driving around and shaking hands and really has new vision and energy. People look at that and say, 'We've got to help the little guy.'"[1]

> — *California Governor Arnold Schwarzenegger (Referring to campaign of U.S. Senator Scott Brown of Massachusetts)*

I n late 2001, my husband was in the process of buying a dog boarding facility. As we toured one of the operations for sale, we noticed a large truck and about 20 dogs being unloaded and prepped for display to potential adoptive families. This was the facility owner's second dog adoption event following the success of a similar event several weeks earlier. At the first event, people had quickly adopted 30 dogs or more, so the owner thought he'd find additional demand for adoptions.

However, almost half of the dogs at the second adopt-a-thon didn't get adopted. Both groups of dogs were true underdogs, having lived in a shelter for months. But why did one group win and the other didn't? The dogs from the first adopt-a-thon came from New York City, and they weren't just any New York City dogs; they were "9/11 dogs." These dogs had lost their owners on September 11, 2001, or people had been forced to give up the dogs because their homes had been destroyed or vacated due to proximity to the World Trade Center. The "9/11 dogs" were considered the ultimate losers! Not only were they shelter dogs, but they were orphaned due to an unfair, tragic, and horrific event.

The people who quickly adopted the "9/11 dogs" acted in alignment with our love of the underdog. Adopting those dogs made them feel like compassionate people—even more compassionate than if they had adopted a "regular" shelter dog. Whether dogs or people, we want to help the underdog—but not all underdogs are created equal.

Do you remember cheering for any of the following people or teams? Singer Susan Boyle. The Butler University men's basketball team playing against Duke in the 2010 men's NCAA championship game. The Chicago Cubs.

Author Steven Kotler wrote "The Playing Field," a blog about the science of sports and culture for PsychologyToday.com. (Coincidentally, he is cofounder of the Rancho de Chihuahua dog sanctuary.) In his article "Why We Love Losers"[2], he noted that we are inexplicably drawn to cheering for the underdog in sporting events and virtually all contests. It's in our DNA, at least in the United States; *anyone* can rise to greatness.

This love of the underdog is intriguing because it violates classic social psychology theory that suggests an important part of our self-worth derives from identifying with successful, high-status organizations and groups. A core tenet of social identity theory asserts that the accomplishments of the groups with which we affiliate are a crucial source of our self-esteem. We are better people (or at least we think we are) when we're aligned with winners. Author Isaac Asimov put it this way: "All things being equal, you root for your own sex, your own culture, your own locality…and what you want to prove is that you are better than the other person. Whomever you root for represents you; and when he or she wins, you win."[3]

This explains the insufferable superiority that New York Yankees baseball and SEC (South Eastern Conference) football fans display; they're obviously burdened with low self-esteem and need to affiliate with winners to feel good about themselves.

All kidding aside, the literature on this topic is clear: when our team wins, *we* win. Have you ever noticed how people talk about their favorite team differently after a victory than after a defeat? Tune in and you'll see them identify with winners in all its selfish glory. According to a small experiment by Dr. Robert Cialdini, the fan of a winning team will exclaim, "We beat Oregon" or "We crushed Michigan." But if the fan's team loses, the pronouns change. "They lost to Ohio State" or "Ohio State won." (Hate me if you must, but I am unabashedly identified with the Ohio State Buckeyes—and yes, some of my self-esteem derives from their accomplishments.)

Research shows that people tend to see individuals of high status as more influential, competent, and worthy than low-status (underdog) individuals or groups.[4] The low-status individuals and groups are more likely to be targets of prejudice and negative stereotyping, and they're more likely to be seen as unworthy and incompetent.[5]

This makes our support for the underdog all the more curious. Why doesn't affiliating with underdogs *hurt* our self-esteem? In one study, sports fans whose favorite teams repeatedly suffer defeat show temporary decreases in mood and testosterone, and they even lose faith in their own mental and social abilities.[6]

This should cause us to sympathize more with Chicago Cubs fans. (The Cubs pro baseball team holds the record for the longest championship drought of any major North American professional sports team.) If you know and love any Cubs fans, I'll let you draw your own conclusions.

THE UNDERWHELMING ASSET

If you're a believer in the accepted "wisdom" that powerful people only listen to other powerful people, or that they don't have any affinity for the "common man," think again. In fact, the scientific literature reveals that high achievers, the "tall poppies," often elicit envy and resentment from others, especially if their achievements are seen as *undeserved.*[7]

Now, our tall poppy friends might not care that others resent them. However, if they're ever in a persuasion encounter pitted against "more deserving" tall poppies, they may lose. What makes certain tall poppies more deserving? Because the influence target presumes they worked *harder* for their success. For example, in the case of a boot-strapping business owner vs. a business owner who inherited a business, the boot strapper has an advantage. (Note to all tall poppies: Make sure your achievements are merited—that you worked like a crazed weasel to achieve them! People notice the difference.)

I interviewed University of South Florida psychologist Dr. Joe Vandello who recently began studying the reasons people cheer for underdogs. (Once you understand why they do it, you'll realize how being the underdog is a persuasion *asset* rather than a persuasion *liability*.)

Studying the appeal of the underdog had not been on Dr. Vandello's academic bucket list. "This research is kind of a sidetrack to what I normally study," he explained. "Most of my research deals with conflict-related themes. But one of my students who was collaborating with me on other projects would often meet me in my office after class. We'd find ourselves talking about sports. We started wondering why people always root for the underdog. After all, it does violate accepted social science theory. I thought there would be a lot of research about it, but interestingly, there's not. So while it's not my main course of study, I'm looking at the phenomena of the underdog."

In one of Dr. Vandello's research projects, he asked students to watch a video clip of a basketball game. The game was from a European championship, so his American viewers had no knowledge of which team was favored to win. The researchers manipulated the background story so that half the viewers were told the team in red didn't have a lot of resources and were not expected to win. The other viewers were told the exact opposite—that the team in *yellow* was the underdog. Both groups watched the same game.

Dr. Vandello's team then asked those in the two viewing groups which team they wanted to win the game. Not surprisingly, the group that was told of the red team's struggles wanted the red team to win, and those who believed the yellow team was the underdog rooted for the yellow team. Then they were asked to cite characteristics of each team.

"We found that they believed the team with fewer resources and less past success had more persistence, guts, and heart than the other team," reported Dr. Vandello. "They thought that the underdog team, regardless of which team they believed it to be, displayed more effort. So, whoever the underdog is," he summarized, "it changes how differently one views events."

Trying hard, as an underdog does, invokes positive characteristics. Other research has shown that people give more positive evaluations to others when their performance is attributed to effort rather than ability.[8]

People love those who try hard more than those who have superior abilities. Plus the underdogs must be good and moral (we might surmise), or they wouldn't try so hard, right?

A JUST WORLD FOR ALL

So how does this impact you as an individual underdog in extreme influence situations? It gives you an enormous advantage. As Dr. Vandello said, most people view the world with the "just world theory," as it's called in social psychology. That is, most people have an innate desire to live in a just world. They want equality and justice; they want the playing field to be level. And some people may want that more than others.

If you follow geopolitics, this explains why the United States will always be the object of disdain as the lone superpower. Many in the world are biochemically incapable of supporting any country with more resources than theirs, especially during times of international conflicts. Attempts to win over world public opinion will always be a "tension convention" because of our resources, so until America becomes a third world country, it won't have many cheerleaders on the world stage. (Knowing that's partially what's required for world love and adoration, I'll forego an international cheering section, thank you.)

"People who are powerful and wealthy probably have an even better sense of this than those who aren't in high-level positions," stated Dr. Vandello. "It gives them the opportunity to say, 'Look, we help others too; we aren't the bad guys.' Social science indicates that people have a general aversion to inequality; they want to correct it. Helping the underdog is one way to correct it. Further, because underdogs have a lot of heart and grit, we see them as good and moral people. Therefore, it makes us feel more moral to help other moral people."

New research to be published in *Psychological Science* supports Dr. Vandello's assertion that the powerful have a pressing need to help the underdog. It's because they may be aware of their own possibly nefarious nature; after all, the research supports the old notion that power corrupts. Specifically, power breeds hypocrisy because the powerful can feel entitled *not* to obey the moral rules of the underdog and the rules they ask others to follow.

In five experiments,[9] researchers assigned 172 subjects high-power roles (e.g., prime minister) and low-power roles (e.g., civil servant). The subjects had to consider a series of moral dilemmas involving stolen bikes, broken traffic rules, and tax fraud. In each of the five experiments, the more high-power characters repeatedly showed moral hypocrisy. They disapproved of immoral behavior (for example, padding expense reports) and yet behaved badly themselves. For instance, when powerful characters were given an opportunity to self-report their success in a dice game, they cheated, reporting that they won more times than they actually did.

The researchers made note of a sense of entitlement—that is, those who believed they were entitled to a high-status position tended to be more hypocritical than those who felt they were not deserving of power.

Current research even shows that CEOs who are highly paid are "meaner than their peers." Researchers from Harvard, Rice, and the University of Utah found that raising executive compensation packages "results in executives behaving meanly toward those lower down the hierarchy."[10]

Maybe some (not all!) of the high-power people who exhibit hypocrisy and an attitude of entitlement are aware of their sense of entitlement and are motivated to help the underdog to assuage their guilt. Maybe they know they should treat others more respectfully and find opportunities to help the underdog as a way to counteract their transgressions.

As an underdog, be aware that people in high positions often want to help—for whatever reasons that aren't always based on good morals.

PEOPLE BUY FROM UNDERDOGS

Recent research has found that underdog positioning also influences consumer behavior. Harvard University researcher Neeru Paharia, Harvard Business School professor Anat Keinan, Simmons School of Management professor Jill Avery, and Boston College professor Juliet Schor conducted a study of consumer products to determine whether underdog positioning works in the consumer goods marketplace.[11] I interviewed researcher Jill Avery to find out if a kind of underdog branding product has the same characteristics as underdogs experience in sports and politics.

Avery noted that an increase in underdog branding as a marketing strategy is happening. "We see brands across a wide variety of product categories (food, juice, beer, car rental, technology, etc.) using underdog brand biographies in today's marketplace," she explained.

"Underdogs are winning at the polls, at the Oscars (example: the movie *Slumdog Millionaire*), and on grocery shelves across America. This is because underdog stories about overcoming great odds through passion and determination resonate during difficult times. They inspire us and give us hope when the outlook is bleak. They provide the promise that success is still possible, a much-needed message in challenging social, political, and economic times.

"During recessionary periods such as these, people feel increasingly disadvantaged, making them even more likely to identify with the struggles of underdogs. Firms appear to be capitalizing on this; today's brands are seeding underdog stories for consumers to use during a cultural moment in history when consumers feel the American Dream slipping from their grasp," Avery concluded.

THE VALUE OF UNDERDOG INSIGHTS

Former Iowa Congressman Jim Ross Lightfoot, who served for 11 years in the U.S. House of Representatives, told me why he liked listening to everyday people—to underdogs. "They knew their subject matter far better than any of the paid representatives, like lobbyists. They had built their business, their farm, or whatever, and knew firsthand all the challenges they'd faced as well as the consequences of actions the government had taken or was proposing to take against them.

"And their enthusiasm was one-hundred percent genuine. In contrast, the lobbyists' enthusiasm was in proportion to the amount they were charging. Farmers have their own language. Some guy in wing-tip loafers charging $700 an hour usually just doesn't get what the regular person wants to convey."

Congressman Lightfoot craved the information that the "regulars" provided. His tactics employed a combination of persistence and stealth follow-up. "More than once, I asked these ordinary people to call back as soon as they were out of the earshot of the lobbyist, then talk to my scheduler and set up an appointment to come back by themselves. Sometimes I would conduct meetings in the late evening. If a flight schedule was tight, I offered to meet them at the airport and did meet with a couple there one time. Many times, a meeting took place the following weekend back in the district because I went home every weekend."

Former Congressman Toby Moffett represented Connecticut in the U.S. House of Representatives from 1975 to 1983. During that time, he was Chairman of the House Sub-Committee on Energy, Environment, and Natural Resources.

Said Moffett, "I came into Congress as a left wing citizen activist; I entered politics through Ralph Nader's Citizen Action. So I had no permanent business supporters. I went to the local chamber of commerce meetings and those guys would annihilate me—blame me for macroeconomic issues and conditions. I did four or five of those, then said, 'I am just not doing this anymore.' But I knew I needed their support.

"Rufus Stilman was a successful industrialist," continued Moffett. "He had some left-wing leanings as well and gave me a great tip. He told me to start meeting with individual company owners, their employees, and their management. He advised me to start helping them individually and relating to them as individuals rather than as members of a larger business organization.

"So I started helping them individually on various casework and technical issues. I became a champion for individual companies, for the little guys, rather than the business community as a whole. For example, the Dexter Corporation was in my district. It's the biggest maker of tea bags in the world. Its leaders were concerned about a tariff issue so I helped with that. By becoming of champion of individual companies more than the business community as a whole, I was able to broaden my base of support."

Former Florida State Representative Leslie Waters was first elected to a seat in the Florida House of Representatives in 2000 by fewer than 250 votes. She's a veteran of the insurance industry where she served more than 20 years as a human resources professional and the leader of Allstate Insurance's employee grassroots program.

Waters knew the power of ordinary people to influence the legislative process. In fact, it was her job to get Allstate employees and agents so excited about insurance issues that they would contact elected officials about seemingly arcane yet vital issues to the industry (e.g., combined ratios, verbal thresholds, product liability, etc.). Not exactly issues with a broad appeal, yet still important.

Once in office, Waters turned to people outside the traditional sources of power for the "story behind the story." She explained, "I tended to trust retired businesspeople. I've found retired people from the phone companies to be very, very helpful. You know, for eight years, the Florida Chamber of Commerce voted me as one of their most pro-business legislators in the state. Nevertheless, the most accurate information I could find was from *retired* executives, not the sitting execs. They have tremendous credibility because they tell you what's *really* going on, now that they don't have economic and other ties to the company."

HOW TO BE
A CARD-CARRYING UNDERDOG

Now that you know that underdog status is an asset, it's important to understand what's required to become a "card-carrying" underdog. Not all underdogs are created equal. Some aren't expected to win and they don't; they fade away. Others are able to persuade powerful people to take up their cause, provide resources, and persuade other powerful people to fight for the underdog. The winning underdogs have certain characteristics that "ordinary" underdogs don't have.

Just proclaiming that you or your group is an underdog won't work. (In fact, that tactic is proven to work against you, which you'll read more about later in this chapter.) Certain conditions must be met before becoming an admired underdog worthy of winning hearts and minds. To be a card-carrying underdog, you have to have few resources, not squander the resources you do have, keep expectations low, don't call yourself the underdog, and use unbound influence tactics.

Let's look at each of these characteristics.

Underdog Card Rule #1: Have Few Resources

Jill Avery's team found that the most successful underdog brand biographies have an external advantage that a better resourced competitor doesn't have. And it must be believable.

In 1946, a group of plaintiffs' attorneys involved in workers' compensation litigation grew into the American Trial Lawyers Association (ATLA). The mission of ATLA members is to advocate in the courts for those wronged by organizations or individuals. ATLA touted itself as the champion of the "little guy," an organization whose members held the powerful accountable and created a level playing field in the courtroom. This sounds like a great organization, one that many Americans would support and cheer for, because after all, they represent underdogs with few resources.

In 2004, ATLA published a book titled *David v. Goliath: ATLA and the Fight for Everyday Justice.* When I show an image of that book to audiences (of all political persuasions), I wait for the inevitable cackles and eye rolls. People know better; the underdog mantle comes with conditions, and the trial bar is not always seen as a champion of the underdog. They just aren't viewed as a group with few resources so the underdog label is not believable.

Trial lawyers did and do fight for the everyday person, but they also brag about their power and strength. Their political resources are astounding, and they let everyone know it. (As you'll read later, you will lose underdog status if you become too proud of your underdog label.)

For example, the American Association for Justice (the new name for ALTA) Political Action Committee (PAC) raised over $6.2 million in 2008 for candidates and lawmakers who support their views. The PAC spent more than $4.6 million in lobbying expenses in 2009, and that was a cut from $5.3 million in 2008.[12]

The late Fred Baron, former president of ATLA, commented on why legislation resolving the asbestos litigation crisis would not be enacted by saying, "I picked up my *Wall Street Journal* last night…and what did I learn? 'The plaintiffs' bar is all but running the Senate.' Now I really strongly disagree with that—particularly the words 'all but.'" That's one way to lose underdog "cred"—claiming to be "for" the little guy but bragging about their political power. That's definitely one way to lose credibility!

Dickie Scruggs is a former attorney who gained fame in the 1990s by using a corporate insider against tobacco companies in lawsuits that resulted in a $206 billion settlement, thus accelerating the steamroller of tobacco litigation. Note his advice on shopping for the right judge at a conference sponsored by Prudential Insurance in 2002:

> The trial lawyers have established relationships with the judges that are elected; they're state court judges; they're populists. They've got large populations of voters who are in on the deal, they're getting their piece in many cases. And so, it's a political force in their jurisdiction, and it's almost impossible to get a fair trial if you're a defendant in some of these places. The cases are not won in the courtroom. They're won on the back roads long before the case goes to trial. Any lawyer fresh out of law school can walk in there and win the case, so it doesn't matter what the evidence or the law is.

Now serving time in an Ashland, Kentucky, federal prison for bribery of state court judges, Scruggs is scheduled for release in 2015.

While trial attorneys represent people who may not be expected to win against powerful interests, not everyone with low expectations is given underdog status. Dr. Vandello's research indicates that when an individual or group with low expectations has a lot of resources, others may perceive their position as fair, and they *lose* the underdog position. So while those being represented by a plaintiff's attorney may not have resources, those representing them do have a lot of resources, and they made sure to let everyone know. This attenuates their underdog persona.

Plus, it doesn't help that many who were (and are) sued, whether the lawsuits are capricious or legitimate, are underdogs themselves—underdogs who don't have resources. This opinion was offered in a blog to the editors of a Business Week magazine article.[13] The writer is commenting on trial lawyers:

> I gave up trying to run a small business in California. With a flat organization (3 managers, 50 employees), I had to spend an inordinate portion of my time preparing for, responding to, and defending lawsuits. As a logistics company to the pharmaceutical industry, we were named as an additional defendant every time anyone had a problem with a drug. Large companies have legal departments to deal with this sort of thing. Lawsuits are an expensive nuisance to them, but don't threaten their survival. Small companies are badly damaged by the tort system, since it is the owner/CEO who must deal with the process. Tort reform is not about protecting multinational corporations. It is about saving small business in this country.

The ATLA's zeal to sue owners of small businesses—the heroes and iconic figures of American lore—contributed to the trial bar's changed image from warrior for the little guy to predator of the hard-working, resource-starved underdog. They lost their underdog card.

Not only did the organization lose its underdog status, but its schizophrenic behavior (helping the little guy yet bragging about its power) didn't help. It led to a backlash from the public that forever changed how the ATLA is perceived.

That perception forced ATLA to change its name. In 2006, ATLA's board of governors voted 91-5 to change the organization's name to the American Association for Justice (AAJ).

Jill Avery offered this warning for would-be underdogs who want to avoid the trial bar's fate: "Your biography must be believable to be persuasive. If consumers find the brand biography to be inauthentic or illegitimate, they won't fall for it. Big, powerful brands that use underdog brand biographies (i.e., Oprah Winfrey, Apple) must constantly reinforce their underdog position to convince consumers it's still legitimate."

Conversely, underdog branding may also backfire if used in product categories where being the underdog may be perceived as having lower product quality and where quality matters. Consumers may not want to patronize an "underdog hospital," Avery wisely said.

Underdog Card Rule #2:
Don't Squander the Resources You Do Have

Remember Dr. Vandello's experiment with the basketball game? Another interesting finding from his project sheds light on how people view underdogs who might have many resources but have low expectations of winning.

When one of the teams has low expectations but high resources, it loses some viewer support. Although low expectations are an underdog trademark, if an entity has low expectations and a great many resources *but squanders them*, it loses its underdog label and support.

Think of how this possibly affected Hillary Clinton's primary contest against Barack Obama. Although touted in 2006 and 2007 as the inevitable front runner for the Democratic presidential nomination, after many primary victories, Obama emerged as front runner and Clinton became the underdog (claiming the mantle herself). And while, as we have learned, the underdog brand is strong and compelling, when resources are wasted, underdog support erodes.

Clinton raised $26 million in the first quarter of 2007, almost three times as much as any politician had previously raised at that point in a presidential election.

By comparison, John Edwards reported at least $14 million for the quarter, New Mexico Governor Bill Richardson, Senator Christopher Dodd, and Senator Joe Biden were in decimal dust territory (as presidential races go), having raised $6 million or less each. Clinton started 2007 as the candidate to beat in the money race. She was widely heralded as the inevitable nominee.

However, Clinton's campaign finance report, published in February of 2008, showed a pattern of spending priorities that some fundraisers interpreted as errors in judgment and management. What expenditures caught attention? To name a few: almost $100,000 for party platters and groceries before the Iowa caucuses, rooms at the Bellagio hotel in Las Vegas at a cost of $25,000, plus $11,000 on pizza, $1,200 on doughnuts, and fees to consultants for (the fundraisers believed) a losing strategy.

In addition, as a part of their Iowa get-out-the-vote project, the campaign had a local supermarket deliver sandwich platters to pre-caucus parties at a cost of $95,384. They also bought lots of snow shovels to make the way clear for caucus goers. Mrs. Clinton came in third in the January 3 caucus. It didn't snow—and her fundraisers noticed.

"We didn't raise all of this money to keep paying consultants who have pursued basically the wrong strategy for a year now," commented a prominent New York donor. "So much about her campaign needs to change—but it may be too late."[14]

Joe Trippi, a senior advisor to John Edwards's presidential campaign, divulged his insights on Clinton's campaign's money management. "The problem is she ran a campaign like they were staying at the Ritz-Carlton. Everything was the best. The most expensive draping at events. The biggest charter. It was like, 'We're going to show you how presidential we are by making our events look presidential.'"[15]

Underdog Card Rule #3:
Keep Others' Expectations of You Low

In 1992, Billings, Montana won the All-American City Award. One reason given for their selection was the community's honesty in admitting it had a sulfur dioxide (SO_2) air pollution problem and its continuous work to resolve the problem. The same year, Billings was listed by the EPA as "the worst city in America for its annual concentrations of SO_2."

In 1995, Exxon's refinery in Billings emitted higher levels of SO_2 than any of its other 124 plants in the country. This occurred because of an exception in a state law, the Hannah Bill, which passed in 1987. The Hannah Bill allowed companies emitting sulfur dioxide pollution in the Billings area to comply with federal standards rather than the more stringent state standards.

At the time, Montana Lt. Governor John Bohlinger was a Republican state representative representing Billings in the Montana state legislature. His legislative district included many towns in close proximity to Exxon's refineries.

"Environmental issues weren't on my legislative agenda," said John in my interview with him. "But my district was affected. I noticed that, when I'd go campaigning, we'd see a lot of people with respiratory ailments. People would tell me, 'You've got to do something about the compromised air standard.' So when I was re-elected, I introduced legislation to get those air standards back to acceptable levels. However, the lobbyists for the petroleum companies were more influential than my speeches and the legislative committee testimony by MDs who were pulmonary specialists. The bill failed to pass. It's hard to fight established interests.

Then John told me to talk to a guy named Vince Larsen for the full story. "You need to call him and get his story because everything changed when he became involved," he said.

Vince Larsen is a "regular," albeit influential and credible citizen who is also a retired petroleum geologist. A fiery and determined man, Vince had followed the SO_2 issue for years. He found it, in his words, "disgraceful" that his industry had demonstrated such little respect for the wellbeing of Billings' citizens.

Around this time, Exxon's national lobbying expenditures totaled over $5.5 million. They raised over $640,000 for their Political Action Committee in 1998. (The Center for Responsive Politics, www.opensecrets.org) (For the record, let me say I see nothing nefarious about organizations raising money via voluntary employee contributions to help elect legislators who support their growth and employees; it's a form of free speech.)

Martin Lobel, a Washington lawyer who represents consumer groups and small oil companies, said this about Exxon leaders in the '90s: "They are probably most effective behind the scenes. They'll get their economists and lawyers to see the IRS and the company will stay relatively hidden. You've got maybe two Ph.D. economists in the entire IRS, and Exxon can hire as many as they want. We were once in a big battle with Exxon on the issue of oil overcharges and there must have been thirty economists on the other side."[16]

Vince knew that a local group, the Yellowstone Valley Citizens Council (YVCC), a dedicated but somewhat unorganized organization, was fighting to get the Hannah bill repealed. It was opposing Exxon but without much progress. During this time, the Council had no website, no opportunity to get a million Facebook friends, no regular communications to supporters, no budget, etc. Vince decided to check them out.

"When I became involved in this issue, the Yellowstone Valley Citizens Council was a bit unorganized and frankly kind of stuck," he said. "The people in it didn't know what they were doing. I told them I would get involved under one condition: everything we said would be sourced and documented.

"After we joined the cause, it was apparent that we had no reliable information to work with except for what was available locally. We knew nothing about the air pollution problems elsewhere. We needed a database so we could compare our area with others with similar problems.

"When I investigated the study of the pounds of sulfur dioxide admitted per barrel of oil, I found that the Billings Exxon Refinery admitted 1.5 pounds of sulfur dioxide per barrel, which placed it at the top of 124 U.S. plants at that time. So Exxon operated differently in Billings than it did in any other city or state. I was interviewed by the paper for this, and of course the headline said 'Critic Assails Exxon Refinery.' Clair Johnson, an excellent reporter for the *Billings Gazette* told me, 'Wow, you sure are going to get calls on this today.'

"And sure enough, I got an anonymous call from someone in Exxon who said, 'You are doing the right thing. I'm with Exxon and close to retirement so I can't speak out.' That really motivated me. The more I worked, the more angry I became. Hell, I had to be put on blood pressure medication for the first time in my life. I was wiped out," he recalled.

Vince appeared before a Senate Health and Welfare Committee hearing at the state capitol in Helena, Montana, to support the repeal of the Hannah Bill. "During the presentation, I dropped the microphone and tripped over the cord. From there, everything went to hell! I learned that gathering of information was easy; getting up and presenting our work before other groups was not.

"We wrote the Billings Chamber of Commerce asking for a resolution to support Bohlinger's legislation, and of course I had lots of documentation to show that Billings had compromised its standards compared to the rest of the country. Nevertheless, the Chamber and some opinion leaders in town just would not touch this.

"John Bohlinger was the only one who would seriously listen to our story. John is a strong, principled, and dedicated legislator who came to our meetings, learned about the issue, and had the courage and conviction to do something about it.

"John was baffled as to how our legislature could be so compromised and pass legislation that would exempt industries in Yellowstone County from complying with state laws that applied to everyone else in Montana. He authored legislation to repeal the infamous Hannah Bill that had exempted Yellowstone County from Montana's ambient air quality standards. His first attempt to repeal the Hannah Bill failed."

As John Bohlinger remembered the debate, he acknowledged that what eventually changed the outcome were the messengers. "Two years later, I spent more time talking to those who were affected by the lack of air quality, the 'regular' people. They had an influence and voiced their concerns. As a result, we successfully repealed the Hannah Bill in 1997 because we simply had more citizen stories to tell than in 1995. What made them compelling was that ordinary people were speaking out, not the medical experts," he said.

While resources, both human and financial, have a huge impact on the outcome of an influence campaign, underdogs with street cred don't have an abundance of either. And that's one factor that contributes to their persuasion quotient. For Vince, despite not having the resources of Exxon, the truth proved to be the paramount resource. He reminded me several times during our interview: "Is what a group is saying the truth? That's what it's all about."

Underdog Card Rule #4: Don't Call Yourself the Underdog

During the 2008 presidential race, the candidates expressed one thing in common: their underdog label. Nearly all of the major candidates claimed the underdog title. Barack Obama claimed that "when your name is Barack Obama, you're always an underdog in political races."[17] New Mexico Governor Bill Richardson noted, "I know I am not the favorite in this race. As an underdog and governor of a small western state, I will not have the money that other candidates will have."[18] Senator Hillary Clinton, behind in the delegate count, embraced the stamp as well: "I'm here asking for your support. I'm the underdog in South Dakota; I've gotten used to that role. Clinton again touts underdog status, proving you can't teach an old dog new tricks."[19]

The Republicans also declared an underdog status. Mike Huckabee, Tommy Thompson, and Congressman Tom Tancredo cited themselves as underdogs. In an interview on Meet the Press, the late host Tim Russert referred to Rudy Giuliani as "the darling of conservatives all across the country" if he were to face Hillary Clinton. Giuliani responded, "Tim, I'm not comfortable being a darling...underdog is better. Underdog from Brooklyn is much better."[20]

Sometimes politicians state the obvious when claiming underdog rank, but why, when trying to prove they are electable, would they boast about being the underdog? We know that people prefer to affiliate with high-status individuals. It might be for their own psychological equilibrium because many underdogs are associated with success. Those who beat the odds are iconic characters or events, whether in history, sports, politics, or folklore: the American Revolution, the racehorse Seabiscuit, the "Miracle on Ice" of the 1980 U.S. Olympic Men's Hockey team, U.S. Senator Scott Brown, who won a come-from-behind victory in the 2010 Massachusetts U.S. Senate race, and lest we forget the classics: Robin Hood and Cinderella.

Dr. Joe Vandello conducted another research project to determine the benefits and risks of projecting an underdog image in the political arena. When the 2008 Democratic presidential primary came to a choice between Barack Obama and Hillary Clinton, he wanted to find out if claiming underdog status proved advantageous.

He asked students to read a speech supposedly given by Barack Obama. The speech ended with the candidate declaring *himself* to be the underdog. To another group, the research team provided the same speech, but removed the underdog language and inserted "I know I'm the front runner in this race." Other study participants read a statement from the media that described Obama's current position as an underdog compared to Hillary Clinton and another statement that described him as the front runner.

After reading the speech excerpts, participants rated Obama on 10 personality traits such as warmth (likeable, trustworthy, humble, warm, friendly) and competence (skillful, wise, credible, capable). As Dr. Vandello predicted, portraying a candidate as an underdog affected how people rated his character. As an underdog, he was seen as warmer than when portrayed as the front runner.

But the most interesting finding of this experiment is this: *where the underdog label comes from had the most impact on how participants perceived the candidate.* A positive underdog effect was more prevalent when Obama's underdog status was bestowed from the outside (in this case, from media reports) than when the candidate claimed it himself.

Here's another example. Bob Benham, the owner of an upscale women's fashion store in Oklahoma City, was a retail underdog who teamed with stores like Sears, Target, and Wal-Mart to persuade members of Congress to change Internet taxation laws. The change would level the playing field for small brick-and-mortar retailers. He didn't wave his underdog card, even though he could have easily done so. And that's what got him noticed.

"When we would meet with members of Congress and their staff," said Benham, "the guys from the big stores liked to talk. Many times the congressional staff would cut them off and ask me what I thought. It happened enough that the National Retail Federation staff made sure that everyone from that point forward could articulate what was happening with Main Street businesses. It stunned me that powerful people listen more to the small business owners than the big guys."

When you're the underdog, it's probably not good to wave the underdog banner because your earmark as an underdog has more credibility if it comes from someone else's lips.

Underdog Card Rule #5: Don't Use the Same Tactics as Big Dogs

The last way to obtain your underdog card is using unconventional tactics to achieve your persuasion goals. Think about it. Although all types of power can accomplish changes in behavior, which power tactics are used most by those in authority? Coercive power, reward power, and position power. However, employing these types of power rarely changes private beliefs, nor do they encourage future interaction or identification with the persuader. They won't create a mutually beneficial relationship. They are actually limiting forms of power because they can be "one strike and you're out" tactics.

The successful underdogs profiled in this book don't have (and didn't try to gain) those types of power. Instead, they developed and continued to use an array of *unconventional* tactics, as you will see.

Author Malcolm Gladwell devoted his May 2009 *New Yorker* column to this very topic. In "How David Beats Goliath: When Underdogs Break the Rules," he cited a study of military battles over the past two centuries and found that David beat Goliath 29 percent of the time. Not bad. But when the underdogs used unconventional tactics, they won 64 percent of the time. What's unconventional? Doing what others are unwilling to do. Acting contrary to "accepted wisdom," "breaking rank," and being "unbound."[21]

LESSONS FROM THE APOTHEOSIS OF UNDERDOGS

When we dissect what being "unbound" means for an underdog today, we have to look at the exemplar for all underdogs, the shepherd boy David and his slaying of the giant Goliath. David isn't "old school"—he's the only school. Indeed, the biblical account is so familiar that secular confrontations between "giants" and "underdogs"—from athletics to national politics—are commonly verbalized in "David and Goliath" terminology.

We read that David was unbound. He did just about everything a warrior was trained *not* to do. Let's review his unusual tactics.

First, he was intrepid. As King Saul plotted strategy, David stepped up to take on Goliath. But like most underdogs, David had his detractors.

"And Saul said to David, 'You are not able to go against this Philistine to fight with him; for you *are* a youth, and he a man of war from his youth.'" (1 Samuel 17:33) (Life Application Study Bible, NIV, Zondervan Publishing and Tyndale House Publishing, 1991.) King Saul was telling David that it wasn't his turn.

"But David said to Saul, 'Your servant used to keep his father's sheep, and when a lion or a bear came and took a lamb out of the flock, I went out after it and *struck it,* and delivered the lamb from its mouth; and when it arose against me, I *caught it by its beard*, and struck and killed it.'" (1 Samuel 24-35) I know nothing about lion killing, but I think that smacking a lion's face and pulling its beard aren't in the training manual. Even before the battle with Goliath, David was unbound.

David also did not wear the same clothing as most warriors. When David determined that he would fight Goliath, King Saul told him to wear armor. After all, Goliath sported a javelin, a spear, and a metal helmet. His entire body was protected by armor, and he was an early adopter of human shields, as he used a shield-bearer to go ahead of him. (1 Samuel 17:5-7) What an awesome sight—what an outward appearance! King Saul was intimidated and believed that David needed to dress similarly. But David wanted to be himself.

"Then Saul…put a coat of armor on David and a bronze helmet on his head. David fastened on his sword and tried walking around, because he was not used to them. 'I cannot go in these,' he said to Saul, 'because I am not used to them.'" (1 Samuel 17:38-39) Underdogs live by the creed "Be yourself—everyone else is taken."

Warfare in biblical times was mostly hand to hand, with some use of weapons such as bows and arrows, slings and stones. Fighting was a dangerous, personal, and bloody business. Familiar weapons included the trusty club, spear, battle axe, sword, sickle sword, bow and arrow, and David's choice, the sling and stone. David knew that he was outsized, and that the usual hand-to-hand combat would not end well. However, stones could be flung by a warrior at 100 to 150 miles per hour.

"Then he took his staff in his hand, chose five smooth stones from the stream, put them in the pouch of his shepherd's bag and, with his sling in his hand, approached the Philistine." (1 Samuel 17:40)

Next, and I love this, the scripture says he *ran* to the battle. No sneaking around trying to mug Goliath from behind. "As the Philistine moved closer to attack him, David *ran quickly* toward the battle line to meet him." (1 Samuel 17:48)

David used his sling shot to plant a stone between Goliath's eyes, which killed him. Then, to put an exclamation point on his work, he cut off Goliath's head. This is perhaps one of the least examined parts of the battle.

My colleague, influence expert Dr. Kelton Rhoads of USC's Annenberg School for Communications, gave this opinion: "What is fascinating is that once David cut off Goliath's head, the Philistines basically forfeited. They were completely demoralized and quit. So there is something about that exclamation point that was a demoralizer. Of course, we should not decapitate our adversaries, but when facing relentless adversaries, consider ways to break their morale. It can prevent or delay another encounter."

The shepherd boy David taught us the lesson. Let's take a look at how these unbound approaches have been used in sports and business.

Underdog Profile: Super Unconventional

On February 7, 2010, Super Bowl XLIV between the New Orleans Saints and the Indianapolis Colts presented an engaging scenario. The Indianapolis Colts were led by quarterback Peyton Manning, said to be one of the most intelligent quarterbacks ever to play the game. They were up against the New Orleans Saints, a good team that has been playing less effectively as the season wore on. However, the Saints emotionally connected with its fans because the team represented all of the struggles and triumphs of New Orleans since Hurricane Katrina. Most sports reporters picked the Colts to win the contest. The Saints were decided underdogs. Their coach, Sean Payton, was thrilled with that status. He told his players that it was a coach's dream to be an underdog when in fact you've got the better team.

Lee Jenkins, writing in *Sports Illustrated*,[22] described it this way:

> At the end of the first half, the Saints were down 10-6. To open the second half, Sean Payton became the first coach in Super Bowl history to call an onside kick before the fourth quarter. He quizzed his players about how they would feel if the play failed, and they told him they would support him. "Coach, we've got your back," one piped up and others nodded. Thomas Morstead's kick bounced off the facemask of Indianapolis player Hank Baskett and into the arms of the Saints backup safety Chris Reis. That prompted a vicious struggle for the ball that lasted so long that Reis said his "forearms were burning."
>
> The decision of the onside kick revealed the fundamental difference between the Saints and the Colts: one team was playing it loose, the other playing it safe. The Saints' onside kick tactic wasn't just unconventional, it was unheard of. But they knew they had to try something to mix it up and get back in the game.

What happens to underdogs who try to use unconventional tactics in business and commerce? Do they ever work? One of the most successful companies in U.S. history has shown that employing those tactics can bring short- and long-term results.

Underdog Profile: Southwest Airlines

If you remember back to September 11, 2001, it was unclear if and when commercial airlines would be allowed to fly again, or how many citizens would be willing to fly on them. The threat of terrorism and a recession made the industry volatile. So naturally, all of the U.S. airlines except one did what so many corporations do well: They began announcing layoffs. That one airline that didn't lay off employees, Southwest Airlines, still has never had an involuntary layoff in its almost 40-year history.

Today, Southwest is the largest domestic U.S. carrier and has a market capitalization bigger than all its domestic competitors combined. This company lives what so many other corporations mindlessly tout—that its people are its greatest asset. The leaders believe it, and thus are not jettisoning their most valuable resources. As President Emeritus Colleen Barrett said, "The warrior mentality, the very fight to survive, is truly what created our culture."[23]

Southwest has always played by the underdog creed and continue to do so, most recently with the "Bags Fly Free" initiative. While other domestic carriers continue in their "me too" management philosophy and copy each other's worst practices (charging for checked luggage, to name one), Southwest alone lets passengers check two pieces of luggage for free while others charge $20 and more to check one piece of luggage. Southwest CEO Gary Kelly said this no-fee policy has helped Southwest increase its share of the domestic market by about 1 percent, or $800 million to $900 million, driving its traffic growth at a time when the domestic market is shrinking.[24]

Underdog Profile: Texas Roadhouse

The Texas Roadhouse restaurant chain, headquartered in Louisville, Kentucky, started with one location in 1993 at the Green Tree Mall in Clarksville, Indiana. While they aren't an underdog in the restaurant industry overall, they can be considered an underdog in comparison to their competitors in the casual dining segment, such as Outback Steakhouse, Chili's, and Applebee's. As of 2010, Texas Roadhouse had more than 330 restaurants. Outback operates more than 900 locations, Chili's more than 1,400, and Applebee's more than 1,900. Texas Roadhouse has become an example of using unconventional tactics that led to double-digit *decrease* in employee turnover, an *increase* in its stock price, and hundreds of thousands of dollars in free publicity.

A few of Texas Roadhouse's accolades include being named the "Number One Steakhouse in America" by *Consumers Choice and Chains* survey, voted "Best Steakhouse Value" by *Consumers Choice and Chains*, and ranked number one in *Nation's Restaurant News* for "Top Growth Companies." *Forbes* Best Small Companies List ranked Texas Roadhouse in the top 40 for two consecutive years, and in 2009, readers of *Consumer Reports Magazine* rated the restaurant chain "Best Value."

The business community generally has a herd mentality. Whether it's the latest management fads, the type of charities they contribute to, or the degree to which they go "green," companies follow one another. Texas Roadhouse, in true underdog fashion, chose not to follow the herd that gathered in the autumn of 2008.

In 2008, to help "resolve" the implosion of the financial markets, insurance giant AIG received taxpayer bailout money of nearly $85 billion. It then spent nearly $450,000 on an incentive program at the St. Regis Monarch Beach resort in California. Shortly thereafter, other stories of incentive travel events in companies that received taxpayer money resulted in a volcanic eruption of anger and rhetorical layups by the media and politicians against the firms.

In the wake of criticism by government officials and a public outcry, thousands of companies cancelled meetings and conferences. The meetings industry then suffered from a drastic reduction in demand for meetings in late 2008 and 2009. The results—dubbed the "AIG Effect"—were staggering. Consider:

- Corporate travel budgets were slashed by an average of 35 percent, according to a survey conducted by Northwestern's Kellogg School of Management in February 2009.

- Overall business travel spending was down by 12.5 percent in the first six months of 2009 compared to the year before, according to the U.S. Travel Association.

- Occupancy at luxury hotels was down 16.3 percent from the previous year, compared with a 10.9 percent decline for the industry as a whole during the first three months of 2009, according to Smith Travel Research.

- The global airlines industry forecast its losses at $9 billion in June 2009, according to the International Air Transport Association, the industry's largest trade group.

The cancellations added up to $2.5 billion in total revenue lost for destinations, hotels, and meeting suppliers, according to a survey by Meeting Professionals International and American Express. The effect on the meeting, hospitality, and travel industries was staggering. What the media and Congress forgot in their oral hysterics were the multitude of hospitality industry workers who benefit from incentive travel: the cab drivers, hotel housekeepers, bartenders, and caterers, who also felt the repercussions along with the big guys.

The travel industry yearned for someone from the corporate world to speak out on behalf of incentive meetings—to defend them—but there were no takers. Until G.J. Hart came on the scene. Hart is the CEO of Texas Roadhouse (TRH), and he wanted to help. Hart knew what the media and political outcry was doing.

Texas Roadhouse was planning its annual incentive meeting to be held in San Francisco. His public relations team, led by public relations director Travis Doster, suggested that G.J. conduct a television interview during the meeting and give the press unfettered access to all parts of the meeting—a five-day, 1,000-person blowout in San Francisco. Hart told him to reach out to their vendor partners, other colleagues, and PR experts for their opinions.

According to Doster, "Not one person we consulted with felt there was an upside to talking to the media, and certainly saw no advantage in giving them access to our meeting. In fact, one group sent me a three-page memo with nothing but negative feedback. No one thought we should do it. So, although I wanted G.J. to move forward, I told him that the consensus feedback was: 'Too much risk'; 'No upside'; 'Don't do it'; 'Big risk to have CNBC come to the meeting'; 'Why would you do *that*?'

"Nevertheless," continued Doster, "G.J. decided to conduct the interview and also to allow the media full access to our meeting. I believe he steeled his resolve when he arrived in San Francisco. When he went into our hotel, he noticed that a few of the hotel restaurants, usually busy places, were closed. When our meeting started, the hotel manager told us the restaurants would reopen for a week and a half due solely to our meeting. The hotel employees approached G. J. and thanked him for bringing the meeting to the hotel because they were able to work for a period that they wouldn't have otherwise."

Hart proactively defended the travel and meetings industry as well as his decision to hold a large meeting in not one, not two, but *five* on-camera CNBC interviews from the San Francisco meeting—at a time when most companies preferred to keep their reward programs out of the media spotlight, or cancel them for fear of an angry public and disgruntled shareholders and politicians.

When asked by the reporter whether he had second thoughts on spending between $2 and $2.5 million on the festivities, he replied, "I'm not sure that was enough. You have to invest in what you claim is important, and our people are important. Maybe we should be spending more."

After the CNBC interviews, Texas Roadhouse stock jumped 22 percent. In addition, it received three national and state awards from the meetings and travel industry.

"Texas Roadhouse stood up and said, 'The media and government can't tell us what to do,' said Jim Feldman, president of the Incentive Travel Council (ITC), a strategic industry group of the Incentive Marketing Association. The ITC gave its first-ever Travel Incentive Award to Texas Roadhouse. "The company held its ground and reaffirmed incentive travel and its reward components. It set a standard for others to not be pushed around by miscommunication from the media," stated Feldman.

Travis Doster was prepared for the negative emails. "When we originally agreed to appear on CNBC, we thought we would get complaints, maybe 30 or 40. Instead, we received zero negative responses and hundreds of positive ones. We never expected this type of response. Most were from industry folks and customers, but some were from people who had never tried one of our restaurants and were now going to patronize them."

Here's one example:

I'm writing to commend the CEO of Texas Roadhouse for being willing to speak about the value of meetings and events. Employee recognition is extremely important, particularly in the hospitality business where turnover is high and customer service is crucial. At a time when so many CEOs are canceling recognition events, I think it's great that your CEO has the courage to publicly comment that these investments are in the success of your company. I therefore intend to become a more frequent customer of Texas Roadhouse and I will encourage others to as well.

Megan Tierney, Senior Vice President
Information Management Network
New York, New York

In contrast to Outback Steak House, Applebee's, and Chili's, each of which has $100 million advertising budgets, Texas Roadhouse does not have a national advertising budget. Instead, it relies upon a localized approach where stores build relationships with local community groups, which then spread the word about the restaurants. Instead of asking franchisees to send them money for national ad buys, they encourage them to spend money locally. Some great national publicity opportunities go unrealized, but that doesn't matter to G.J. Hart.

In September of 2009, when many restaurants were closing their doors and halting expansion plans, Texas Roadhouse built a new restaurant. But it wasn't your typical restaurant. It was financed with company funds but would bring no financial return to TRH. Doster explained, "We opened a Texas Roadhouse restaurant in Logan, Utah, the first and only in which 100 percent of the proceeds go to Andy's Outreach—a philanthropic organization we established to assist employees impacted by unforeseen events like natural disasters, severe illnesses, personal injuries, etc. Andy's Outreach was started due to one of our loyal employees who passed away, and his family didn't have funds for a proper funeral and burial. We created it as another philanthropic arm of the company, and we now have a restaurant in which all profits go to Andy's Outreach.

"I told G.J. that the Logan, Utah, restaurant's opening day was a good opportunity for some positive national media exposure," continued Doster. "Well, he quickly reminded me, 'That's not why we opened the restaurant.'" Unconventional, indeed.

Does all of this impact the bottom line? Texas Roadhouse has seen its employee turnover rate reduced by 15 percent over the past two years, while nearly 90 percent of its customers say they'll return to the restaurants, and 71 percent say they eat at a Texas Roadhouse at least twice a month. Far from being a persuasion disability, being an underdog can impart "underprivileged power."

Cheering for the underdog is about the transference of achievement. We want to believe in them because of what it means for us.

THE UNDERDOG'S CHECKLIST
How to Gain Power

✓ Check your resources. More resources = greater expectations. Greater expectations = less likelihood of underdog positioning.

✓ If your lack of resources is unfair, beat that drum.

✓ Make sure your underdog biography is believable. (Oprah Winfrey and Apple have to keep reminding people of their humble origins.)

✓ To maintain the underdog label, don't squander the resources you do have.

✓ If you're labeled an underdog, reinforce that you worked hard for what you have.

✓ If you're not an underdog, if you're a "tall poppy," make sure your achievements are seen as deserved. Work it!

✓ Don't brag about your underdog mantle—let someone else brag for you.

✓ Become unbound! Underdogs are more likely to win when they use unconventional tactics.

CHAPTER 2

Tactic #1:

Build Your Street Cred

"Those who play by the rules and work hard go to the top of my list."

— *Former Congressman Jim Ross Lightfoot*

"The track record and reputation matters. If I have a question mark in my mind, it takes longer to get there with me."

— *Jo Ann Davidson, Former Ohio Speaker of the House and Former Co-Chair, Republican National Committee*

"Whether a potential employee, friend or spouse, the right person is most often the one you choose in the first ten minutes. More often less than a minute."

— *Robert Lanier*

"**A**ll humans make snap judgments, and the busier people get, the more they rely on these snap judgments," said Dr. Kelton Rhoads, who teaches influence psychology at the Annenberg School for Communications at

31

the University of Southern California. "People revere these decisions when they refer to having 'a gut feeling' and 'an excellent sense of intuition.' Come to think of it, when have you ever heard anyone say they *don't* have excellent intuitive ability? *Everybody* has awesome intuitive powers; just ask if you doubt it.

"In our culture, we are uniquely set against the concepts of 'bias' and 'prejudice,'" Dr. Rhoads continued. "But in point of fact, all human brains function on the basis of 'bias,' which consists of thinking of shortcuts that allow us to arrive at a decision without a lot of mental effort and on the basis of applying past learning and judgments to present situations.

"For good and ill, bias and prejudice are efficient. Humans are indeed 'cognitive misers,' and powerful people are no different. They are perhaps even *less reflective than average*," said Rhoads, "because they're generally overwhelmed with time constraints and social pressures."

Based on Dr. Rhoads, everything you do accumulates. So knowing about your past actions, statements, and even those you affiliate with allow top dogs to whirl you in their mental food processor and develop an opinion that influences whether they will grant you access and time. But what kind of mental shortcuts do they use?

I've found they're partial to the following five characteristics:

- your reputation,
- your presentation,
- your possible suffering,
- your playing by the rules, and
- your being unbiased.

Then, if you pass that test, others will listen to the merits of your argument.

YOUR REPUTATION: THE PAST IS PROLOGUE

As I interviewed powerful individuals whose minds were changed through underdog influence, almost all listened to the underdogs not just because of *what they said* but because of *who they were*. Without my asking specifically about the person's reputation or credibility, this factor rose to the top as a key characteristic for high-achieving underdog influencers.

Here's a sampling of unfiltered comments made by big dogs as they told me their stories:

> "If I have heard good things about you or the group you are affiliated with, that helps."

> "I had heard that she had a good reputation in the community, and I knew her husband."

> "They were well-known and well-respected religious leaders in my district."

> "She was very credible and a well-known person in the area."

> "He was a nice guy, well respected in the business world."

> "I did not know her, but I was very aware of her organization."

> "I never met her, but the woman was credible to me because she tried to find other avenues for help."

> "I knew about her through my staff who went to church with them."

Can you discern the pattern? It reveals that *reputation* matters. A good reputation becomes a shortcut to determining the merits of your argument without weighing it in a mindful way. It substitutes for consideration because accessing someone's reputation is easier than plodding through data and arguments. Dr. Rhoads added jokingly, "In fact, I abused this bias tremendously as a college student. It was always my goal to get a high score on the *first* test to set my 'reputation.' Then subsequent mediocre work during the rest of the class was viewed through the rose-colored lens of that first test."

Former Ohio Congressman Clarence Brown who served in the U.S. Congress for 17 years admitted, "I was not noted for my interest in the environment." However, a woman in his district, Claire Mae Fredrick, approached him about the Cedar Bog nature area that would become depleted if a highway were built through it. She wanted Congressman Brown to get the Cedar Bog area declared a nature preserve, which would then prevent the highway bypass project.

"I was an Eagle Scout, I got my Bird Merit Badge, but I wasn't deeply interested in this Cedar Bog issue. I got elected on economic issues, not environmental issues. Claire Fredrick was a biology teacher at the local college. I knew *of* her but didn't have any kind of relationship with her. I knew she had a good standing in the community. And I knew her husband was the county coroner," he said.

Congressman Brown decided to take on her case based not only on what she said but on her reputation. He and his staff investigated the situation, agreed with her views, and worked to gain a federally protected nature preserve status for Cedar Bog. In fact, he worked *against* his political party who favored building the highway. Mrs. Fredrick's reputation brought the issue to his attention, and he allocated resources to fulfill her request.

The most scrutinized part of one's reputation is whether the person is deemed trustworthy or not. And while you might think the term "trustworthy" is easy to define, Dr. Rhoads explained that 'trustworthiness' is highly relative. "Would a placard-carrying member of PETA (People for the Ethical Treatment of Animals, a radical group opposing meat eating, fur, hunting, etc.) consider the editor of *Field and Stream* to be trustworthy? Probably not. So elements of 'Are you on my side?' and 'Do you agree with my morality?' fit into the equation.

Noted Dr. Rhoads, "We heard this a lot during the years Bill Clinton was president. I'd hear my students say, 'I don't approve of his personal morality, but his policies are great.' A lot of Americans who would think thrice before leaving their daughter alone in a room with President Clinton nonetheless thought he was a wonderful guy to have in office.

"So we make allowances for certain types of untrustworthiness *and* are exceedingly harsh on others," Dr. Rhoads cautioned. "But which do we allow and which do we excoriate? We tolerate untrustworthiness that conveniently lets us have the world the way we want it. And we rain down hell on forms of untrustworthiness in those who oppose our world view."

YOUR REPUTATION: THE FIRST IMPRESSION IS FINAL

The research indicated that people who are adept at correctly reading others aren't smarter than those who can't. They just spend a lot of time with people—which is exactly what powerful people do. As former Congressman Lightfoot noted, "We listen to a lot of people and get good at telling whether someone is honest or not."

Powerful people are among the highest-paid listeners around. After all, listening is essentially how they spend their time. From board meetings to special interest group meetings to committee hearings to town hall gatherings to constituent meetings. That makes mastering first impressions a major piece in the underdog influence puzzle. The more time people spend listening to and interacting with others, the more skilled they are at accurately making snap judgments.

Snap Judgments

David Funder, professor of psychology at the University of California at Riverside, noted that snap judgments are reliable judgments, especially among people who spend a lot of time with other people.[25] This doesn't apply to those who belong to 72 online communities and don't interact outside of their computer screen. Rather, it depends on spending time with human beings, in person.

His studies have found that two observers often reach a consensus about a third person, and their assessments accurately match the third person's assessment of himself or herself. "We can be fooled, of course, but we're more often right than wrong," Professor Funder commented.

Psychologists have noted that snap judgments occur when clues hit us simultaneously and form a final impression. What do you think when you receive the following signals: A man with a soggy handshake? A woman with a mellifluous voice? Anyone with excessive tattoos? A woman with dagger-like fingernails? Those who wear a Rolex watch? Admit it—you form a laser-like impression based on those signals.

Many like to think that they don't judge books by their cover, but indeed people do. They can't help it. And those judgments can be amazingly accurate.

"I couldn't care less what people say about how they judge others," said Dr. Frank Bernieri, an Oregon State University professor who conducts experiments in nonverbal communications. "I'm interested in what takes place instantaneously, reflexively, subconsciously and immediately."[26] According to Dr. Bernieri, impression making is all over in the first 30 seconds.

In one of his experiments, untrained subjects were shown 30-second video segments of job applicants greeting interviewers. The subjects rated the applicants on qualities such as self-assurance, competence, and likeability. Then trained interviewers conducted 20-minute interviews with the same job applicants and were asked to complete a four-page evaluation of each applicant. The evaluations of the trained interviewers who spent 20 minutes interviewing the applicants did not differ from those of the untrained observers who watched 30 seconds of videotape!

"Yes, people do judge books by their covers. First impressions predict final impressions," Dr. Bernieri noted. First impressions lead to what social psychologists call the "confirmation bias." He said, "In social psychology, there is an amazing amount of literature and research showing that once we have any expectation— any working theory, any working hypothesis—we are biased in the way we process information. We go out of our way to seek confirming evidence. However, in our minds, we think we're being analytical and processing the whole time. So by the time we finish, we think our judgments are based on the data."[27]

Image

The workplace is particularly brutal to those who make an unfavorable first/final impression. According to Megan Hustad, author of *How to Be Useful*, your image is most relevant when first meeting your co-workers. If you make a poor first impression, it's almost impossible to adjust upwardly others' expectations of you.

This reminded me of the co-worker I was introduced to years ago. After pleasantries were exchanged, she made sure I knew she had pet snakes and that she slept with them. I'm all for workplace diversity, but this initial mental image threw me. It got worse when she brought the molted snake skins to the office and proudly displayed them on her bulletin board. Let the reptilian rights crowd come after me, but I just couldn't get over imagining her sleeping with her snakes! My co-workers and I never viewed her as a serious professional, and she left the company a year later, I hope to a more reptilian-friendly workplace.

Digging deeper into the nuances of first/final impressions, Amy Cuddy of Harvard Business School, Susan Fiske of Princeton, and Peter Glick of Lawrence University have developed a new model to further delineate how we quickly judge others. All over the world, it turns out, people judge others on two main qualities: warmth and competence. Are they friendly with good intentions? Do they have the ability to deliver on those intentions?

As human beings, it makes sense that we would abhor cold, incompetent folks. But Cuddy and her colleagues found that we respond with ambivalence to other personality blends, too. For example, warm and incompetent people elicit pity and benign neglect; competent but cold personality types foster envy and a desire to harm. Thus, warmth and competence becomes the winning combination.[28]

Appearance

Woe be to those underdogs who don't manage their first impression! It can certainly doom their top dog's desire to help. Here's more evidence why this is true.

For this book, I conducted a focus group with prominent D.C.-area lobbyists. Given the leveling of the playing field for persuasion tools available (e.g., grassroots lobbying, Political Action Committees, social media opportunities, and more), I asked the lobbyists how they typically gain an advantage over their opponents. As one candidly admitted, "Well, something that doesn't cost much but is very effective is how you present yourself. I love it when environmental lobbyists and their grassroots advocates meet with a legislator right before I do. Typically, they don't leave a good first impression. Their appearance is unprofessional, so I always look better by comparison."

Based on this lobbyist's experience and Dr. Bernieri's findings, could the environmental lobbyists be perceived as less organized, less competent, and less responsive than those who have a more orderly appearance? If the people they want to influence don't share their same values and hence don't give them the benefit of the doubt, this is a distinct possibility. You can take a chance that your first impression works if you have a sympathetic or like-minded audience, but that's not the point. Because you're focused on persuading those who have views averse to ours, you're wise to play the percentages. That means *managing* your first impression so it works to your advantage.

Rick Scott would agree. Elected to be Florida's governor in November 2010, he's the former CEO of Columbia/HCA, at one time the largest hospital company in the nation. In 1996, Time magazine listed Scott as one of the 25 most influential Americans. He has since founded Solantic, a string of 23 urgent-care facilities, and he also runs an investment company. There, he listens to a lot of "pitches" (formal and informal) from people who want him to invest in their enterprises. In his experience, the younger the person, the more important it is to make a favorable "first/final impression."

As Scott advised, "How people getting started present themselves is extremely important because they don't have a track record. Young people who do present themselves well can get a lot accomplished."

I was reminded of this dynamic when I delivered a training workshop for a leading national nonprofit organization. Day one consisted of persuasion training while day two was a visit to the State House to meet with state representatives and senators. One workshop participant (who showed up without registering, which should have been the first warning) was wearing a "picnic casual" outfit of shorts and a baggy top, complete with the ubiquitous water sandals in case the room flooded. My client and I worried. What if this person visited the State House with us the next day? If he did, what would be his future wardrobe choices? When one of the organization's leaders reminded him about wearing "traditional business attire" to the State House, he took offense, stating, "I think legislators appreciate the novelty of different attire." Actually, they don't—unless different attire makes your message more vivid (like doctors wearing white lab coats). So my client adroitly counseled this individual not to participate in the State House visit unless he was willing to don traditional business attire. The possibility of his wearing "picnic casual" again wasn't worth risking the organization's carefully protected brand.

Yes, it's crucial to dress appropriately for the situation and let your personal style come through. You can do that and *still* show respect to those you are petitioning. In fact, failure to do so communicates that you care more about yourself, your comfort, and your "style" (and I'm using that word extremely loosely) than the person you want to persuade. Remember, it's about *them*, not *you*.

Here are additional research findings about one's appearance:

Those who show skin and tattoos are recommending themselves for low-level positions. (That said, if you're pursuing a job in the tattoo industry or a position in a highly creative industry, having tattoos are an advantage.)

- More skin = less power.
- Men with long hair are viewed as creative.
- Women with medium-length brown hair are judged as outgoing.
- Women who show cleavage are judged poorly at work

As the speed of life and transactions increase, style and clothing become a person's visual vocabulary. Exhibiting care and style with your visual vocabulary conveys two things: (1) meeting with others is worthwhile and (2) you are a person of interest. Your appearance announces to the world that you have assumed command of yourself, which communicates confidence. And showing you have confidence in your message can sway *people even more than your expertise can.*

Confidence vs. Expertise

If you wonder why media pundits who failed to predict the 2008 economic crisis are still employed and giving advice, the reason has to do with how people view confidence—another factor in understanding the final/first impression.

Recent research by Don Moore of Carnegie Mellon University indicates that people prefer advice from a confident source, even to the point of being willing to forgive a poor track record from that source.

In Moore's experiment, volunteers were given cash for correctly guessing the weight of people from their photographs. In each of the eight rounds of the study, the guessers bought advice from one of four other volunteer "advisors." The guessers were given information on how confident each advisor was. For example, one advisor would say there was a 70 percent chance the person's weight was 170-179 pounds, a 15 percent chance it was 160-169, etc. A more confident advisor would focus on one weight range and say there was a 100 percent chance the weight was within the 170-179 range. Here's the catch: In each round, before they chose their advisor, the volunteers saw each advisor's expressed percent of certainty but not the associated weight ranges.

What happened? From the start, the more confident advisors found more buyers for their advice. This caused the advisors to give answers that were more and more precise as the game progressed. Any escalation in precision disappeared when the guessers had to choose whether or not to buy the advice of a single advisor. Indeed, in the later rounds, guessers tended to avoid advisors who had been wrong previously, but this effect was more than outweighed by the bias shown toward confidence. Moore said that following the advice of the most confident person often makes sense due to evidence that precision and expertise go hand in hand. One indication is that people give a narrower range of answers when asked about subjects with which they're more familiar.[29]

However, Moore observed that sometimes this link breaks down. With complex but politicized subjects such as global warming, for example, scientific experts who stress uncertainties lose out to those who deliver a more emphatic message. Moore argued that in competitive situations, this tendency can drive those offering advice to increasingly exaggerate how sure they are.

Charisma

For more from the "it's not what you say, it's how you say it" school, look to Dr. Alex "Sandy" Pentland of MIT whose research focuses on measuring charisma. Before you dismiss the idea that charisma can be measured and cue up New Age music, read on.

While at a party, Dr. Pentland and his colleague Daniel Olguin placed recording devices on several executives. These devices recorded data about their vocal tone, gestures, proximity to others, and more throughout the evening. Five days later, the same executives presented business plans to a panel of judges in a contest. Without reading or hearing their presentations, Dr. Pentland correctly forecast the winners with 87 percent accuracy by only applying data collected at the party. How did he correctly predict the winners? By measuring the intangibles—what he calls "honest signals"—that are powerful predictors of persuasion.

Pentland referred to "honest signals" as signs that cause changes in the recipient of one's communication—the influence prospect. It's a term that describes nonverbal cues people use socially to coordinate their behavior themselves. These cues include gestures, expressions, and tone of voice. His team looks at how much you face those you're talking to, how close you stand to them, and how much you let them talk. He called his approach "obtaining a God's-eye view" because the "honest signals" can't be faked. In fact, when people become aware of them and try to consciously change their delivery, they become more self-conscious and hence less persuasive.

Dr. Pentland's team also found that successful people are more energetic than the average person. They might talk more, but they also listen more, and they spend more face-to-face time with people. They pick up cues from others, draw them out, and get them to be more outgoing. He noted that it's not only the signals they send that make them charismatic; it's what they elicit from others. "Positive, energetic people have higher performance. We're proving that," said Dr. Pentland.

While people may intuitively know that charismatic team players are more successful, it's been thought of as an imprecise attribute, making it a "nice" but not "necessary" quality to develop in our teams. However, Dr. Pentland stated, "Because we can measure it, social intuition is no longer magic; it's now quantitative science." Therefore, it can be trusted.[30]

Dr. Pentland's evidence corresponds with advice from Randy Colvin, associate professor of psychology at Northeastern University in Boston. He agrees that it's best to let those "honest signals" come through and not mask one's intentions. Doing so is counterproductive. Colvin has found that "the people who are easiest to judge are the most mentally healthy. Their exterior behavior mimics their internal views of themselves. What you see is what you get."[31]

People like other people who are easy to read—what I like to call "blurtatious." As Dr. Bernieri reminded us, "If people look at you and think they're seeing right into you, then they tend to like you. If you have a poker face, if you're reserved, then you're a more difficult read. People seem not to like that."[32]

Many work environments sanitize individuality, which can attenuate persuasion. You know them when you see them—the excessively "professional" employee who communicates devoid of emotion or "unapproved" expressions. I'm all for appropriate professional behavior, but I've met some workers for whom I'm afraid if their face peeled off, you'd see a circuit board.

Bottom line? If we can't read someone, we like that person less than those we can read. And if we like them less, we are less apt to say, "yes" to what they propose.

YOUR SUFFERING

Once you've managed your "final" impression, you can have even more credibility if you demonstrate suffering, especially suffering for your beliefs. Let me explain with a story.

Former Florida State Representative Janegale Boyd is the president and CEO of the Florida Association of Homes and Services for the Aging. Although Boyd wasn't an expert in state retirement system law, she told me about a woman who compelled her to quickly become one. At the time, if a state employee died at the "wrong time" (within a few days or weeks before becoming vested in the state retirement system), the family received no death benefits.

"One day, a woman called and poured her heart out to my staffer," explained Boyd. "Her husband, a correctional facility guard, had died of a heart attack a couple of days before being vested to receive full retirement benefits. When the woman called staff in three other state offices, she was told, 'This is the law; we can't change it.' I was outraged about this situation. I knew the law needed to be changed.

"The woman's appeal was desperate and highly personal," continued Boyd. "I learned that she and her husband were good citizens who paid their taxes. She didn't want to get welfare despite being eligible for it. Knowing that helped persuade me to take action because I understood she wanted to do the most honorable thing. She was credible because she had looked at various ways to work through the system. Further, she was caring for her disabled daughter and her mom who had Alzheimer's.

Boyd took this woman's concern to the Department of Retirement to see about changing the law that would make her husband's retirement payments retroactive. After sitting down with officials at the Department of Retirement, Boyd introduced a Special Claims Bill that would make spouses of people who died within days of being vested eligible for full retirement benefits. "Today, any person whose spouse dies within a year of retirement is eligible for the money owed. This woman made it happen. And I never met her until the bill was introduced," she concluded.

To me, one of the most puzzling yet encouraging aspects of credibility is suffering. Yes, people ascribe credibility to those who have been hurt, which seems to contradict what's known about expertise and evidence as credibility boosters. But to be encouraging, it reinforces that we are indeed human beings rather than automatons. And on the dark side, it explains the victim mentality and ability of "smart" people to make stupid decisions based on the (self-proclaimed) victim status of others.

Suffering infers credibility. I was reminded of this when reading the results of a February 2009 Harris Poll. In the poll, people were asked to name their heroes and state why they were considered heroes. Among the reasons mentioned most often were these:

> *"Doing what's right regardless of personal consequences"* (89%)
> *"Not giving up until the goal is accomplished"* (83%)
> *"Overcoming adversity"* (81%)

Translation: *heroes suffer.* Everyone likes a hero; everyone wants to help a hero. So if you have legitimately suffered, you need to let your top dog know.

YOUR PLAYING BY THE RULES

Top dogs have an innate desire to help those who play by the rulebook. Doing so proves you're a moral person, at least to a degree. And as Dr. Vandello stated in

Chapter 1, underdogs are usually viewed as more moral than others. Therefore, by helping moral people, we capture some of their good qualities, if only psychologically.

"I am the only living human being who has cut the IRS budget and lived to tell about it," bragged former Congressman Jim Ross Lightfoot from Iowa. In the mid-'80s, Iowa experienced a farm credit crisis. Farmer after farmer dealt with high interest rates that forced them to go bankrupt and sell their farms. In many instances, Iowa bankers told farmers they would simply write off the bad debt, no questions asked. However, the IRS learned about that arrangement and decided to count the forgiven loan money as income. Soon after, they received a "love letter" in the form of an income tax bill.

As Lightfoot recalled, "We received tons of desperate calls and letters, many times right before someone's farm was going on the auction block to pay the IRS. It got so bad, I had my district office staff go to their homes and spend the night with them, they were so distraught.

"I was especially moved when a young man walked into my district office and told his story with tears rolling down his cheeks. He'd done everything right, his outstanding farm loan was forgiven, he got a new job, he was putting his life back together, and then he got a $42,000 bill from the IRS!

"I was enraged. So I pushed through a piece of legislation stating that farmers were exempt from paying taxes on their forgiven loan amounts. It was just for farmers and specifically for the situation in Iowa during that time. "Those who play by the rules and work hard go to the top of my list," he declared.

What did the play-by-the-rules farmer have in common with Janegayle Boyd's underdog? They both suffered!

Bob Benham, whom you read about in Chapter 1, played by the rules and suffered, *and* he went on to persuade key lawmakers to his point of view by employing the playing-by-the- rules concept. Here's what happened.

Today, some products and services purchased over the Internet are taxed, depending on which jurisdiction the online retailer operates from. But in 2000, a debate fired up between those who wanted a totally tax-free Internet and those who wanted to level the playing field to a degree between online retailers and physical stores. According to a June 2000 article in *The Wall Street Journal*, "The road to a tax-free Internet looked smooth and clear in Congress. Then an oddball coalition came along." That oddball coalition shifted the debate and made Internet taxation a reality. The same article reported that "…this turn of events can be explained in large measure by people such as Bob Benham."[33]

Bob owns an upscale Oklahoma City women's fashion store, Balliet's. In the late 1990s, Bob witnessed Internet sales chipping away at his profits and those of other Oklahoma brick-and-mortar retailers. He became more concerned when people wanted to exchange items purchased online or alter the clothing they bought on the Internet. "I joked that we do virtual alterations on all Internet purchases. You need a good sense of humor to keep this thing in perspective," Bob said.

Instead of seething, Bob took action. He began meeting with numerous members of Congress and their staff. He sent more than 300 personal communications to members of Congress urging them to support the Sales Tax Fairness and Simplification Act. As it turned out, one of his biggest challenges was persuading his own representative, Congressman Ernest Istook.

"Congressman Istook is a pro-business guy drawn to positions that reduce taxes or prevent new taxes. I had two meetings with him. He was opposed to Congress even being engaged on this issue—very opposed. But he didn't know about the unfairness of the current tax structure in lost sales tax revenue to his district. I told him stories of customers coming to our cosmetics counter to learn about new products from our staff and then ordering them online. Now, we retailers promote Oklahoma City and happily contribute sales tax to Oklahoma City, but this situation was unfair."

Bob especially drew Istook's attention—and that of other members of Congress—by saying, "We retailers sponsor the Little League teams, buy tables at charity events, hold fashion shows to benefit nonprofits. When was the last time a dot-com did a charity fashion show in your district?" They realized that Bob's company played by the rules and gave back to the community while online stores received financial benefits without any participation. These retailers suffered by doing the right thing—and that wasn't fair.

These days, more goods and services purchased on the Internet are taxed, thanks (or not, depending on your viewpoint) to the fairness argument of Bob Benham.

He helped those who disagreed with him see the issue differently. In doing so, he became the apotheosis of all aspiring underdogs. His efforts were even chronicled in a front-page, above-the-fold issue of The Wall Street Journal and featured his portrait captured in the Journal's classic grainy style.[34]

YOUR BEING UNBIASED

It's easy to get so emotionally attached to your cause that you forget there's another side to the story—your *opponent's* side. Many unsuccessful underdog persuaders are just chemically incapable of seeing the other side (the "yaktivists" and "madvocates" come to mind). But bias exists, and those who reside on the other side of the road feel just as strongly as you do. It's also easy to assume that a strong argument showcasing the best evidence carries the day. But in fact, research shows that using logical arguments as a tactic can backfire.

Political scientists are starting to catch up with what social psychologists have long known—that fact-based arguments only work with certain people and in certain situations. People might think they're smart and deliberative if they believe that logic and facts sway them. But if that were true, let's face it, no one would ever smoke, eat too much, or drink too much.

Here's evidence. In a series of studies in 2005 and 2006, researchers at the University of Michigan found that when misinformed people, particularly political partisans, were exposed to corrected facts in news stories, they rarely changed their minds. In fact, they often became even more strongly set in their beliefs. Conveying facts, they found, did not "cure" misinformation. Like an underpowered antibiotic, facts could actually make misinformation even *stronger*.[35]

My friend and mentor, the wise Vickie Sullivan, has often reminded me that "in every heresy, there's a grain of truth." That's what ineffective underdogs can overlook when presenting a case. They can't imagine any truth in their opponents' arguments, so they clobber them with tendentious facts about why their perspective is the best.

Your top dog is not only exposed to your carefully honed arguments and evidence; he or she also hears counterarguments, thus requiring you to present both sides of your position. Early experiments on the effects of one-sided versus two-sided presentations from researchers Linda Golden and Mark Alpert show that two-sided presentations are more effective under two conditions: 1) when your persuasion prospect is exposed to subsequent counterarguments, and 2) when your prospect is initially opposed to your point of view.[36]

In addition, the cerebral abilities of audience members influence which type of arguments you should use. Is your top dog highly educated? If so, use two-sided arguments. People with education and status tend to be more persuaded by two-sided arguments. In contrast, those with little education tend to be more influenced by one-sided presentations.

Congressman Mike Honda of California admitted that hearing both sides of an argument creates a favorable influence environment for him. "The most successful influencers tell me the context of their situations without prejudice. They give both sides. When I ask professional lobbyists what the other side says and they can't tell me, that informs my decision-making process. Some lobbyists are truthful, some are not."

The objectivity of an outside expert influenced Jim Buchy, former Ohio State Representative and Director of the Ohio Department of Agriculture. He said, "The Ohio Department of Natural Resources wanted a program that would provide money for farmers to insert buffer strips around their land for stream runoff. The goal was to stop runoff, which I agreed with. But I wasn't in favor of the government paying the farmers to do what they should do on their own.

"A knowledgeable agronomist who was politically astute proved to be more objective than others with similar expertise," Buchy continued. "He impressed me because we had a similar philosophy, but sometimes he gave me answers I was unhappy with. In contrast, another individual I dealt with regularly on Ag issues showed such an evident bias that I couldn't get any objectivity from him. The credible agronomist guy told me that we could use the budget money to educate small farmers to be more personally responsible. The personal responsibility angle resonated with me. I finally supported the initiative after opposing it in the beginning."

Contrary to what popular culture preaches, it's *not* all about you. So to gain the credibility you need, you have to give your top dog *both* sides of the argument.

YOUR CREDIBILITY:
ONCE LOST, FOREVER LOST?

What if, before you knew better, you did exactly the opposite of what successful underdog influencers do to build and maintain their credibility? Say you now have little or no credibility. Can you ever get it back? To all whose credibility has fallen short, Dr. Rhoads offered this encouragement: "Credibility is seldom irrevocably lost if the player is committed to rebuilding it. Part of the rehabilitation depends on what elements of credibility have been lost. Trust is harder to rehabilitate than ignorance or incompetence, for example.

"But credibility is a dynamic concept," he explained. "I'm sure you've heard that 'once credibility is lost, it's lost forever,' but nothing could be further from the truth. A person's or a corporation's or a nation's reputation is in constant flux, waxing and waning depending on moves that are made.

"So when the wheels come off your credibility and you end up in the ditch, don't give up. You lose the credibility game only if you end the game once you hit the ditch."

THE UNDERDOG'S CHECKLIST
How to Build Your Street Cred

✓ Be aware that all people—especially busy, powerful people—use mental shortcuts based on their biases. "Powerful people are likely less reflective than average people because they're generally overwhelmed with time constraints and social pressures." (Dr. Kelton Rhoads)

✓ Don't forget that your past is prologue—what you do accumulates. Your reputation presents a mental shortcut for those who don't know you and who are averse to your position. How are you proactively managing your reputation to get what you want in five or ten years?

✓ Remember that top dogs listen to others. A lot. That makes them adept at reading behavior and assessing credibility.

✓ Make mountains out of moments. You've got 30 seconds to show warmth and competence. The first impression is the final impression.

✓ Be confident. Because people tend to be "cognitive misers," confidence matters as much or more than expertise.

✓ Dressing appropriately for the occasion shows consideration of your top dog. Clothing is your visual vocabulary.

✓ Incorporate legitimate suffering for your cause or belief system into your message whenever possible.

✓ Let others know how you followed the rules. Fairness resonates with top dogs because they have an innate desire to help those who stick to the rulebook. It gives you credibility as a moral person, and by helping you, they view themselves as more moral.

✓ Get your opponents' arguments out there as well as your own and be as unbiased as possible. Remember, "In every heresy, there's a grain of truth." (Vickie Sullivan)

✓ Be blurtatious. People like others who are easy to read.

✓ Don't end your credibility journey if you land in the ditch. You can gain it back if you commit to rebuilding it.

CHAPTER 3

Extreme Influence Tactic #2:
Be Vivid

"I looked up in the gallery and saw them looking down at me, and thought, 'Moffett, what the hell were you thinking?'"

> — *Toby Moffett, former U.S. Congressman*

"When you are trying to convince someone who is opposed to your ideas, it becomes necessary to meet face to face."

> — *Dewey Reynolds, Virginia Association of REALTORS*

"Half the brain is devoted to processing visuals. To not use that ability is to simply throw away precious real estate."

> — *Dan Hill, Founder and President, Sensory Logic*

A t the risk of sounding like an infomercial, what if you knew of a persuasion technique that was scientifically proven to be a crucial element in changing someone's mind? Wouldn't you want to use it? Every one of our successful underdogs knows the secret. Typically, professional protestors don't know about this element or don't choose to use it. But a simple, highly effective way to persuade others is to engage in *vivid* communications.

THE ONE THING: FROM VOICE TO VICTORY

If you do nothing else, the one thing you must do to persuade a top dog is *be vivid*. What (I can hear you asking) does *that* mean? And why is being vivid a crucial communications technique in changing people's minds?

Merriam-Webster's Dictionary defines *vivid* as "producing a strong or clear impression on the senses: sharp, intense; specifically producing distinct mental images." People tend to both *remember* and *act on* information that's conveyed in a dramatic way. When confronted with a compelling anecdote, people can be strangely insensitive to factual information that indicates an anecdote may reflect an exception rather than a rule.

Since the ancient Greeks first began recording persuasive techniques, influencers have relied on vivid examples and stories to change hearts and minds. Following the Greeks was British philosopher Sir Frances Bacon, who observed:

> *The human understanding is most excited by that which strikes and enters the mind at once and suddenly, and by which the imagination is immediately filled and inflated. Then begins almost imperceptibly to conceive and suppose that everything is similar to the few objects which have taken possession of the mind...*[37]

Translation: One vivid encounter colors—and has more power—than all other relevant input.

For example, while doing your research on which type of dog to rescue, you learn that German Shepherds are extremely smart and protective. So you contact German Shepherd rescue groups and search for this breed at your local animal shelters. But then your spouse exclaims, "Oh, no, not a German shepherd! My sister was bitten by our neighbor's German Shepherd 23 years ago. The medical bills were over two thousand dollars. They're dangerous dogs! We can't get a German Shepherd!"

Research suggests that, after hearing this story, you won't be rational and merely add that anecdote to your research on the behaviors of German Shepherds. The vividness of your spouse's story makes it difficult to discount, so you give it more weight than it merits when considered with all the other data you collect.

Consider these three scenarios.

(1) A friend tells you about the night she got hit by a drunk driver who ran a red light. She said she can remember looking down and seeing the spreading stain of her own blood soaking her white dress. (2) You're watching the half-time show of Super Bowl XXXVIII and you witness entertainer Janet Jackson's "wardrobe malfunction" in real time. (3) On a summer evening in southern California, you smell smoke. You go to the window and see orange flames engulfing the nearby hillside.

All three scenarios have this in common: they're vivid! Social scientists say vividness invokes one or a combination of these three elements: (1) imagery-provoking (the blood-stained dress); (2) emotionally interesting (the wardrobe malfunction); and/or (3) proximity or closeness (fire on nearby hillside).[38]

Compared to pallid and abstract accounts, aren't these examples more likely to motivate a behavior like joining Mothers Against Drunk Driving (MADD), writing to the Federal Communication Commission (FCC), or cutting the dry brush on your hillside?

VIVID STORIES CHANGE HEARTS AND MINDS

Remember how the September 11, 2001, terrorist attacks caused massive changes in human behavior? Those attacks didn't happen in the Middle East where they can be relatively common. Reading about incidents "over there" rarely motivates people on the other side of the world to contribute to an international relief organization for the affected people.

Yet the terrorist attacks of 9/11 in the U.S. affected thousands of people directly and millions indirectly *and emotionally*. How many of us contributed to a 9/11-related charity, gave blood, or helped in some heartfelt way? We did something because the event happened in our own front yard. It was *vivid*. The event also caused millions of people to drive when they normally would have flown, despite the statistically lower risks of flying. Indeed, if terrorists had crashed more full planes during the rest of 2001, statistically Americans would still have been safer traveling in planes than in cars. Yet the 9/11 attacks came about, in Sir Francis Bacon's words, "at once" and "suddenly," in the eyes of the vast majority of the population. This tragedy was unexpected and sudden.

The vividness of events definitely affects the causes we donate to. According to a tally by the Center on Philanthropy at Indiana University, Americans stepped up and donated $1.3 billion for Haiti disaster relief, which was about equal to their contributions after the 2004 Asian tsunami. However, it trails the amount Americans gave in the same timeframe after the September 11 terrorist attacks ($2.3 billion) and Hurricane Katrina in 2005 ($3.4 billion). As Una Osili, director of research for the Center, said, "Lower giving for Haiti could be the result of the recent recession."[39] I'd venture to say that the lower amount of giving for Haiti was related to the more vivid nature of the September 11 attacks and Hurricane Katrina; they are "closer to home."

IS ALL VIVID INFORMATION EQUAL?

In 1982, a kind of war was instigated among psychologists over the concept of vividness. Several social psychologists reviewed 47 studies from the influence literature and found little support for vividness as a persuasive device.[40] This thrust a portion of the influence research world into a tailspin, resulting in two camps: the vividness-doesn't-work-even-though-you-thought-it-did camp and the vividness-does-SO-work-and-I'm-positive-it-does camp. Almost 30 years later, it turns out they were both right—in a way.

Social scientist Rosanna Guadagno and her colleagues recently performed a meta-analysis on the vividness effect, examining 63 studies conducted over the past several decades.[41] They found that vividness does indeed persuade. However, they also discovered that *vividness has to be correctly engaged* in order to accomplish the goal of persuading. That means it's not a tactic you can just slap into place and expect a persuasion miracle. As always, the devil is in the details.

Let's examine what Guadagno's team found. First, vividness has to be "figural," not "ground," to affect attitudes and behaviors. That means the vivid descriptions must forward the main theme that's being made, not amplify flashy but irrelevant details of the background. Referring back to your friend's collision with the drunk driver, the image of a spreading red blood stain on a white dress provides testimony to the damage caused by drunk driving. If she had remembered something irrelevant—for example, that her attending paramedic looked like George Clooney—this vivid but irrelevant detail wouldn't forward the argument that drunk driving is a social evil that must be combated. In fact, the image of George Clooney might even *distract* from the main theme and weaken the argument! Haphazardly expressed vividness that's off topic can actually be detrimental to persuasion.

Second, the researchers found that of the three elements of vividness (imagery, emotionality, and proximity), one far outweighed the others in effectiveness—*proximity*. Apparently "location, location, location" is more than a real estate mantra. Especially persuasive vivid examples are ones that happen in *your* front yard—or in the front yard of the person you're trying to persuade. So the brush fire that's *just outside your window* becomes particularly persuasive in getting you to act compared to a fire burning miles to the north. Your friend's story of her spreading blood stain becomes particularly vivid because it happened to *your* friend. And the story about the aggressive German Shepherd may resonate because it was *your* spouse's sister who received the bite. But what about the Janet Jackson incident of brief nudity on TV? Although some may have been outraged enough to fire off a letter to the FCC, my response was "who cares?" A sense of being "close to home" didn't exist in this case.

VIVID = PROXIMITY POWER

As these examples show, people tend to pigeonhole the proximity element of vivid communications as a happening "close to home." While that's true (and will be examined later), don't overlook the fact that proximity *includes the distance between the requester and the influence prospect.* The research on vividness reveals that being near your prospects increases the probability of influencing them.

Those familiar with psychological theory might know the famous 1974 Milgram experiments. Some think those experiments demonstrated the power of authority figures; others believe they reveal the strength of proximity in influence situations.

In these experiments, subjects were asked to give electric shocks to those who didn't grasp certain material (confederates, to be sure, not innocent victims). When an experimenter and subject were in the same room, about 65 percent of the subjects obeyed the experimenter's command to give 450-volt electric shocks to the "poor learner." However, when the experimenter left the room and gave his commands by telephone, only 20 percent were obedient to the 450-volt level.

Milgram also changed the proximity of the subjects to the victim. When the subjects were seated right next to the victim, only 40 percent of them obeyed and shocked the victim to the 450-volt level. Thus, if the experimenter was close to the subjects, his authority was deemed strong, but if the victim was close physically to the subjects, then the victim's protests overrode the demands of the experimenter. Location, location, location![42]

In another experiment, Bibb Latane and his colleagues developed a theory of social impact. Its premise is that people who are proximate have more influence. Proximity increases social impact, such as obeying someone's request to sing loudly, give money to a charity or political cause, tip in large amounts, or expend effort for the group. Likewise, in a group, social loafing—that is, letting others do the work— is *minimized* when members are physically close and contributions to the group can be clearly identified.[43]

Corresponding with this finding, not one of the underdogs in this book changed the minds of their top dogs using remote influence tactics. It's one thing to make noise (electronically) and another to get a "yes" from a recalcitrant opponent. While today's fascination with remote technologies is rampant, it's wrong to think that because of the prevalence of electronic communication, being in front of your prospect should be jettisoned. To change the mind of a top dog, it's vital to engage the power of proximity.

Researchers have even found that people are more likely to respond to emails based on the geographic proximity between the sender and receiver![44]

That said, researchers have found that *once you have already formed close relationships,* technology can aid team cohesion and personal connections in helping *sustain* the feelings of commitment and cooperation. But the stumbling block for many aspiring underdog influencers is thinking their electronic communications will change someone's mind. The research simply doesn't support this compared to proximity power.

Dr. Kelton Rhoads has counted seven proximity power advantages for the underdog who understands that influence is a face-to-face contact sport. Proximity makes it easier to:

- capture your top dog's attention
- show that you care
- observe his or her understanding
- monitor and counter negative feedback
- read nonverbal reactions and adjust accordingly
- demonstrate a willingness to make an effort to communicate
- begin to establish a personal relationship (another tactic used by most of our underdogs; see Chapter 7).

We are social beings. When we see someone, we can look for what Dr. Pentland referred to as "honest signals," discussed in Chapter 2. And those honest signals are vivid.

FACE FIRST

More than 100 studies exist showing the powerful effect of face-to-face discussion on social cooperation.[45] Researchers believe these results come from the commitment people feel when they make social contracts face to face *and* from the good feelings that accrue from being part of group interaction.

Upward influence necessitates collaboration, and only a few moments of face-to-face contact can have marked effects on an interaction. For instance, in one of the earliest studies of competitive games, subjects were instructed to "win as much as you can for yourself." When they could communicate with their game partner, 71 percent of the time they made choices that helped both players. They cooperated on only 36 percent of the trials when they couldn't talk with their partner.[46]

In their study, Kerr and Kaufman-Gilliland showed that group members who were given five minutes to discuss an investment game with one another were far more likely to cooperate with the others than group members who didn't have this opportunity. This effect was not duplicated when group members merely heard the group discussion and weren't able to participate.[47]

I doubt that a company will go bankrupt by relying on virtual teams, but those that have high-performing teams working in proximity to each other have an advantage. More than 50 years of peer-reviewed research has demonstrated that proximity is associated with numerous emotional, cognitive, and behavioral changes that affect work processes for the better.

"Virtual work teams" may be a misnomer because the evidence overwhelmingly shows a plethora of shortcomings with distributed work teams. Lack of proximity is a fact of life in the work force today, but it represents a less than excellent choice for productivity, team cohesion, spontaneous cooperation, and creativity.

Here's an example of how "face first" works in getting voters to the polls. In a rigorous analysis of get-out-the-vote drives (GOTV) conducted by candidates, interest groups, and political parties, Alan Gerber and Donald Green analyzed various GOTV techniques.[48] They wanted to find out what made someone who was ambivalent about voting go to the polls and vote. These days, numerous techniques are used to drive the vote, such as the dreaded "robo-calls," blast emails, direct mail, personal phone calls, and so on. The companies who sell those services tout that their particular service succeeded when turnout is high. (Of course, in the case of low turnout, the candidate "could not inspire his base" and those firms admit no shortcomings in their services or products. Their tactics only work when the candidate wins, right?)

Gerber and Green found that out of nine possible GOTV techniques, face-to-face canvassing produced the highest ratio of voter turnout per contact—one vote for every 14 face-to-face contacts. The worst? The dreaded "robo-calls" with only one vote per 20,000 contacts—and, no, that's not a typo. No wonder the robo-calls keep coming. You need 20,000 of them to get one person to vote!

Remember Dr. Sandy Pentland's quantitative research on charisma in Chapter 2? Though his experiments, he learned that 30 percent of the variation in MIT freshmen's political views was a function of their face-to-face exposure to others' opinions. And Minnesota Governor Tim Pawlenty noted the value of face-to-face outreach in a *Connect Business* magazine interview by saying, "It's easy to talk about budgets here while looking at them on spreadsheets, but not so easy going out and looking into the faces of the people they affect. That emotionally impacts me. I try to take those kinds of conversations seriously."[49]

VIVID ENCOUNTERS AFFECT VALUES

You might think that vivid communications work only when requests are minor, not with decisions that involve deeply held values. However, this is not the case.

In 1979, before government bailouts of big corporations became fashionable, Chrysler Motors came to Congress for help. In big financial trouble, the company lobbied for a bailout in the form of a government loan. The request was "decimal dust"—a measly $1.5 billion—compared to the government's 2008 bailouts.

Former Congressman Toby Moffett's vote on this bailout was due, in part, to vivid representation by members of his local autoworkers union (UAW). His philosophy, while liberal, also contained a libertarian streak that embraces limited government. (Some in the Libertarian Party believe government services should be limited to law enforcement and national defense, period.) The Chrysler bailout offended Moffett's libertarian sensibilities.

As the day of the vote arrived, he was leaning toward voting "no" on the bailout, exactly the opposite of what his UAW members wanted him to do. He arrived on the House floor to cast his vote and looked up at those seated in the House Gallery. His union members sat there, all wearing their UAW t-shirts. The people he saw there changed his mind.

"I glanced up into the House Gallery and saw dozens of UAW workers from my district looking down at me. I thought, "These people are the reason you're here, Moffett. *What are you thinking?*" He proceeded to vote in favor of the bailout.

Here's another example of vivid communications that have changed values. When Kentucky State Representative Tom Burch became chairman of the Kentucky House Health and Welfare Committee, the committee was considering three abortion bills that would have limited or eliminated a woman's right to an abortion. Burch had a definite point of view about the abortion issue.

"I was a poster boy for the Kentucky Right to Life group," he said. "I went to their meetings. I didn't know anything about the pro-choice side of the coin, but I did know I didn't like the anti-abortion activist's tactics." Dona Wells, executive director of an abortion clinic in Louisville, Kentucky, had come to Burch's office in 1986 when he'd just become the new chairman of the House Health and Welfare Committee. At the time, two abortion bills were being considered: one required a 24-hour wait and another completely outlawed abortion. Representative Burch recalled how Wells approached him.

"The legislative session was beginning, and Dona Wells visited me several times in my office in the capitol to discuss abortion. I was concerned that women were being pressured to have an abortion. Dona told me that all the women who went to her clinic for an abortion talked to a counselor before the procedure. She said if a woman appeared ambivalent about her decision to have an abortion, the procedure didn't occur. Telling me I needed to see for myself, she asked me to visit the clinic she ran in Louisville.

"I went to Dona's clinic on a Saturday to observe. Her description of the clinic's practices was consistent with what I saw. In particular, seeing that the women weren't being pushed into anything made an impression on me. They appeared to be in command of their situation. The biggest stress they experienced was running through the gauntlet of those nuts demonstrating outside," Burch said.

Observing patients in the clinic's waiting room had a profound effect on him. It clearly helped advance the point Wells was making—that women at abortion clinics weren't being cajoled or pressured into having abortions. Remember, for vivid information to work, it has to be relevant or it won't advance your efforts. As a result of Dona's efforts, Burch moved from being an award-winning pro-life advocate to a pro-choice advocate.

In another example, former Congressman Jim Ross Lightfoot served 11 years in the United States Congress. His philosophy favored fewer government programs and lower taxes. Consistent with his philosophy, he had never supported a particular government-sponsored Job Corp Center in his district. As he explained, "When I managed a small manufacturing company in Texas, I had negative experiences with such centers. I felt that the people who ran them didn't care about their clients, and that it was sloppily run." His mind was changed when a constituent talked to him about the accomplishments of the Iowa Job Corps Center. "He kept badgering me, telling me I needed to visit and see what they were doing. So I went, thinking it would be a wasted day. But I found that the staff people truly believed in the program, which trains people and gets them into new jobs." Getting a direct, vivid feel for this Job Corps Center influenced this Top Dog's decision to support the program. Congressman Lightfoot changed his mind after observing the Job Corps operation in his own front yard *and* after a key face-to-face conversation about it.

Using imagery and visualization adds to vividness that can powerfully persuade. In the following examples, simple props such as a coffee can and a plastic bag of sugar dramatically tipped the scales for two underdogs.

THE SUGAR SHOW

As a retired registered dietician from the health department in Lexington, Kentucky, Carolyn Dennis was way ahead of the curve. In 2005, she began persuading elected officials that childhood obesity was an issue that impacted educational outcomes and school behavior, long before it came into vogue. Her task in 2005 was to convince Kentucky State Representative Jimmy Higdon that restricting the sale of high-sugar, high-fat foods in Kentucky schools was good for kids. Carolyn was blazing a trail. Most legislation like this didn't come about until the end of the decade after activist groups had witnessed how other like-minded groups had dealt with "big tobacco" and used those tactics with "big food." Further (and no offense to my Kentucky friends), Kentucky isn't known for its trend-setting legislation; that's usually reserved for California.

The bill was introduced in 2003 but failed to pass in 2003 and 2004 due to strong opposition from the Kentucky Grocers Association, the soft drink industry, and the state's school principals association.

This meant Carolyn had an especially tough persuasion task. Representative Higdon was not only opposed to the bill, he had publicly come out *against* it. He changed his mind. "I had been a strong, vocal opponent of the bill when it was debated in 2003, but she continued to talk to me about it."

In addition to Carolyn Dennis, Higdon heard from others. "I had constituents in my district—ladies who worked in school lunchrooms—who were opposed. I also heard from the Kentucky Grocers Association and lobbyists from the soft drink industry, who were, of course, opposed."

Carolyn decided to use one simple visual tool to boost her persuasiveness. As Higdon remembered it, "Carolyn brought in a Ziploc bag containing eleven and a half cups of sugar—the amount of sugar ingested in one month by someone who drinks one twenty-ounce Coke or Pepsi a day. She also carried a Mountain Dew bottle that was empty except for eighteen teaspoons of sugar, the amount of sugar in one twenty-ounce drink. That was pretty amazing. She told us the average male in Kentucky drank *five* Mountain Dews a day!"

Carolyn's success was amplified because she used proximity—that is, she met with Higdon repeatedly in person. Her adept use of the Ziploc bag of sugar—the main culprit—brought out additional images and advanced her main argument, clearly required for vividness to work.

Research points out that the more emotion your information evokes, the more vivid and persuasive it is—and it can produce unexpected results as the next example shows.

ONE VIVID EXAMPLE VS. SIX YEARS OF STATISTICS

A national expert on child safety issues, Dr. Gary Smith is director of the Center for Injury Research at Nationwide Children's Hospital in Columbus, Ohio. He first became an advocate when he saw the impact that needless childhood accidents had not only on the children and their families, but on the professionals who care for them.

After publishing more than 80 peer-reviewed articles, he realized it was futile to do research, publish articles, and then have them sit on a shelf in a nicely bound journal. Taking his findings out into the world was critical. As he explained, "We call it 'translational research' in our profession. For us, the goal is getting the information back into the community. I try to live that by helping facilitate informed public policy and making it real. I'm surrounded by professionals who do that every day; that are why I love what I do. We know we are making a difference."

Dr. Smith's entry into underdog influence came about through a "normal" day in the ER. He was on a team treating a child who came into the emergency room after a car accident. The child had not been wearing a seat belt. "I was a resident at the time. As the doctor in charge examined this boy, I was holding his head and noticed blood coming out of his ears. I calmly told the doctor that, and he screamed at me: 'Of course! Why do you think that's happening? He's dying, for God's sake!'

"I realized in that riveting moment the sadness and stress that needless accidents bring to the professionals who care for injured children. The doctor was angry at the whole reason this was happening—something so preventable. I know that doctors and nurses really care. With all our skill, training, and technology, sadly, we can't help everyone."

This realization stuck with him. Years later, Dr. Smith became involved in a legislative hurdle in the Ohio legislature as part of a coalition promoting mandatory bike helmets for children. "Of course, there were the usual opponents who questioned whether this was the appropriate role of government versus parental responsibility. In addition, the police were worried about getting a bad reputation by giving tickets to children for not wearing helmets.

"We battled this in three legislative sessions over a six-year period. We had lots of facts and figures to support our position, but in all that time, they weren't compelling enough to move the bill.

"Then in 1990 and 1995, the University of Cincinnati conducted what they call an 'Ohio Poll' on various public policy issues. They surveyed parents and found that seventy-five percent of them throughout the state supported mandatory bike helmets for children. They even segmented it by gender, race, political party, income, and so on. All levels, all segmented groups, supported the initiative. So that helped legislators see we had something that their constituents supported.

"At the district level, the Safe Kids Coalition conducted meetings and petition drives to make it personal and reinforce the message. Everything changed, though, when we had a young man who had been brain damaged as a result of a bike accident come to testify. He'd been riding his bike downhill and had lost control. He fell and struck his head. His parents testified first about how they had literally brought home a stranger from the hospital. Silence in the room. Then this young man spoke before the committee. While he was talking, we could hear the sound of a horn honking outside. That visibly upset and distracted him. He fought hard to regain his concentration as he read his remarks about his personal struggles in halting sentences. Then he talked about trying his best to hold down a job, but found that tremendously difficult. Still, he didn't want government handouts.

"I knew we were making progress when one of the conservative legislators on the side of less government turned to the committee chairman and said, 'Mr. Chairman, in all my years, I have never heard a more moving testimony. Who could vote against this bill?' Finally, we got the bill passed."

Dr. Smith added, "You know, we have crackerjack epidemiologists who can crank out numbers, but having a real person in front of everyone brought it home. You just have to marry the two pieces. Whomever you're trying to persuade has to feel the emotion of your point of view. We'd used facts and figures for five years and gotten nowhere."

YOUR HEART CAN CHANGE YOUR MIND

In another example, former Congressman Ron Mazzoli of Louisville, Kentucky, told about an individual who changed his mind about landmark legislation on which he was initially undecided. Again, he was persuaded by emotionally vivid information.

The Americans with Disabilities Act (ADA), passed in 1990, is a wide-ranging civil rights law that prohibits discrimination based on disability. ADA covers employment, public accommodations, public facilities and transportation, and telecommunications. It affords similar protections against discrimination to Americans with disabilities as the Civil Rights Act of 1964 accomplished, which made discrimination based on race, religion, sex, national origin, and other characteristics illegal.

Congressman Mazzoli was not completely in favor of it. He explained, "At one of my town hall meetings, I saw a man with severe cerebral palsy in a wheelchair. A woman with him held an alphabet board. He eventually came to the front of the meeting hall and pointed to letters on the board. He struggled to point to each letter on the alphabet board, yet was able to request that I vote for the ADA.

"I asked my staff to research the pros and cons on this bill. After that, I became a co-sponsor."

Mazzoli admitted that if he hadn't seen Arthur Campbell face to face (proximity) and experienced his emotionally vivid message, he might not have voted for the bill and would certainly not have been a co-sponsor. Arthur went on to help other disabled people by getting a job at the Center for Accessible Living, an independent living center that provides housing information, peer counseling, personal assistive services, and advocacy for people with disabilities in Kentucky and southern Indiana.

OBSTACLES TO PROXIMITY POWER

In our examples of vivid communications, the first step is to engage proximity—to simply show up, face to face. Indeed, that's how each of our underdogs achieved their influence goal. But if this works so well, why isn't it used more often? In part, because of authority traps.

For one reason, people have a tendency to either fall into or (subconsciously) *fear* falling into what psychologists call "authority traps." The quality of authority is subconsciously signaled by a person's title, type of clothing, height, type of car, and other "trappings of authority," down to the number of carpet tiles in the person's office. Subconsciously (or consciously), we take in these cues. These trappings of power and position subtly say that the person we're talking to is smarter, nicer, wittier, and better than we are. How would he or she have achieved this status otherwise?

Coming into contact with authority cues can suddenly and mysteriously make us less persuasive. No, we don't actually lose our subject knowledge, conviction, or communication skills, but the cues can cause us to *feel* less convincing, even though there's no rationale for it. Clunk. We've fallen into an authority trap.

Psychologists discovered this trap from observing astute, sincere people become not just nervous but almost inept when they tried to "influence up." Let me share a vivid learning moment that demonstrates the power of authority to bring us to our knees.

I was hired by a major insurance company to teach their executives how to persuade their member of Congress to support issues specific to that company. These weren't national issues that affected lots of people but were technical ones that might get a mention in insurance industry trade journals. With little controversy associated with these issues, I assumed this assignment would be fairly easy.

As a part of the event, I was asked to sit in on the meetings between the executives and their Congressional members. But these executives weren't just *any* executives; they were members of the Million Dollar Round Table (MDRT). The Million Dollar Round Table is an international, independent association of more than 31,500 members—a prestigious group making up less than one percent of the world's life insurance and financial services professionals. MDRT members are known for exceptional professional knowledge, strict ethical conduct, and outstanding client service. Implicit from its name, MDRT members sell a lot of financial products, and they aren't shy.

The mission of these particular MDRT members was twofold: first, to thank their elected representatives for their support for legislation that benefited one of their financial services products, and second, to ask for their votes on a highly specific, technical amendment that applied only to their company. And for the meeting I witnessed, the legislator had already publicly committed his support of the amendment, so the MDRT members were simply reinforcing an existing commitment. Plus, they outnumbered the lawmaker three to one!

Naturally, I thought these folks would be able to guide this unsuspecting legislator around on a leash due to their business expertise, but more so because of their natural sales talents. I experienced one of many learning moments when I witnessed the inauspicious start to the meeting. The leader of the group had made his millions selling life insurance and had become an officer in the company in charge of the sales force. This guy possessed both the "street cred" and the organizational clout to make him a persuasive communicator.

Except that he wasn't. As he began to speak, his bottom lip started trembling and his neck gave him away; he was breaking out in hives and we could see them spreading from his neck to his face. I thought, "How can this be happening? This guy sells life insurance, and a lot of it, for God's sake! What's wrong? Get it together and stop breaking out in hives!"

Yet this accomplished, successful leader suddenly lost his skills—and possibly some brain cells—in the presence of a person of position and power. He'd fallen into the authority trap.

WHY DO WE FALL INTO THE TRAP?

Whether it is requesting a raise, presenting a new project, interviewing for the big job, or asking for someone's vote, it's common to mysteriously lose our ability to communicate with confidence when faced with a person of higher authority. Research shows that in these situations, we subconsciously react in ways that sabotage our autonomy. Here are two examples:

- Researchers arranged for a man to violate the law and jaywalk on a busy city street. Half of the time, he dressed in a traditional business suit; the rest of the time, he wore "business casual" attire. The researchers counted the number of people who followed him across the street. They observed a 350 percent increase in the number of people who followed him when he was wearing a business suit from the number who followed him when he was dressed in casual attire. Clothing can be an authority trap.[50]

- Communication researchers found that people often subconsciously shift their vocal tone and speech to be in sync with those they perceive to be in authority. One study analyzing interviews on CNN television's "Larry King Live" show found that King adjusted his vocal style when talking to people such as Bill Clinton, George Bush, and Barbara Streisand. Yet when interviewing people of lower status (at least in his eyes)—including Dan Quayle, Spike Lee, and Julie Andrews—he kept his normal vocal style. In fact, the vocal styles of the interviewees actually shifted to match his![51]

Whether out of fear of disapproval or deference to someone's real or apparent authority, we tend to lose our own self-confidence in the presence of a person who seems to have more of it than we do.

To make matters even more difficult, most underdog influencers usually meet on the top dog's turf (translation: big office, gatekeeper, business suit, extravagant furnishings, and other cues of authority). Many of our underdogs meet their influence target in a state capitol or Capitol Hill office to make their cases. The architecture of most state capitols is Greek Revival or neoclassical style, built more for the gods the Greeks worshipped than the common folks. Often grand marble statues lord it over our underdogs as they walk into these grandiose buildings. A bit intimidating, to say the least.

Overcome the Obstacles

How can you avoid the power of the authority trap? Let's consider three actions that have worked for others: (1) getting out of your own head; (2) letting duty motivate you; (3) sticking your neck out a little at a time.

Get Out of Your Own Head

Because the authority trap is based on fear made up in your head (even though it may be subconscious), you can get out of your head where the fear resides by focusing elsewhere.

Some researchers use the term "hyper self-awareness" to describe the dynamic of being too focused on yourself. If you're performing a task you don't feel expert in, the anxiety of being in a new situation or around new people creates a loss of confidence and a drop-off in communication skills. So calm down and resist the drain of authority traps. Emulate successful underdog influencers and think less about yourself and more about the position you've come to champion.

Let Duty Motivate You

I've heard that "courage is fear that has said its prayers." Kathleen McGowan, writing in *Psychology Today*, profiled several people who demonstrated face-to-face courage. She concluded that the courage to confront is not about fearlessness but about duty. A sense of duty forces people to take action who otherwise would not.[52] McGowan provided the example of Kenneth Pedeleose.

Kenneth Pedeleose was an analyst at the Defense Contract Management Agency, which monitors federal military contracts where he oversaw contracts. He was concerned about the high prices for spare parts, such as $714 for rivets and $5,217 for brackets, as well as serious safety violations on projects. In fact, he and other engineers signed the reports to members of Congress who made decisions about military operations.

Pedeleose said he was sickened by what he saw and couldn't let the safety violations go unreported because he would have been, in part, responsible for a plane crashing. He was in the position to affect change and had the knowledge to call attention to what he witnessed. He was not honored for his whistle-blowing; rather he was suspended twice in four years and had to fight to get back pay. He estimated that he's spent 2,000 hours over the years uncovering fraud and abuse and defending himself against backlash. How did he get the courage to speak out?

"Bravery played into it, but I calculated my arguments so I had a high chance of success," he explained. "It means more when you can prove what you are saying."[53] His story illuminated a widely misunderstood truth about courage. It's motivated not by fearlessness but by a strong sense of duty.[54]

STICK YOUR NECK OUT
A LITTLE AT A TIME

Todd Kashdan, a psychologist at George Mason University, stated, "Being courageous is really a large number of moments in which, in the face of feeling uncomfortable, you still went forward."[55] Set up small behavioral experiments for yourself, he suggested. "We spend so much time experimenting with foods, with different ways to organize our houses, and so little time experimenting with all the ways we can act as a person."[56]

So if you are challenged with being more vivid, try sticking your neck out a little at a time. Soon you'll be comfortable with courage.

THE UNDERDOG'S CHECKLIST
Becoming More Vivid

✓ Meet with your top dog face to face. Remember, this is a tactic that every one of our underdogs used. Not one of them persuaded using remote influence tactics. Memorize the seven "proximity power" advantages and engage them.

✓ Use vivid images to help your top dog visualize and understand what you want to get across.

✓ Make it proximate (relevant to their lives) so they care enough to take action. Do your examples and stories happen in or near your top dog's "front yard"?

✓ Be sure your vivid examples and stories advance your main theme and aren't irrelevant details. Being imagery-provoking, emotional, and proximate means nothing if you're not supporting your main theme.

✓ Recognize authority traps for what they are and realize they don't magically decrease your knowledge or ability to persuade.

✓ Stop thinking about yourself and what others think about you and instead focus on your mission so you can calm your nerves and escape authority traps.

✓ Feel a motivating sense of duty about what you're trying to accomplish and whom you're helping by getting agreement from your top dog.

✓ Go forward and stick your neck out in uncomfortable ways until you're comfortable being courageous.

CHAPTER 4

Extreme Influence Tactic #3:
Get Grit

"Nobody ever drowned in his own sweat."

— Ann Landers

"My skill is being unstoppable. Most people would give up. But not me. I could see myself doing it for the rest of my life."

— Kate Hanni

"You get committed to your cause, but then discouraged because more powerful people come behind you, so you just have to be persistent."

— Frank Amend

"I never thought about giving up."

— Bob Benham

"We heard people whisper outside the committee hearing room that they were surprised that we alarm guys really thought that we could take on Ameritech."

> — *Bob Bonifas*

"I always thought, 'There is a way to reach this person.' It's just figuring out which approach works best. And persevering."

> — *Carolyn Dennis*

Underdog persuasion consists of more than one conversation, one email, or one meeting. Underdog influencers don't become discouraged easily. Their work is neither instant nor glamorous. It's gritty. Know it, stow it, show it, sow it. There are many disciplines on the road to underdog influence, but the road of grit has no detour.

For the record, here's how long it took some of our underdogs to change the minds of their prospects:

Bob Benham – 120 meetings (and counting) and "countless" phone calls

Bob Bonifas – 100 meetings in Washington, D.C.

John Boyd – 26 years

Patrice Dell – two years

Kim Delevett – four years and 18 meetings

Kate Hanni – four years and over 300 meetings

Amy Kremer – 53 tea parties

Vince Larsen – three years

Brad Neet – one year

Cathy Pickett – four years

Dr. Gary Smith – six years

Bob Stone – two years and two months

Joel Ulland – two years

Dona Wells – 16 meetings

The advice to persevere is nothing new. In 1869, Francis Galton published "Hereditary Genius," his investigation into the factors underlying achievement. His method was basic: He gathered as much data as possible on dozens of men with "very high reputations." His sample included poets, politicians, and scientists. He noticed that success wasn't a matter of just intelligence or talent. He summarized that achievement was only possible when "ability is combined with zeal and the *capacity for hard labour.*" That's the zinger—hard labor. The research on why prodigies fail finds that, with many, success comes too easily. They are ill prepared for what happens when the adoration goes away, their competitors catch up, and their progress is thwarted.

What's new is that researchers are finding that Galton's "capacity for hard labour" must be *directed*, and directed for more than the time it takes to update a Facebook page. It's not about positive *thinking*, it's about positive *doing*…and doing and doing and doing.

University of Pennsylvania psychologist Angela Duckworth became intrigued by the science of achievement after observing how her college classmates fared once out of their Harvard enclave. She noticed that the most successful people in her Harvard class chose a goal and stuck with it while others just flitted from vocation to vocation. She found that the less successful graduates were just as smart and talented as the high-achievers, but they often changed course to do new things without sticking long enough at any one area to become really good at it.

When Duckworth returned to school to earn her Ph.D., she approached Dr. Martin Seligman, the father of the positive psychology movement and director of the University of Pennsylvania's Positive Psychology Center, to investigate achievement. She interviewed high achievers in fields from investment banking to journalism, medicine, and art. What did she find? That *tenacity* was just as important as smarts. "Certainly a fair number of people were brilliant, ambitious, and persevering," she said. "But a lot were not geniuses in any way—just really tenacious."[57]

While grit lives in the same mental neighborhood as motivation and self-discipline, it's on a distinct property—and not many researchers have driven down that lane.

One of the main challenges for scientists trying to document the influence of personality traits on achievement was the vague standard definition of traits. Duckworth wondered if traits that are more precise would be more predictive. Her research on high achievers focused on aspects of conscientiousness that have to do with long-term stamina, such as maintaining a consistent set of interests. It downplayed aspects of the trait related to short-term self control, such as staying on a diet. In other words, a person with grit might eat too many M & Ms now and then, but won't change careers every year. "Grit is very much about the big picture," explained Duckworth.

After developing a survey to measure this narrowly defined trait (which you can take at www.sas.upenn.edu/~duckwort/images/17-item%20Grit%20and%20 Ambition.040709.pdf), Duckworth set out to test the relevance of grit. Initial evidence suggested that measurements of grit can often be just as predictive of success, if not more, than measurements of intelligence. For instance, in a 2007 study of 175 finalists in the Scripps National Spelling Bee, Duckworth found that her simple grit survey was better at predicting whether or not a child would make the final round than an IQ score.[58]

She also found that among more than 3,500 participants attending nine different colleges, task follow-through was a better predictor than all other variables (including SAT scores and high school ranking) of whether a student would achieve a leadership position in college. Follow-through was also the single best predictor of significant accomplishment in science, art, sports, communications, organization, or other endeavours.[59]

You'd think that the cadets at West Point would be naturally gritty, wouldn't you? They're among the best and brightest in their high school classes, and they survived the competitive admissions process. Although West Point admission is highly selective, approximately five percent of cadets still drop out after the first summer of training, known as "Beast Barracks."

The U.S. Army has searched for the variables that best predict whether cadets will graduate, using everything from SAT scores to physical fitness tests. But it wasn't until Duckworth tested the cadets of the 2008 West Point class using a questionnaire with statements such as "setbacks don't discourage me" that the Army found a measurement that worked well. Duckworth has repeated the survey with subsequent West Point classes, and the result is always the same: The cadets that "make it" are those measuring high on the grit scale.[60]

"I bet there isn't a single highly successful person who hasn't depended on grit," stated Duckworth. "Nobody is talented enough to not have to work hard, and that's what having grit allows you to do. Maybe it's more fun to try something new, but high levels of achievement require a certain single-mindedness."[61]

Author Jonah Lehrer took a similar view of grit in his article for The Boston Globe, "The Truth About Grit." He wrote, "It's about picking a specific goal off in the distant future and not swerving from it."[62]

Dr. Martin Seligman noted that gritty people are more likely to meet their goals than others because they're resilient when setbacks occur. "Unless you're a genius," he said, "I don't think you can ever do better than your competitors without a quality like grit."[63]

NO GRIT, NO GLORY

This research reminded me of a gut reaction I had after the 2008 election. President-elect Barack Obama's campaign team announced that his massive campaign volunteer corps would become Organizing for America (OFA) and maintain the campaign momentum by pressuring members of Congress to support Obama's agenda. Maybe it's because I'm blessed to teach "black belt" varsity grassroots team members across the country that I sensed this effort, although innovative and intriguing, might not meet its expectations. From what I observed, many (not all) of the fervent Obama supporters didn't have what the most impressive underdogs I've known possess: grit. As the Chinese military proverb reminds us: "The more we sweat in training, the less we bleed in battle."

Sweating develops grit. Among Obama's supporters, I just didn't smell a lot of sweating that would translate into upward influence later. In observations featured in Politico, I wrote that maintaining a Facebook page for Obama, going to a town hall meeting or rally, or asking a friend to vote for Obama, was decidedly different than persuading a powerful member of Congress (who may be philosophically opposed to Obama's agenda) to vote for his position.[64] I suspected that, while a devoted following would indeed "show up" in the influence game, many of his supporters wouldn't have the fortitude for the industrial-strength persuasion that's required with members of Congress.

Fast forward to a National Public Radio broadcast on March 16, 2010. The topic? "Can Obama's Grass Roots Sway Midterm Elections?" The consensus of insiders such as Steve Rosenthal, a veteran grassroots organizer who was once the political director of the AFL-CIO, and other volunteer team leaders conformed to what I had predicted. They concluded that the same degree of enthusiasm for candidate Barack Obama had not translated into influencing members of Congress.

In March 2010, Mara Liasson of NPR reported that many of Organizing for America's (OFA) volunteers have had a hard time convincing even their neighbors to support Obama's agenda as president.

> Donna Miller was a team leader for the Obama campaign in Wisconsin. When the campaign morphed into Organizing for America, she stuck with it. Her experience illustrates why, even when OFA has field staff and volunteers on the ground, it's become harder to energize the president's supporters.
>
> "Part of that has to do with expectations," Miller says, adding, "A lot of people just had really, really high expectations that things could be done really, really quickly and happen overnight. And they're finding out that the process of politics is pretty ugly."
>
> Nothing looked uglier to some of the new Obama voters than the push to pass health care legislation.
>
> It wasn't just that the legislative process looked too much like politics as usual. It was also that it didn't deliver. Rosenthal says that also disillusioned Obama's core supporters and made it harder for OFA to motivate them.
>
> "Some of it's been watching Congress spend a year debating health care and still seeing nothing happen," Rosenthal says. "So for most Americans, if

you spent a year on the job and didn't have anything to show for it at the end of the year, you probably wouldn't be working in that job for very long."[65]

The revealing phrase in Rosenthal's comment is "for most Americans." Our underdogs have spent years working toward their goals undaunted. *They aren't like most Americans.* Contrast them with the de-motivated Obama adherents who, after just one year of debate on a "little" issue like health care reform, became de-motivated. No grit, no glory.

While volunteering for Obama's campaign, did the OFA members suffer much hardship? Probably some made sacrifices and had obstacles to overcome, but I'd guess the majority did not. It looked like they had a lot of fun at those rallies. One volunteer viewed her experience this way: "Oh, my goodness; I'm sitting around a lot of people that I have so much in common with, especially politically, and I'm just forming bonds…bonds that I really feel will last a lifetime." Simone Simpson of Las Vegas said the experience took her back to her youthful days at Camp Cedar Point.[66] Simone and others attended Camp Obama, a campaign volunteer training "camp" geared toward young volunteers, which brings up a piece of the grit puzzle—youth.

As you will see later in this chapter, *unless one has experienced early loss*, youth naturally renders less grit than older folks do. And we know that Obama cornered the youth voter market. So it's not terribly surprising that his most ardent followers during the campaign haven't shown up in the same way in the struggle to influence the big dogs in Congress.

Before you become violent with me, I'm not saying that all young people don't experience hardship and thus don't possess grit. I'm saying that, all else being equal, those who've struggled have grit, and depending on how they processed their hardships, they will achieve more than those who've had it easy. It's just that hardship keeps showing up as you get older, so when you do the math, older individuals are likely to have more tenacity and perseverance than younger people. Remember, one of the prerequisites of "grit" is hardship and strife. While you may not want to join the adversity club, evidence reveals that it creates grit, an element of underdog achievement.

Let's look at a few examples of underdogs who displayed grit. Then we'll dig into how grit is developed.

THINK CONGRESS IS A HARD SELL?
TRY THE MILITARY

One of the institutions perhaps least amenable to underdog influence would be the U.S. military. While it's known for fantastic innovations in technology and operations management, those changes have to come through a chain of command; they typically don't come through underdogs.

The military environment can create people who are afraid to propose new ideas—that is, if you fail to obey orders, you and possibly your team can be penalized. Sometimes those penalties linger throughout your career and limit advancement. Your transgressions follow you. So while the military does embrace innovation, the path to innovation is rocky and reserved for the intrepid.

Undeterred by this perception, Bob Stone undertook a two-year campaign to modernize the nation's military installations. Bob had flunked out of MIT but was later re-admitted and went on to obtain his master's degree in chemical engineering. His most recent accomplishment is being named to management guru Tom Peter's list of the "Top 41 Entrepreneurs of the Decade" for his role in reforming the management of U.S. military bases.

The following story includes excerpts from Bob's book, *Confessions of a Civil Servant: Lessons in Changing America's Government and Military* (used with permission) and email correspondence with Bob.[67]

Bob served 24 years in the Department of Defense, concluding his career as Deputy Assistant Secretary of Defense. His role was to oversee base operations and put together a budget for construction, which at the time was five percent of the defense budget.

In describing the environment that made change difficult, Bob said, "You know the five-hundred-dollar ashtray everyone has heard about? It cost that much because we had to make one that was theft-proof. The previous model actually had a cool logo, which made it very desirable. People would steal it from the planes.

"So many policies, laws, and regulations existed that people were behaving with apparent insanity. The people who made the deal for the five-hundred-dollar ashtray were fired, but they were rehired when it was discovered they were just following orders.

"Other examples of craziness arose from the bases. The safety czars at the Pentagon required Army recruits to take a military driving test and get a military driver's license even though they'd all gotten state licenses when they turned sixteen. That rule had been under attack since 1964 but never was addressed until our Model Installation Program was initiated.

"Every base had a 'self-help store,' a military Home Depot of sorts, where all the materials were free. Staff could take out materials on loan and return them. The inspector general wrote up a four-star general for violating a rule that prohibited power tools from being lent to the military. Mind you, these people are trusted with bombs and machine guns, but not power tools.

"My favorite crazy rule required painters on the tank repair line at the Anniston, Alabama, Army Depot to get written approval from the base chemist before using a can of spray paint that was past its shelf 'pull date.' The chemist applied a computer-generated label that stated that the can had been 'revalidated.' This rule broadcast to all who heard it that they were expected to check their brains at the door when they came to work.

"More than just crazy rules, the Pentagon system seemed designed to ensure that people in the field who knew what needed to be done couldn't act until they'd gotten permission from people in Washington, D.C., who didn't have a clue. Jim Eddings, the base civil engineer at Kirtland Air Force Base in Albuquerque, New Mexico, saw some leaky roofs and wanted to have them repaired before they deteriorated or damaged material stored inside. But he had to get approval from the deputy assistant secretary of the Air Force, who had no way of knowing whether the roofs needed repair except from what Eddings told him."

Crushed Morale

Bob believed that inefficiencies like these had crushed the spirit and output of the three million people who lived and worked on military bases. He became inspired to start a campaign after reading Tom Peters's book *In Search of Excellence.* His goals? To make the U.S. military installations places where commanders could have more autonomy in decision making and create a culture where the troops felt comfortable—beyond the current standard of "minimum acceptable level of comfort and quality." (And yes, that's accurate.)

This type of change would require nothing less than a cultural earthquake.

The woeful state of the military and troop morale had become such a major issue in the 1980 election that the new Reagan administration had rushed through the biggest military pay raise in years, along with billions of dollars to increase readiness. But, as Bob recalled, "The 'minimum essential' culture still ruled the Pentagon, especially in the offices of the comptroller and the inspector general."

During the next two years, he presented his case to Pentagon insiders to no avail. "The Department of Defense was focused inward—on doing what the secretary of defense and the House and Senate committee chairs wanted. Their focus was like bees protecting the queen bee. They didn't care what was going on outside the hive; just 'protect the queen!'"

Time to Use Underdog Tactics

Bob then traveled to the military bases one by one to find out what the Pentagon could learn from the base commanders. "When I was traveling to the bases, it was obvious the base commanders were the cream of the crop. Highly educated, they had received many promotions. But, culturally, everything in the military is headquarters-focused. People read what the Secretary of Defense is doing. From the time they are brought in, they learn from the mentor's knee not to make anyone higher up look bad, so they don't want to expose anything. Whenever a new problem surfaced," explained Bob, "the drones put out new restrictions to protect the queen bee from these blights."

He also realized that no matter how sensible this initiative was, as he put it, "There was only one little thing in our way: I didn't control any installation. The military commanders did, and they didn't trust the Office of the Secretary of Defense one bit." Bob had to go on the road and sell his program to four-star generals. He needed their agreement to establish a model installation at one of their bases.

Selling to the four-star generals proved difficult for several reasons. "They had a general mistrust of the Office of the Secretary of Defense, my predecessor had a terrible history, and there was a real worry on their part. They thought I had a scheme to take over all the bases, find one single best way to operate them, and then mandate that all bases operate in exactly the same way."

They also wanted to see if one of their colleagues, Air Force General Bill Creech, was on board. If he were in favor, then the other branches would probably play along. (As you'll read in Chapter 6, Building Your Pack, there's usually one pack member who can accelerate your cause. General Bill Creech was that person for Bob Stone.)

"Creech had massive credibility. He was the creator of the biggest turnaround in the military since Grant, or at least since MacArthur. He was the natural leader of the Air Force, although he was never made chief of staff because of, I believe, procurement politics."

Upon Creech's death in 2003, General John P. Jumper, Chief of Staff of the Air Force, said, "No single officer has had greater influence on the Air Force in recent times than General Bill Creech. He transformed the way the Air Force conducts warfare."

Creech turned around the languishing Tactical Air Command and oversaw the development of much of today's modern air weaponry, including the F-117 stealth fighter. A former Thunderbird pilot of the 1950s, he also was known as "The Father of the Thunderbirds" for rescuing the Air Force's aerial demonstration team from a congressional chopping block after four of its pilots were killed on January 18, 1982, near Indian Springs while on a training exercise.

Bob met with Creech, and the general loved the idea. "When Creech came on board, the others followed." After doing his homework, Bob was ready to present the Model Installation Program to the Deputy Secretary of Defense, William Howard Taft IV.

As previously noted, underdogs have to use different tactics than their high-powered associates. One of Bob's tactics was as simple as wearing a baseball cap. "Taft had an informal council with a highly bureaucratic name, the Defense Council on Integrity and Management Improvement on the Model Installation Program. Meetings usually included a series of mind-numbing briefings. I wanted the audience to be wide awake for my briefing and to remember it. So, we created a baseball cap with the Department of Defense's logo. Emblazoned on the logo was 'Excellent Installations: the Foundation of Defense.' I was told that if I wore that cap to the briefing, Taft would never forget it. I think this was a first for the Pentagon."

During the meeting, Bob told Taft about the "craziness from the bases." He explained that "government-issue reflective vests cost twenty dollars, but base commanders could buy them locally for a dollar twenty-nine each."

Taft's controller, who outranked Bob by two levels, was not impressed. "We can't manage by anecdote. These are anecdotes," he observed.

"Oh, but what wonderful anecdotes they are," Taft replied.

From that point on, Taft became Bob's "godfather and protector." As Bob explained, "He saw me as someone who would bring good publicity to the department. In fact, major newspapers commended Taft's leadership, stating that he was 'bringing common sense to the Pentagon.'" And Bob won approval to establish the Model Installation Program.

Bob Stone's grit helped transform the U.S. military and, in turn, the morale of thousands of troops. In 1986, David Packard, chairman of the President's Blue Ribbon Commission on Defense Management, wrote this in his final report to the president:

> Despite formidable bureaucratic obstacles, I believe that a center of excellence approach can tangibly improve productivity and quality...By according installations commanders much greater latitude to run things their own way, cut through red tape, and experiment with new ways of accomplishing their mission, commanders and their personnel have found more effective means to do their jobs, identified wasteful regulations, and reduced costs while improving quality. The program has shown the increased defense capability that comes by freeing talented people from overregulation and unlocking their native creativity and enthusiasm."[68]

Later in this chapter, you'll see how to develop grit. However, some people naturally have more grit than others, largely due to difficult experiences they probably wish they hadn't had.

ADVERSITY DEVELOPS GRIT

Researchers have found that prior hardship is required for displaying grit later in life. The University of Virginia's Jonathan Haidt has argued that adversity and setbacks are necessary to lead a happy, fulfilled life. He called it "post-traumatic growth."

J.K. Rowling, author of the Harry Potter books, told a class at Harvard, "Failure stripped away everything inessential. It taught me things about myself I could have learned no other way." She was newly divorced and could barely support her daughter, but she committed to her dream of becoming a published novelist. In 1994, while her daughter slept, Rowling would plop her in the stroller and wheel her to the nearest café to get a few quiet moments to write about the boy wizard. You know the rest of the story. Rowling once received welfare payments, but her wealth now exceeds the Queen of England's. She ranks #937 on *Forbes'* list of the world's richest people.

Systematic studies of highly successful individuals reveal that a history of hindrances are the *rule* rather than the exception. Researchers at the Cass Business School in England found that entrepreneurs are five times more likely to suffer from dyslexia than the average citizen. Virgin Atlantic mogul and adventurer Richard Branson has dyslexia; so does real estate nabob Barbara Corcoran.

"My entire career has been one long attempt to prove to the world once and for all that I am not stupid," said Corcoran, who turned a $1,000 loan into an eponymous real estate empire that she sold 25 years later (in 2001) for $70 million. "As pleased as I am for my success in the moment, I'm still thinking I've got to prove something." Her childhood home was happy, but school was not. Being dyslexic, she didn't read until seventh grade. "I don't think you ever heal the wounds of your deficits as a kid, but [my wound] has been my greatest advantage."[69]

Sometimes Adversity Sparks Unexpected Power

Kate Hanni is the quasar of our underdog stars. She was a top-shelf realtor in the Napa Valley, having sold more than $40 million in real estate in 2005. While working as a real estate agent, she was showing a house to a prospective buyer. The "buyer" threatened to rape and kill her. He fled after she told him her son's father had died several years before, pleading, "If you kill me, my son will have no parents and will kill himself." Hanni said she funneled what she learned from that adversity into starting what has become one of the largest nonprofit consumer rights organizations in the country—that is, changing how customers get treated by the airline industry.

How and why did this come about?

On December 29, 2006, Kate was stranded on the tarmac in a small jet. *For nine hours.* According to Hanni, during the long wait, she began psychologically unraveling, flashing back to the attempted sexual assault. She remembered that her therapist urged her to confront her fears. Today, she credits that ordeal with helping her "deal with those fears in an amazing and transformative way." The ordeal of being stranded "riveted in my mind how horrible the feeling of powerlessness is," she said. "In a different but still important way, being stranded on an airplane for a long time is being powerless, and I decided, at least in this case, I could do something about it."[70]

While she was stuck, Hanni began collecting phone numbers of fellow passengers. After the nine-hour ordeal concluded, she started calling fellow passengers as soon as she got to her destination. She and 40 of the people among the 138 stranded passengers drafted a passengers' bill of rights, and she asked her congressional representative, Mike Thompson, D-CA, to sponsor the legislation. To support the effort, Hanni's husband, Tim, started a stranded passengers blog—http:// strandedpassengers.blogspot.com.

Hanni's work became super-charged on February 14, 2007. Amid a severe ice storm in New York, thousands of airline passengers became trapped for as long as 11 hours on grounded jets at New York's John F. Kennedy International Airport. Most of the stranded jets were operated by JetBlue Airways. The Valentine's Day fiasco at Kennedy fueled weeks of television and newspaper headlines as well as Congressional hearings. Hanni was featured prominently in the media frenzy, and the coalition's rolls exploded from 3,500 members to 12,500 members.

With the support of more disgruntled passengers, the coalition gathered stories from troubled travelers—each more horrific than the last.

"Who can ever forget the Dog Poop Plane?" Hanni asked. That was the flight on which a panicked dog defecated on a stranger in the next seat. Also legendary is the Barf-Bag Flight during which a woman, ill after hours of confinement, threw up into a vomit bag and was angrily told by a flight attendant to hold the bag because she had no place to discard it. "As hours go by," explained Hanni, "lavatories become filthy and in some cases reach capacity. On one flight, waste overflowed onto the feet of nearby passengers. One unfortunate lady was wearing flip-flops."[71]

After collecting and cataloging stories, the coalition successfully convinced members of Congress to introduce a new Passengers' Bill of Rights. A rule enacted in December of 2009—it took effect in late April 2010—now allows passengers to deplane from stranded domestic flights after three hours.

Founded One of the Largest Non-Profit Consumer Travel Organizations

Today, with more than 27,500 members, FlyersRights.org is the largest nonprofit consumer organization in the United States representing airline passengers. Kate's efforts have garnered tremendous recognition. She's received prestigious industry honors, including:

- 2010 Huffington Post's #1 game changer in travel

- 2009 Forbes/Conde Nast trailblazer

- 2008 Forbes Executive Woman (named among the top 25 most influential executive women in travel)

- 2007 Nielsen Business Ratings (named among the top 25 most influential people in travel)

- 2007 Travel Weekly (named among the top 33 most influential people in travel)

In a four-year period, Kate has given more than 3,000 interviews to national print and broadcast media representatives. Hardly a day goes by that Kate or FlyersRights.org isn't quoted by a major media outlet. Indeed, no story about stranded flyers has been written since then without commentary from Kate Hanni. (You'll find more details at http://www.katehanni.com)

Hanni credits Ed Mierzwinski, consumer program director of the U.S. Public Interest Research Group (PIRG), with helping her make connections in Congress. But she definitely had to show grit to get *his* attention. She made an appointment to see Mierzwinski at U.S. PIRG's D.C. offices, but the first meeting didn't go well. He didn't take her seriously, she was sure. He informed her that PIRG could do little to help the coalition and said that, "the most we can do for you is send out a letter to Congress," she recalled. Yet Kate proved to be an intrepid Underdog. She followed up with Mierzwinski by email and sought his advice on how to handle new developments. "Within a month, he started letting me use an office there," she noted. Hanni has come to consider Mierzwinski her mentor.

I interviewed Ed Mierzwinski, the formerly skeptical consumer program director at the U.S. PIRG, and asked him about Kate's evolution from underdog to leader of a movement.

"It's really quite simple," Ed replied, recalling her grit. "Kate was working on passenger rights, which I'd long felt was an important issue, but no one else was working on it, and we didn't have the resources to tackle it. Also, she was passionate and committed and entrepreneurial, and she wouldn't take no for an answer from anyone. Basically, I thought Kate had the potential to win and that her issue was important to consumers.

"Remember, Lois Gibbs was once a housewife who started by herself, organized her neighbors, and successfully fought the state of New York bureaucracy and the Hooker Chemical toxic legacy of the Love Canal. Now, more than twenty years later, she runs a highly successful anti-toxics coalition.

"Four years ago, Kate and her coalition families were just victims of a lack of passenger rights—and now she's the leader of a movement that's made great strides toward reform. I see parallels. She's figuring out that you need to be a long-distance runner, not a sprinter, to win in this town. That's an important thing to know!"

Hanni's grit has enabled her to face the reality of her battle. The exhilaration of the last four years has been balanced by the knowledge that those opposing the bill had more money, experience, and power than her coalition and its allies. Since the beginning of her campaign, she made more than 60 trips to the East Coast raising funds from coalition members. In 2007, she raised $50,000 for air travel, expenses, and the salaries of two part-time staffers.

Being in the Public Eye Requires More Grit

The media attention she's gleaned has had some frightening consequences. Kate had to contend with five stalkers, including a cab driver "who fell in love with my hands." He started calling after the *San Francisco Chronicle* published a story about Hanni featuring photographs of her hands.

Even my interview with Hanni kept getting interrupted. She had to file a report with a law enforcement officer because her family's computer had been hacked into. She later filed a lawsuit against Delta Air Lines and an aviation consulting firm for hacking into her email and personal computer. Hanni made these allegations in a lawsuit and is seeking $11 million.

In August 2009, Hanni discovered the hacking, which involved thousands of emails dating to June 2008. Some emails were stolen and other materials on Hanni's computer were damaged. Her PC and America Online email account were both accessed illegally, with AOL and Microsoft support technicians confirming the breaches, said her attorney, Jason Gibson.

A consulting firm in Dulles, Virginia, called Metron Aviation was also named as a defendant in the suit. Gibson said Hanni and a former Metron employee were communicating via email about data collected regarding airport and airline delays. According to the lawsuit, Metron confronted that employee in September and said Delta—a client of the firm's—was angry he'd been working with Hanni. In that discussion, the employee was shown copies of his emails with Hanni, which had been sent from a Delta email account. The Metron employee got fired. He plans to file a separate wrongful termination lawsuit in Virginia, according to Gibson.

Kate's family, including her wine consultant husband, Tim, and their children, have made sacrifices. For example, the family took out a $200,000 line of credit on their Napa home to pay bills so she could work full time on this campaign.

Another of Kate's sacrifices has been giving up time with her rock band, the Toasted Heads. In the midst of all this, she did rewrite the lyrics to the 1965 Animals' hit song "We Gotta Get Out of This Place," turning it into a theme song for stranded passengers.

ADVERSITY + LOSS = INDUSTRIAL-STRENGTH GRIT

In addition to adversity, researchers have found that early loss can be a common grit instigator. Loss of health, enterprise, loved ones, opportunity—all of these represent hardships requiring perseverance.

John Boyd is a fourth generation Virginia chicken and soybean farmer. Like Hanni, Boyd experienced his share of adversity, and he has also experienced loss. Those two dark occurrences create industrial-strength grit. Today, Boyd continues to influence up to obtain what could be one of the largest civil rights settlements in history.

In 1995, Boyd founded the National Black Farmers Association (NBFA)—now having more than 94,000 members—with its national office located in a small room at the front of Boyd's farmhouse. From there, and on numerous trips to Capitol Hill, he has persuaded previously disengaged members of Congress to support legislation for his cause. What is it? He wants to ensure that African American farmers who file settlement claims against the government for lending discrimination receive payment for damages.

Boyd can trace his family line as far back as the founding of the small towns around South Hill, Virginia. His father was raised on a farm with 12 brothers and sisters; his grandfather, Thomas, also farmed the land; his great-grandfather was born a slave on the Boyd plantation just outside of South Hill.

Where did John Boyd get his grit? "Frankly, it started from a personal interest," admitted Boyd. "But now I advocate for the farmers who didn't get what they deserve."

Here's his story, gleaned from my interview with Boyd and from a *Washington Post* article titled "A Quest to Be Heard."[72]

"When I was 28 and my farm was nearing foreclosure, I applied to the U.S. Department of Agriculture for operating loans. Year after year, they were denied or delayed. A white farm service loan officer literally tore up my application in my face and started cursing at me. I noticed he chewed tobacco and had a tobacco spittoon not far from his desk.

"I looked at him and said, 'You're not going to process my application, are you?' He didn't answer me, but he spit tobacco on my shirt. At that point, I felt like less than a man. I couldn't hit him; I knew what would happen to a black man hitting a white federal employee.

"That took me to my lowest point," said Boyd. When he went home, his wife asked if they got the loan. "I had to tell her no and that broke up our family. We argued about the farm and our debts. That's what people don't realize, Amy. This tears up families."

Boyd told his wife he refused to let the farm go, but to no avail. "Our marriage fell apart and the government then started seizing my land," he said. An employee from the United States Department of Agriculture (USDA) drove a "For Sale" sign in his yard. Boyd took his chain saw and sliced the sign in half, but his anger didn't lessen the threat of foreclosure.[73]

During the 1980s, he watched as some black farmers began a movement to persuade the USDA to engage in equitable lending practices, but it didn't make progress. In 1997, Timothy Pigford, a black farmer from North Carolina, filed a class action lawsuit against the USDA, alleging that between 1983 and 1997, the agency systematically treated black farmers unfairly in its decisions to allocate price support loans, disaster payments, operating loans, and farm ownership loans. Then Secretary of Agriculture Dan Glickman was the defendant.

The government settled in 1999 for $50,000 for each claimant. However, thousands of other black farmers were unaware of the *Pigford v. Glickman* class-action lawsuit and missed the filing deadline, and the USDA disqualified thousands of other farmers. John led the effort, known as the Black Farmers Late Claim Bill, to ensure that some 80,000 black farmers would receive compensation.

Since then, other farmers have pushed to reopen the case because they missed deadlines for filing. About 70,000 said they didn't know that a settlement for damages was even available.

"I received my settlement, but discrimination ruins lives. It brought out the burn in me." That's why John Boyd became an Underdog Influencer.

One day in 2000, John drove three and a half hours to Washington, D.C. to find legislators who would meet with him. A week later he went again, and again the week after that. Over the next eight and a half years, Boyd continued his fight.

"I've had very few formal, scheduled meetings. I know where the legislators go. I know when they're going to vote, and there's only one way to get there and that's through this damn tunnel. So, I'd hang out in the tunnel breezeway and I catch them there. In fact, that's where I caught then Senator Obama and Senator Joe Biden, believe it or not. Obama urged me to keep speaking out on this issue."

Grit Bears More Fruit

Boyd explained how he not only scored a victory but made a champion out of U.S. Senator Blanche Lincoln, who was previously on the fence concerning his cause. "Senator Blanche Lincoln of Arkansas was undecided on the proposal to include money in the budget ensuring that African American farmers who filed settlement claims would receive the money they're entitled to as a part of the 2008 Farm Bill. She has a lot of farmers in her state affected by this—a couple thousand. I had hard numbers to back that up. These are real people—the deacon in the local church and others. These people vote.

"My goal was to get her support. If she couldn't support it, I wanted her to reach out to Agriculture Secretary Tom Vilsack for his support. I was very laid back. I didn't press her. I didn't tell her I'd picket her if she didn't support us.

"I kept following up with staff and developed relationships with the gatekeepers because I know they have the representatives' ears. I went back to Lincoln's staff six or seven times over a couple of months. The only thing I asked for was to let me know honestly whether they were a thumbs up or a thumbs down on the legislation."

Not only did Boyd gain Senator Lincoln's support, but on August 12, 2009, Lincoln co-sponsored legislation to ensure settlements for African American farmers who filed claims as a result of the 2008 Farm Bill.

Boyd and his association were successful in convincing President Obama to include $1.25 billion for black farmers in his 2010 budget to settle claims against the USDA, one of the biggest civil rights settlements ever. Congress was given a March 31, 2010, deadline to approve the funds. Lawmakers left Washington on March 23 for a two-week break, missing the deadline for approving them.

Boyd was unsuccessful in trying to get the Administration to declare the settlement an emergency, a move then Senate President Harry Reid and then House Speaker Nancy Pelosi supported. But John was undeterred: On November 19, 2010, the U.S. Senate approved a $1.15 billion measure to fund the settlement reached between the Agriculture Department and minority farmers. The U.S. House of Representatives approved it on November 30, 2010.

On December 10, 2010, President Barack Obama signed the bill that will provide compensation to thousands of black farmers who say they were discriminated against by the federal government when it came to loans and subsidies. About 30,000 black farmers are eligible for the settlement. "The president said 'You are here; now how does it feel?' I told him it was bittersweet because I still think about the names and faces of those who died and who aren't here to see this day. I'm glad to see the president sign the bill and deeply saddened by those who died waiting for justice," said John.

Suppose, like John Boyd, you've lost your enterprise. Or you've gone broke. That's a serious knock against the achievement dimension of your life.

According to Robert Emmons, a psychologist at the University of California at Davis, we have four basic dimensions to our lives: achievement, spirituality, community, and legacy. Our psychic immune system kicks in when we have a loss in one of these dimensions. Perhaps you lose something in the achievement realm, and then the remaining three get stronger.

You can see this at play with underdogs who have survived loss. The legacy dimension of their lives becomes their cynosure. Failure builds grit because it can initiate a search for meaning, shifting from temporary pleasure to the kinds of happiness that endure.

GETTING GRITTY:
DON'T RUMINATE, ACTIVATE

In a 1989 study, New York psychologist J. Marvin Eisenstadt reviewed the history of 699 eminent, high-achieving Americans—those whose works garnered a mention in encyclopedias of the day. He found that 45 percent had lost a parent before age 21. Only two other groups in the general population show that level of orphanhood—juvenile delinquents and depressive or suicidal psychiatric patients.

Encountering loss can force psychological growth, confidence, and will, all of which are components of grit. Eisenstadt noted that Paul McCartney and John Lennon both lost their mothers as adolescents and concluded that "loss of a parent is a trauma that imposes pressure on the child to 'recapture paradise lost.' This ideal state, he believes, can be re-established through creativity in ideal works of art, in science, literature, etc., or in the will toward power as a political leader. Through the search for an ideal in society, a political leader can become the father of a society in which a father is what one longs for."[74] The underdogs described here fit the mold of grit through loss.

Kim Delevett is a Vietnam War refugee who lost her biological mother, extended family, and motherland when she was two-and-a-half years old. Cathy Pickett was raped and contracted HIV. John Boyd had his farm taken away and his marriage shattered. When she was young, Carolyn Dennis's father suffered so many debilitating strokes that he was moved to a nursing home. Her mother had bipolar disorder, which her father had shielded from her. At age 12, she dropped out of high school and ran away from home. Eventually, Dennis obtained her GED, put herself through college, and earned bachelor's and master's degrees in nutrition.

Eleven days before his scheduled triple-bypass surgery, Frank Amend was laid off. Three years later, he was diagnosed with a debilitating kidney disease. During that time, he pursued a job and raised a family. Bob Stone flunked out of MIT but was readmitted later. Dr. Gary Smith lost some mobility when he was afflicted with polio at age seven. Bob Benham was losing business due to unfair competition. Patrice Dell lost an active childhood because she suffered numerous illnesses. They required her to wear an intrusive medical device during her junior high and high school years, bringing taunts and jeers from her classmates. Chip Thayer had lung cancer. Kate Hanni survived an assault.[75]

But what makes one person who suffers loss a tenacious overachiever and another a juvenile delinquent or suicidal psychiatric patient? The distinction is emotional mastery and a lack of excessive rumination. (The word "ruminate" comes from the Latin for chewing cud, referring to the way cattle grind up, swallow, regurgitate, and re-chew their food.)

Yes, everyone gets shaken by their failures. Some welcome it as a learning and grit-developing experience while others engage in unhealthy rumination. They keep swirling thoughts around in their mental food processor. In fact, Dr. Martin Seligman said this is one reason why women experience depression at higher rates than men—that is, they ruminate, analyze, commiserate, and obsess more over issues than men do.

When a woman gets fired from her job, she often wonders why and what she did wrong. She spends a lot of time thinking. A man in the same situation creates distractions. He might drink, become boisterous, and try to momentarily forget. Seligman believes that rumination run "ayuck" can be dangerous because it feeds depression. Taking action, however, tends to break up the depression cycle. Evidence is streaming in that supports the role of rumination in the variance in depression rates between men and women.

Yale University psychologist Susan Nolen-Hoeksema, Ph.D., has extensively tested her theory that rumination cascades a host of negative effects. When she asked women in a study to indicate what they do when they're depressed, most said, "I tried to analyze my mood" or "I tried to find out why I felt the way I did." The majority of men said they did something they enjoyed such as playing a sport or a musical instrument. Or they made statements such as, "I decided not to concern myself with my mood."

In another laboratory project, men and women were offered a choice of two tasks when they felt sad. They could list words that best described their mood (a task that focuses on being depressed) or rank a list of nations in order of their wealth (a distracting task). Seventy percent of the women chose the emotion-focused task, listing the words that described their mood. With the men, the percentages were reversed.[76]

Another of Nolen-Hoeksema's studies, conducted with Judith Parker, Ph.D., and Louise Parker, Ph.D., found that rumination predicted major depression among 455 people ages 18 to 84 who had lost family members to terminal illnesses. Those who ruminated more often became depressed and stayed depressed, based on their follow-ups 18 months later.[77]

A community survey Nolen-Hoeksema conducted on 1,300 adults ages 25 to 75 backed those results. It found that ruminators develop major depression four times as often as non-ruminators do: 20 percent versus 5 percent. (The results were significant even for ruminators who weren't deemed depressed at baseline.)

In addition to meditation and prayer, Nolen-Hoeksema concluded that doing distracting tasks is critical to reducing ruminating behavior. She also suggested:

- Jettisoning unhealthy or unattainable goals.

- Taking small actions to begin solving your problems.

- Revaluating negative perceptions of events and your high expectations of others.

- Developing multiple sources of self-esteem. (If your esteem is based primarily on your work, your kids, your spouse, or your hobby, you'll be weak in the face of misfortune.)[78]

But what if you can't point to any major tribulations or loss in your life? Are you doomed to live a gritless life? Not if you can use your opponents to develop your grit.

USING THE OPPOSITION
AS A GRIT COACH

Even though our underdogs might not want extra hardship during the battle, they use it as a motivator rather than a source of discouragement. Injustice and opposition seem to encourage grit.

You met Vince Larsen in Chapter 1. As he volunteered on the Yellowstone Valley Citizen's Council (YVCC) to reform the clean air regulations in Yellowstone County, Montana, the treatment he received from those opposed to the clean air regulations fueled his "burn," as John Boyd called it. Explained Larsen, "From the information we were able to gather, it became virtually impossible for our polluting industries to continue to proclaim that they were operating responsibly and in compliance with our air quality standards. The more they resisted, the harder we all worked.

"Days and months just disappeared. I can honestly say that I've never worked as hard on anything—even on those geological projects in which I had an economic interest—as I did on the SO2 issue. I made presentations to heads of labor unions, senior citizens, the League of Women Voters, two high schools, environmental groups at Montana State University Billings, the Billings City Council, and to several members of the Chamber of Commerce, where for the first time, I was directly insulted."

During one public meeting, the politicians and one of Montana's U.S. senators were dancing around the clean air issue. Vince finally walked up in front of the audience, looked directly at the Exxon refinery manager, and asked, "Why can't Exxon operate here in the same way Conoco does?" His reply? "Because we don't have to." The more Vince learned about Exxon, the angrier and more motivated he became. But three years later, Vince's grit had prevailed and the people of the Yellowstone Valley breathed easier—literally.

In his article "Confessions of a Late Bloomer" in *Psychology Today*, Scott Barry Kaufman cited obstacles like our underdogs faced as major instigators of grit. He wrote: "Running into roadblocks at any age can force psychological growth, and while that takes time, it ultimately spurs the development of ego strength—the emotional stability, will, and confidence that confer resilience. In wrestling with adversity, individuals learn skills important to success. So those with the greatest challenges can wind up winning from behind.[79]

GETTING GRITTY: OPTIMIZE

Another aspect of resilient thinking calls for fostering optimism—not in the style of the fictitious self-help expert Stuart Smalley on NBC-TV's *Saturday Night Live* ("I'm good enough, I'm smart enough, and doggone it, people like me!"), but by paying attention to the truly positive in your life *and* by giving yourself options.

When you think negative thoughts, rather than gazing in the mirror and chanting to the universe or telling yourself how great you are, do a Perry Mason and put the negative thoughts on trial. Rebut them to prove the belief is unwarranted. As a result, the thoughts simply become false evidence rather than a life sentence.

What's the key? *To metabolize failure and not take it personally.* Psychologists know that when people think their achievements are predicated on their DNA more than on their ability and hard work, they will be brittle in the face of adversity.

The U.S. military develops grit on an epic scale. At the John F. Kennedy Special Warfare Center and School at Fort Bragg, the vast U.S. Army base just outside Fayetteville, North Carolina, soldiers train for two to three years to join the Special Forces. Only 20 percent of the candidates make it through the first time. Their final stage of training involves Survival, Evasion, Resistance, and Escape, or SERE for short. For three weeks, they live primarily outdoors at Camp Mackall where the SERE exercises take place.

The stress that SERE students experience rates among the highest ever tested scientifically. According to researchers who have studied SERE students, changes in their levels of the stress hormone cortisol reach higher levels than skydivers on their first jump, pilots landing on an aircraft carrier for the first time, and patients prior to heart surgery. The result of that stress, instructors say, is that soldiers become inoculated against the real thing.

Coinciding with the psychologists' findings on the role of optimism in developing grit, Gordon Smith, a SERE instructor who earned his status through 26 years in the Special Forces, said, "I tell the students, if you have a guy with all the survival training in the world who has a negative attitude and a guy who doesn't have a clue but has a positive attitude, I guarantee you that the one with the positive attitude is coming out of the woods alive. Simple as that."

During SERE training, the biggest obstacles are psychological. They feel trepidation at the unknown, stress over things beyond their control; anger at being in this predicament. On the battlefield, soldiers might experience guilt over comrades who didn't make it. One of the master sergeants and the chief instructor at SERE acknowledges that these emotions are normal, but potentially spirit-crushing. So if you dwell on the negative, you can become depressed and indecisive. The stress will submerge your confidence.

Throughout SERE, instructors focus on the psychology of survival. Instead of allowing fear and anxiety to become destructive, trainees learn to use those emotions as a positive force of motivation—to avoid being cavalier and leaving themselves vulnerable to the enemy, to rise to the myriad challenges they face.

Of course, maintaining a positive attitude in the face of countless setbacks and seemingly insurmountable odds is difficult, to say the least. When you're in survival mode, it's important to keep improving your situation while practicing optimism, if only by fractions. John, a master sergeant and chief instructor at SERE, said, "You need to celebrate small victories: 'I caught a fish today,' 'I've avoided getting sick,' 'I have enough water to last a few more days.' You're looking for any reason to hope."[80]

Just as grit requires perseverance and a positive attitude, it also requires a burning desire. It takes having "the fire" as this parable reveals.

DO YOU HAVE THE FIRE?

A young violin prodigy was walking down the street en route to his next violin lesson and pondering if he should pursue a life in music. He dreamed of performing before packed concert halls, of fan adulation, of collaborating with the brightest minds in music. His teacher and others told him he had great potential. But he knew he'd have lots of competition, and he wondered if all the hard work he faced would be worth it.

While walking, he came upon a violin teacher—the most famous violin teacher in the world. Scarcely believing his luck, he stopped the great teacher he idolized and asked if he could play for him. He said his family and teachers thought he had potential, but he'd love to get the master's opinion. If the great teacher told him he was wasting his time, he might abandon his dream of a career in music.

The great teacher nodded silently for him to begin. As the young musician played, beads of sweat appeared on his forehead. When he finished, he was certain he'd given his finest performance ever. But the great maestro only shook his head sadly and said, "You lack the fire." Devastated, the young musician returned home and announced his intention to abandon music. He put his violin away and never touched it again. Instead, he followed "plan B" and entered the world of business. He liked it, he was good at it, but he didn't love it like he once loved music. However, he turned out to have such a talent for business that in a few short years, he was richer than he'd ever imagined.

Almost a decade later as he walked down another street in another city, he again spotted the great teacher. He rushed over to the master and said excitedly, "I'm so sorry to bother you, and I'm sure you don't remember me, but I stopped you on the street years ago to play my violin for you. I just want to thank you. Because of your advice, I abandoned my greatest love, the violin, painful as it was, and I became a businessman. Today I enjoy great success, which I owe to you. But one thing you must tell me. All those years ago, how did you know that I lacked the fire?"

The great teacher shook his head and said, "I didn't. I tell all who play for me they lack the fire. And if they do have the fire, they don't listen!"[81]

Do you listen to the naysayers? Are you easily discouraged? Or do you have the dedication and passion that grit requires?

THE UNDERDOG'S CHECKLIST
Have You Got Grit?

Although Woody Allen said that 80 percent of success is showing up, our underdogs have shown that upward influence success isn't only about showing up—it's about showing up *with grit*. So how do you get grit?

✓ First, flick any belief in "instant gratification" off your shoulder and realize that it may take years to reach your goal. Commitment to your cause is key.

✓ Get out of your own head. Think less about yourself and more about those you're fighting for. Each of our gritty people cited the welfare of others as a motivation for persevering.

✓ Use your opponents as motivators.

✓ Don't ruminate over previous defeats and shortcomings. Act. Do something.

✓ Remember that your skills are not the sole source of your achievements. (Those with this belief risk the inability to improve because they believe their skills are inborn, and they therefore can't improve them.)

✓ Celebrate small victories.

✓ Welcome the struggle.

✓ Metabolize failure—don't take it personally.

✓ Don't worry about living a life of perfectly balanced quadrants. Most underdog influencers (and high achievers) focus on one issue or cause.

✓ Remind yourself how you persevered through other tough situations. The skills and behaviors that brought you through earlier challenges haven't disappeared.

✓ Remember, if someone can talk you out of doing it, you don't have "the fire."

CHAPTER 5

Extreme Influence Tactic #4:

Eyes Up into the Top Dog's World

"When I have had to say 'no' to people, it's usually because people do not have the big picture."

> — *Colleen Barrett*

"Understanding someone's moral system is one of the best ways to persuade. Being validated as a moral person makes you feel like a hero, doesn't it?"

> — *Dr. Kelton Rhoads*

"Save your passion to motivate your troops rather than spending it on your influence target."

> — *Patrice Dell*

"Many times I had to ask myself, 'Who do I hurt in the short run, and who do I hurt in the long run? Can they recover?'"

— *Former Congressman Clarence Brown*

Extreme influence calls for empathy—thinking less about yourself and more about the person you want to persuade to your point of view. That means looking at upward influence attempts in the same ways they do.

The pattern that emerges from doing this reveals six lenses through which they view underdog persuasion attempts. (These may be different than how they would think through requests from peers or those who outrank them; the discussion here focuses on requests from underdogs.)

The six lenses are:

1. Passion: It's not the panacea. Big dogs are *not* enamored by excessively passionate underdogs except under narrow circumstances.

2. Heroics: Give them this gift. Top dogs want to be perceived as heroes.

3. Environment: Keep your eyes up. Be acutely aware of your top dog's surroundings.

4. Values: Learn and understand what they value. If you share common values, that's a big plus.

5. Filters: Fit their way of thinking. Top dogs need your request to align with their established ways of thinking—their own filters.

6. Pressure: Leave some things unsaid. Top dogs want you to know when to stop pressing them.

PASSION: IT'S NOT THE PANACEA

One of the most old-fashioned and overrated pieces of advice for any influencer, especially underdogs, is to be passionate about your cause. Some consider it the answer to all influence challenges, saying, "Just be passionate and you win." If that were true, people would easily get what they want by pushing the passion button. But when has zeal alone ever won the day?

Because "being passionate" is easy on the ears, many underdogs stop there with their influence tactics. But before you send me flaming emails, remember that you're an underdog focused on *upward influence* with someone who is *averse* to or *unaware* of your concern. You can't use the passionate "yaktivist" approach (making lots of noise with no results) or the passionate "madvocate" method (getting mad and screaming for attention) because upward influence requires different techniques—those you're learning throughout this book. Always remember that upward influence isn't a peer-to-peer situation and passion isn't the panacea.

In each interview I did with top dogs, I asked them what *doesn't* work when someone tries to influence them. I heard words and phrases like "too emotional," "can't see the other side," "fist bangers on the desk," "pushing me to make a decision quickly," and so on. Aren't those behaviors also passionate? Don't those individuals feel just as passionately about their cause as those whose request is accepted? Sure they do. What's different? The underdogs who succeed have adroitly used their passion to make their big dogs feel good about helping them.

I'm not advising that you lose the power of your own conviction; I'm suggesting that you exercise self-control. Passion is best used judiciously when you can make the big dogs feel like *good* dogs. When you're on the wrong side—that is, you're not helping your influence prospects win friends and be perceived as good guys—your passion can easily be interpreted as anger.

What I found interviewing top dogs is that passion works *if you make your top dogs feel like they're riding the highest white horse.* That is, passion can be persuasive when a top dog is made to feel like a good and moral person. It also works *if your big dogs can make more allies by acquiescing to your request.*

Don't let feeling proud of your passion work against you, especially in extreme influence situations. Your passion can also make you seem unpredictable and people don't like that.

In psychology, there's an interpersonal fit of human interactions referred to by terms like *fluency* and *flow*. That comes into play when someone's personality and behaviors fit our expectations. It's easy to understand these qualities; we're socially coordinated with them; and we're even able to anticipate that person's future actions. This meshes with Chapter 3's discussion on being blurtatious— that is, people want to be able to read you because it makes their lives easier and, in turn, makes you more likeable. If they can't read you, they simply don't like you as much.

For example, after the 2004 U.S. presidential election, voters who said they didn't agree with George W. Bush's policies claimed they voted for him because "he was a person of strong conviction" or because "he was a straight shooter" or because "I knew where he was coming from." To many, his candor seemed refreshing in a world of packaged sound bites and talking points. They believed they could read him, and that ease of understanding makes their lives easier.

The positive feelings developed from socializing translate into trust and liking, two qualities that pave the road to persuasion. What's more, being able to easily interpret someone and predict that person's behavior feels good mentally and physically. It requires less work and, fair or unfair, human thinking *is* hard work. (This has been tested by reviewing the brain waves of people asked to solve hard math problems and comparing those brain waves to when the same people put their hands into a bucket of ice water. The brain waves were the same both times, indicating that thinking is *physically* painful!)

However, when underdogs demonstrate passion, it doesn't help because, as my interviews reveal, top dogs view it as anger and deem their future behavior unpredictable. When your influence prospects don't know what to expect, they *like* you less, *trust* you less, and are less likely to say, "yes" to your request. What's the key? To pack away your passion and exercise self-control (see Willpower as a Persuasion Tool). This is true under most circumstances with one exception—when your passion makes your prospect look like a hero.

Willpower as a Persuasion Tool

If you tend to become passionate about your cause, you may need to develop more willpower. But the research clearly shows people don't have an endless supply of this trait, which is perceived to a positive one in the American culture.

I define willpower simply as doing the opposite of what you feel like doing. Therefore, it's good when people refrain from gluttony, overspending, gossiping, and endlessly watching reruns of TV's "Jersey Shore." Self-control can be defined as a form of self-regulation that gives you the power to inhibit your dominant tendencies so you can achieve rewarding long-term outcomes.

Social situations require more self-control and effort than you might think. For example, to rein in your passion, you have to sometimes suppress your desired reaction (rolling your eyes or raising your voice at your big dog) in favor of acceptable behavior that lends itself to a long-term working relationship. (See Chapter 7, which indicates relationship building is a key upward influence tool.) Overly passionate underdogs need to heed the latest research. It shows that people actually have a reserve of self-control and willpower, but the amount is limited.

In a research experiment conducted by Dr. Joseph Ferrari of DePaul University, participants were randomly assigned to two groups. Those in both groups were told they'd participate in two tests. The important difference between the groups came in the amount of self-control demanded of them— that is, the experimental group was told to do something that would require self-control while the control group was simply asked to do a task. For example, both groups had to watch a funny film, but those in the experimental group were told to suppress their emotions while the control group was given no instructions about how to react. In another example, people in both groups arrived at the lab hungry, but the experimental group was instructed to eat radishes and resist a tempting plate of cookies. The control group was allowed to eat the cookies or the radishes or both, whatever they liked.

The groups were then asked to complete a follow-up task included solving complex anagrams, drinking an unpleasant but harmless sports drink, and drinking free beer, knowing a driving test would follow. The people in the experimental group failed at the second task. As a result, the researchers concluded that self-control is a muscle that gets tired, just as a physical muscle that gets depleted can't be endlessly deployed.[82] (This could be why, in nightclubs everywhere, an epidemic of poor human mating decisions are made after midnight. Everyone is just tired.)

Another study showed that after coping with a stressful day at work, people were less likely to exercise and more likely to engage in passive activities like watching television, playing video games, surfing the Internet, and so on.[83] Now, please don't think I want to make willpower demonstrations an Olympic sport. I do believe, however, that passionate outbursts usually stem from a lack of self-control, so make sure your willpower tank is full before running full speed into top dog encounters. This means that to prevent your passion from becoming a persuasion pothole, you need to be mindful of how you expend and *replenish* this valuable reserve.

In his book *Change Your Brain, Change Your Body,* clinical neuroscientist, psychiatrist, and brain-imaging expert Dr. Daniel Amen wrote about what he calls a "brain reserve." This refers to the amount of healthy brain function you have available to deal with stressful events or injuries. The more reserve you have, the better you can cope with the unexpected; the less you have, watch out. When a stressful situation occurs, the more likely you are to polish off the macaroni and cheese or drink more alcohol than what's consumed on a Def Leppard tour bus.

Dr. Amen wrote that keeping blood glucose levels at an even level throughout the day improves your self-control abilities. After all, self-control requires that you make a concerted effort to focus your attention, your thoughts, and—related to this discussion about passion—your emotions. People with healthy blood sugar levels also manage stress better than others who do not.[84]

Here's the good news: *Willpower seems to get stronger with use.* For example, increased willpower runs rampant in military training where recruits learn to overcome one challenge after another. And psychological studies show that doing something as simple as using your non-dominant hand to brush your teeth for two weeks can increase your willpower capacity.

Whatever the explanation, consistently doing an activity that requires self-control seems to increase willpower. This reflects a greater ability to delay gratification, which is associated with success in life. Build up your willpower muscle and see how increased self-control can assist in your efforts to persuade top dogs.

Making Your Willpower Available When You Want It

Follow these tips to ensure you don't become unhinged like the front door of a doublewide during a crystal meth drug bust. (They're adapted from an article on self-regulation failure by Dr. Timothy Pychyl.)[85]

Be future-oriented. Motivate yourself by thinking about what's possible, what will happen long-term if you can just get a grip in the here and now. Resist giving in to "feel good" motivations. Feeling good is temporary; self-mastery is eternal.

1. Self-control is a muscle. Take on a self-regulating task and stick to it. It can be as simple as improving your posture or waving and smiling to those who cut you off in traffic instead of using other gestures.

2. Get plenty of sleep. A good night's sleep keeps restoring your ability to exercise self-control.

3. Tapping into self-control late in the day isn't as effective as early in the day. (Again, making poor mating choices at midnight comes into play here!) Be strategic and don't try to accomplish too much in the late hours.

4. Expressing positive emotions increases self-control, so find things to be grateful for. Frequently write down your feelings of gratitude and humorous discoveries in a journal.

5. Get up and move. Physical exercise programs lead to decreased smoking, alcohol, caffeine, and junk food consumption, and even reduced impulse spending and TV watching. It even softens any tendencies to leave dirty dishes in the sink!

HEROICS: GIVE THEM THIS GIFT

Astute underdog persuaders seek ways to give the "gift of heroics." It's critical to help top dogs see that, by helping you, they're doing the right thing and making new friends, too. Here's the evidence: No fewer than half of the powerful people interviewed told me they changed their minds about an issue once they realized that agreeing to the request meant they'd be one of the "good guys." In fact, many used these exact words: "I felt I was doing the right thing."

Another popular response was "I felt I was the only person who could help them." Many temporarily abdicated a value system of less government or a need for personal responsibility or something else if, by changing their mind, they could take the moral high ground. That way they could be, as Dr. Rhoads said, "...on the side of the angels." He affirmed, "Understanding someone's moral system is one of the best ways to persuade. Being validated as a moral person makes *you* feel like a hero, doesn't it?"

This is true for top dogs, too.

The Heroics of Leslie Waters

State Representative Leslie Waters responded to this gift of heroics and became a powerful leader for a cause she previously knew nothing about. As she told the story, "Janet Goree, a woman in her early forties, told me her son-in-law killed her granddaughter due to shaken baby syndrome. You know, a baby's brain is like an egg yolk and shaking the baby shakes up the brain inside. Anyway, Kimberlin West, Janet's granddaughter, died only a few years after the shaking incident.

"I remembered Janet as the 'grieving grandmother' who had gone through so much in response to this death. Not only did her granddaughter die, but her grandson had eye problems and other disabilities. Everyone knew of this woman—the medical association people, the pediatric association people, and so on. You know, legislators may do some things to garner a favor—what goes around comes around—with so many bleeding-heart issues that would come your way.

"This woman was on a mission. She wanted me to help her get new legislation in place to help prevent shaken baby syndrome. Janet had met with other legislators who'd turned her down before meeting with me. Honestly, my first thought was, 'How can we regulate something like this?' Then I learned that she'd worked for agencies that helped kids who were sexually abused. There, she was training others on how to spot and prevent sexual abuse of children. She also was a leader on that issue at national level, so she set a good example. Janet walked the talk," Leslie said. (Sound familiar? It's that "street cred," you read about in Chapter 3.)

"So, I let her use my office as a headquarters. She'd camp out here because nobody else wanted to touch the issue. The first year, we got a House Resolution passed that brought awareness to the issue. A year later, we passed the Kimberlin West Act, which was named after her granddaughter. This Act required hospitals and other birthing facilities to distribute literature about how to avoid shaken baby syndrome to new moms leaving the hospital. Why a new mom would want to bring home a baby after seeing those materials, I don't know. It probably puts the fear of God in them, but we're requiring it anyway.

"I'm a Republican, and the GOP doesn't like mandates, but I thought, 'What the hell?' So in 2004, we instituted childcare personnel mandates that require a childcare professional to have this information.

"My affiliation with Janet and this issue helped me become known with other children's health groups in the state. It widened my base because, coming from the insurance industry, I was previously the devil to them," Leslie concluded.

Clearly, Underdog Janet Goree gave Big Dog Leslie Waters the gift of heroics. Despite Leslie's lack of awareness and involvement in children's health issues, Janet changed how Leslie thought about them. As a result, Leslie became a hero to a large newfound constituency.

The Heroics of Richard Swett

Former Congressman Richard Swett also became a hero by helping a small business person who in turn helped save U.S. soldiers' lives in the Persian Gulf War.

Congressman Swett attended Yale University and became an architect. Active in the Democratic Party, he began a political career that led to his election to the U.S. House in 1990. "I served on the Energy, Science, and Technology committee. Our committee's goal was not to pick winners in the technology field, but to give people options," he said, retelling a time when he did just that.

"During the first Gulf War, our troops had trouble avoiding 'friendly fire.' An engineer from my district came to my office and said he could fix the problem our troops were having avoiding friendly fire. Now, I didn't have any prior relationship with this guy—I didn't know him from Adam. He said he went to Army officers with a device he invented, and they wouldn't let him demonstrate it. He was a small business owner who had no resources to get in front of this audience.

"The device was a battery-coated laser ray that could be discerned by a fighter jet's fire and not allow the weaponry to penetrate the armor. He came to my office and set something that looked like a Maxwell House coffee can on my desk. He talked about in a way that was compelling and convincing. Because he had a small operation, he told me he could both produce this device quickly. He could also assure the military it wouldn't fail in the field. I really believed he had the knowledge and confidence to make it work.

"He impressed me but I knew I had to do a background check on him after our meeting. Obviously, I'm going to learn about his business to make sure I'm dealing with a credible person. I also wanted to make sure his company was not a Mickey Mouse operation so I checked him out. After doing that, I got the right military personnel to allow him to make a presentation. He landed a contract worth millions of dollars—his first government contract ever. Before long, his device was put on the equipment and we were able to identify *our* guys from the bad guys. It was his first government contract ever.

"This man was persuasive in part because he helped me visualize how his product worked from a technological perspective. Plus, he could put this device into effect in two months versus the six to twelve months it typically takes for new military tools." Congressman Swett was a hero for facilitating the delivery of a device that saved the lives of our military heroes in the field and helped a constituent build his business.

So, your passion can work in your favor if you can make your prospects heroes and help them win over more allies without alienating existing ones.

ENVIRONMENT: KEEP YOUR EYES UP

You can better understand your top dog through the practice of "eyes up," referring to looking above and beyond what's obviously in front of you. In this case, it's being aware of your top dog's environment.

All of the underdogs you're reading about are highly observant of their influence targets' environments. By keeping their eyes up, they use what they see to adjust their messages and avoid accidents—just like performance racecar drivers.

Eyes Up at the Performance Driving Center

To give my husband a unique gift, I bought him a two-day stint at the BMW Performance Driving Center in Spartansburg, South Carolina, thus embarking on one of the potentially most dangerous, relationship altering, and wildly fun adventures of our married life. (Shameful but unpaid plug: *you have to go there.* More than 10,000 people attend the Performance Driving Center each year. If you go, you won't regret it: http://www.bmwusa.com/Standard/Content/Experience/ Events/PDS/Default.aspx)

It seemed like a fun idea at the time—the two of us working as a team for two full days, driving at high speeds together, performing driving maneuvers that otherwise would have resulted in divorce. I'm happy to report we survived, and my husband Randy even won the class driving maneuvers and speed contest, aptly titled "The Rat Race." He now bears the BMW-bestowed title "King Rat," which has conveniently become his "get out of jail free" card whenever I innocently offer driving tips. (I did finish third in the slalom course.)

Despite (or perhaps because of) the swerving, the smoking and squealing of tires, the slamming of brakes, and the potential for whiplash, our fantastic instructors kept reminding us of one thing: "Keep your eyes up." As I was taking each hairpin turn, contorting my face as if that would help me avoid flipping the car, I kept hearing one instructor's southern drawl through the walkie-talkie in our car. "Amy, girl, get those eyes up! Don't look at the pylons! Plan your future, plan your future!" In fact, the "Eyes Up" reminder was even imprinted on the door mats at the entrance to each classroom (which I noticed because I was disobediently looking down).

Paul Mazzacane, one of our accomplished driving instructors, has won numerous awards for racing. They range from an NHRA (National Hot Rod Association) title to two Sports Car Club of America titles and two autocross championships. Paul further explained why the "eyes up" philosophy is crucial to good driving (and it's not, God forbid, about looking out the windshield versus looking at your Blackberry; it's about looking farther down the road).

As Paul said, "This 'eyes up' is an old driving philosophy we've taught for some time. It's based on the fact that we drive with our eyes, not our hands. The car goes where you're looking.

"Statistically, we know that people look thirty feet in front of their cars. Think about that. A car that's going sixty miles per hour is traveling at ninety feet per second. Now, we also know that it takes one second for your foot to move from the accelerator to the brake. If you're looking only thirty feet ahead instead of ninety, there's nothing you can do to stop that car or avoid an accident if you don't have your 'eyes up.'

"We harp on looking farther out a lot at the Performance Center because not doing it is the biggest mistake people make. Speed alone gets blamed for a lot of accidents, but many times, if the drivers had been looking far enough ahead, they would have had enough time to slow down and avoid the crash."

Paul agreed that the "eyes up" practice is not only advisable for driving, but for life and work too. "You can't look at the obstacle; you have to look at the goal—where you want to end up."

Eyes Up in Iraq

Values are ingrained beliefs that drive attitudes, and attitudes drive behavior. That means if you want to understand someone's behavior, look at his or her environment. This story gleaned from a *Wall Street Journal* article[86] provides an excellent example.

In 2007, the U. S. Military in Iraq needed to create alliances with what we might call local community groups, better known in Iraq as tribes. This task was left to 46-year-old retired Army Major William "Mac" McCallister.

Mac was prescient in seeing the need for these relationships. In 2003, as an active-duty soldier, he advocated that the U.S. military engage the local tribes to stabilize Iraq. In a 2003 memo to his military bosses, he had written that "coalition attempts to bypass traditional tribal authorities and deal with the local population will fail."

His ideas were rejected, and he retired, but returned to Iraq in 2004 to work for two private contractors. He never stopped studying the tribes, reading books, and asking the sheiks about the tribal rituals.

In 2007, the Marine Corps wanted to select gifts for tribal sheiks in Iraq who had helped U.S. forces fight radical Islamists. By this time, McCallister had spent years in Iraq studying the tribes' myths, histories, and ancient legal system. After some investigation, he decided on the best gift: a Mameluke sword. All Marine officers carry the swords, and they date back to 1804 when a Marine lieutenant led a group of Arabs in a successful attack on pirates and was given a sword by an Ottoman pasha.

The problem was that the swords were not allowable as gifts because their value surpassed the government gift limit. Yet he did come up with the perfect gift idea. How? He kept his eyes up.

In 2003, when he was serving in Iraq, McCallister had sat in on a meeting with an influential Fallujah sheik. He witnessed the tribal leader singing a song about the different kinds of pain a warrior feels when he is wounded by different weapons, comparing the sword, knife, and gun. He surmised that, "anyone who sings about that stuff has a different take on the rules of warfare."

This led to his realization that the military needed to better understand the values of the tribes, but at the time, there was no one in the military command in Iraq with expertise on that subject. "When I suggested we find one, people looked at me like I had something growing out of my head," Mac recalled. After that turning point, developing alliances with tribal leaders was seen as "necessary" not "nice" to their achieving long-term change in the region.

As an example, Mac noted that the military's cultural training focused largely on telling troops what not to do, how to behave in the least offensive ways. While the advice was okay, its focus on passivity made U.S. troops look, well, passive. In contrast, the Iraqis are products of a volatile and passionate culture, and they respect others who demonstrate the same temperament.

"The Iraqis expect the grand gesture. It's one of their rituals," said Mac. "You show them no respect when you don't offend," recalling that tribal sheik meetings start quietly, then escalate into screaming matches before the discussion returns to normal decibel levels.

The Marines took McCallister's advice about being less passive. In June of 2007, General Allen, known to pride himself on staying calm, was meeting with the governor of Iraq's Anbar Province in a hotel restaurant in Amman, Jordan. General Allen told the governor he needed his help to reopen Anbar's criminal courts, which had shut down after threats of violence caused many judges to quit. The governor wasn't moved by General Allen's plea.

Then General Allen slammed his fist on the table, causing silverware and glasses to clang. He yelled at the governor, imploring him to get the courts open and have the first trials in Anbar by August 1. The trials started shortly after that "conversation," and the Anbar governor regularly referred to the meeting with General Allen as a turning point.

General Allen then applied McCallister's formula: he communicated in a way that was understood by his top dog. This happened because Mac McAllister had viewed the experiences of the sheiks from *their* vantage point, not his. The tribal leaders didn't tell him "please become a bit more emotional when you ask for something. Oh, and by the way, we like to sing about weapons, so having any catchy tunes about them wins you points, too!" Instead, he observed and acted. He then integrated their style of communicating into the U.S. approach, which created rapport, goodwill and, most important, successful persuasion among the tribal elders and leaders.

When you have a risky "we've-never-done-that-before" idea, presenting your idea in concert with the value system of the big dogs needs to happen in a way that supports their deeply held beliefs.

Eyes Up on Capitol Hill

Earlier, you read about John Boyd's grit. He is a smart underdog because he also kept his eyes up and used what he observed to win the support of a previously recalcitrant U.S. senator. Here's what happened.

When John first started working the black farmer's settlement issue on Capitol Hill, U.S. Senator Chuck Robb of Virginia "was my best friend on the Hill," according to John. "He sponsored the original statute of limitations waiver that would allow black farmers to get the money entitled to them from being denied loans." But everything stopped when a new senator from Virginia came into office.

"When former governor George Allen was elected U.S. Senator from Virginia, there was a 360-degree change. The staff didn't return our phone calls—we got no attention at all. When Allen was the governor of Virginia, we tried to get his attention to this issue but he didn't pay any attention then either. We picketed outside the Virginia State House and received some media coverage, but nothing from him," John recalled.

Yet John kept his eyes up and recognized an opportunity to connect with Senator Allen. In August of 2006, Senator Allen was on the campaign trail speaking to a group of supporters. In the audience was a volunteer for his opponent (who later became U.S. Senator) James Webb. This volunteer named S.R. Sidarth had attended several Allen events. An active Democrat entering his fourth year at the University of Virginia, Sidarth had been assigned by Webb to trail Allen with a video camera to document his travels and speeches, a common campaign tactic. At one event, Allen evidently recognized Sidarth, an African American, and pointed at him. "This fellow here, over here with the yellow shirt…macaca, or whatever his name is…he's with my opponent. He's following us around everywhere. And it's just great," Allen spouted as his supporters laughed. After announcing that Webb was raising money in California with a "bunch of Hollywood movie moguls," Allen said to the crowd, "Let's give a welcome to macaca, here. Welcome to America and the real world of Virginia!"[87]

Suddenly, calling Sidarth a racist name had far-reaching repercussions for Allen personally and professionally. It also gave John an opening to speak out. "As we know, Senator Allen uttered a racial epithet that got him some negative press. He had tried to do some outreach with African American colleges and it didn't pan out. So I went to him and told him I could get him some African American support. I had two meetings with him and his chief of staff for African American outreach. I told him I knew he was in trouble, and he would need to apologize for what he said. Then everything would be fine.

"I also asked him why he was meeting with me as a U.S. Senator but hadn't when he was the governor of Virginia. He replied that he thought I was a radical, a crazy. I told him I wasn't but I'd done the picketing to get media attention for the cause."

After that, Allen not only gave his verbal support to Boyd and his issue, but with Senator Charles Grassley of Iowa, he co-sponsored the Boyd Claims Remedy Act. The introduction of this legislation provided momentum for John's cause. You'll find details about the battle that John fought—and won—in Chapter 4.

VALUES: LEARN AND UNDERSTAND WHAT THEY VALUE

I've heard it said when it comes to child rearing, "values are caught, not taught." That also is apt for underdog influencers. Rarely will your big dog tell you his or her values; you have to listen for them and apply what you have learned to your persuasion request. Let me tell you how Frank Amend, a heart disease survivor from North Carolina, learned about the values of his Congressman.

The Value of Self-Responsibility

An active volunteer with the American Heart Association, Frank was on a mission to get his member of Congress to co-sponsor the HEART for Women Act. This would allocate resources to study and treat heart disease and stroke in women. The bill authorized Medicare to conduct additional education awareness campaigns for older women. They would provide gender-specific information for clinicians and researchers while improving screening for low-income women at risk for heart disease and stroke.

Who could oppose that goal, right? How about a member from a state that depended on the tobacco industry, like Congressman Walter Jones of North Carolina? "Unfortunately, Representative Jones had never voted for us on any issues, including the STOP Stroke Act or increased National Institutes of Health (NIH) funding. We just wrote him off. When I had met with him previously, I was discouraged because he got us off topic and then turned over our information to his health issue specialist," Frank recalled.

This time, though, Frank thought that meeting him in Washington D.C. would be simple, in part because his wife's cousin was working in Representative Jones's office. Not so. "I met with his staff person during one of our lobby days in Washington. Frankly, she was fairly brusque with me. Afterward, I sent an email, thanked her for her time, and told her I just wanted to follow up with him to see if he needed additional information and to keep in touch.

"I knew I had to figure out the key issue for him. I heard his staff say he was concerned about personal responsibility relative to heart disease and stroke, that individuals should take the reins by taking responsibility for their own health," Frank said.

That's when Frank got it. After hearing the "personal responsibility" angle, he knew he'd have to couch all of his best evidence through that value. Congressman Jones was concerned about how to provide the education that would lead to personal responsibility and still save money. So Frank constantly reminded the Congressman's staff that, in his words, "people can't be personally responsible if they don't have the data and education!"

Eventually, Representative Jones committed to the legislation by not only co-sponsoring the bill, but adding his name to a "Dear Colleague" letter asking his legislative colleagues to support the HEART for Women Act. Why? Because Frank had tuned in to Congressman Jones's concerns. He showed that the Congressman could align with his value of personal responsibility by supporting the legislation.

Like Frank, Carolyn Dennis also carefully listened to her big dog's objections. Doing that allowed her to better frame her request to regulate the availability of junk food in schools.

The Value of Individual Choice

Carolyn is a retired registered dietician for the Lexington-Fayette County (Kentucky) Health Department where she was employed as a diabetes educator. About 10 years ago, she started seeing more and more evidence of the rising rate of childhood (Type 2) diabetes. "When you say diabetes to me, I see familiar faces," she noted.

"I did have trepidation before meeting with State Representative Jimmy Higdon because he was so adamantly opposed to our bill. He owned a grocery store and said, 'Parents buy plenty of junk food, so why did it make any difference to regulate what they could buy in school if their parents didn't even care what they ate?'"

When she heard him say that, Carolyn caught onto his value system. She correctly surmised that he was opposed to regulating adult behavior, so she adjusted her request and framed it in terms of the behavior of children, not adults.

"I focused my discussion on children. I said I wasn't pushing a bill that would regulate adult behavior. Then I found out who his key influencers might be—which legislators or constituents he tended to be tight with. That helped me understand where he was coming from. And really listening to him helped me come up with fresh ways to come back at his objections. I thought, 'There is a way to reach this person.' It's just figuring out which approach works best with them. And persevering.

"I quickly learned to listen and ask—up front—how others feel about an issue. I had to calm down and hear *why* they were opposed to it."

Plus Carolyn, like our other underdogs, made her prospect a hero. As Representative Hidgdon said, "Carolyn held true to the bill's main objective—to cut the sugar intake of students while they were in school. *I got the feeling I was doing the right thing.*"

Representative Higdon, agreeing with Carolyn despite his initial skepticism, voted to regulate the presence of vending machines in schools. The bill passed the Kentucky legislature and was enacted into law in 2005.

Shared Values Equals Shared Admiration

Many times, we ascribe positive attributes to others when their value system aligns with ours. And as you have read in the previous stories, expressing these common values can frequently change minds. What else explains why one of Hillary Clinton's most vitriolic opponents during her husband's presidency would suddenly, during the 2008 Democratic presidential primary campaign, reverse his opinion and laud her "impressive command of many of today's most pressing domestic and international issues"?

Richard Mellon Scaife, heir to the Mellon banking fortune, funded many of the multimillion-dollar campaigns in the 1990s to dig up damaging information about Bill and Hillary Clinton. In fact, he donated $1.8 million to *The American Spectator* magazine for what become known as the "Arkansas Project," which was an excavation of their personal peccadilloes in Arkansas. In March of 2008, he joined his paper's editors for a 90-minute meeting with then-presidential candidate Hillary Clinton.

"I have a very different impression of Hillary Clinton today," he wrote in an opinion article[88] in *The New York Times* after the meeting. "And it's a very favorable one indeed." Quite a change of heart. How did he arrive at his newfound admiration for Mrs. Clinton? He wrote that it was her command of the facts and answers to their questions that were "thoughtful, well-stated, and often dead on."

To the contrary, the real reason he may have been impressed was buried later in the article. It read: "During the meeting at *The Tribune-Review*, he found common ground with Mrs. Clinton on the need to pull troops out of Iraq; on the bumbling federal efforts to rebuild New Orleans after Hurricane Katrina; and on the 'increasing instability in Pakistan and South America.'"[89] In this case, appealing to one's value system trumped the pure facts.

My colleague, Dr. Rhoads, wondered if Scaife revised his opinion based on his shared values with Mrs. Clinton. "What Mr. Scaife called 'facts' are actually *values-based positions.* He saw that he and Mrs. Clinton were on the same page regarding Iraq, Katrina, and Pakistan. Once a person arrives at the right conclusions, then we admire their brilliant reasoning and command of the facts," he said.

FILTERS: MAKE YOUR REQUEST FIT THEIR WAY OF THINKING

Suppose your task is to get a "hated" idea accepted by a top dog. This is when you'd turn to a method similar to mirroring that person's values. You'd make your request appealing by ensuring it aligns with the top dog's own filters, as in this Southwest Airlines example.

Filters of Customer Sensitivity and Corporate Values

Southwest Airlines was incorporated in 1967 with the goal of "giving more people the freedom to fly" through lower costs and spectacular customer service. It originated the concept of low cost, no frills travel; it now carries 65 million passengers every year.

Although it was incorporated in 1967, numerous David vs. Goliath legal battles delayed its first flight until June 18, 1971. This long battle to get off the ground permeates its "warrior" culture that embraces employee input and "coloring outside the lines."

Southwest's President Emeritus Colleen Barrett joined the airline in 1978 and rose to its presidency in 2001. Colleen has received more than 40 awards including the Horatio Alger Award, an award given by Horatio Alger Association of Distinguished Americans to those exemplifying success in spite of adversity. And for two years straight, she made the Forbes.com's "100 Most Powerful Women" list.

If you ask Southwest team members about Colleen, they'll tell you she "has the pulse of the customer" and is the "keeper of the Southwest culture." In her career there, she has overseen management, leadership, and budget responsibilities for everything from corporate communications to marketing to customer relations to labor and employee relations.

When I called to interview Colleen, her love for the people of Southwest was evident the minute she answered the phone. "You know, Amy, I like the concept of your book, that ordinary people can change minds, but we don't have 'ordinary' people here at Southwest," making her point quickly.

"I don't like to be a naysayer, but it's my job to bring up the negative and question people who have new ideas. I consider myself one of the consciences of the company. I'm a pretty good judge of our customers' reactions. I'm always sensitive to that and filter everything through that. Our brand is clear and because I've been there since the beginning, I know when a new idea might disconnect with our brand.

"When I have had to say 'no' to people, usually it's because they just don't have the big picture. There are lots of 'nice to-do' projects, but Herb (Herb Kelleher, founder of Southwest Airlines) taught us to manage for the worst times in the best times. That's a core value of our company. We just don't do the 'nice to-do' projects if they don't make sense. For example, in the early days, the Texas Aeronautics Commission that regulated us when we were an intra-state carrier told us to raise our fares because we weren't charging enough. But we don't operate that way," she explained.

For Colleen, even the initiatives that seem like a natural fit for Southwest's reputation for friendliness and fun have to go through her filter. One of her public relations managers came up with a fun idea that would reinforce the Southwest culture inside and outside the company, believing it would give Southwest free national exposure.

"In fact, this manager came to me with an idea that I hated—I totally opposed it. She said it was 'the opportunity of a lifetime,' which is what she said about everything, by the way. But she knew what type of information I needed to make a decision."

Her idea? To film Southwest employees and customers during normal airport operations for a reality TV show. Each episode would showcase the highs and lows that passengers and crew face behind the scenes of the Southwest Airlines. Viewers could follow pilots, flight attendants, and airport employees as they were dealing with compelling passenger stories and weather delays while trying to meet everyone's schedule.

Colleen wasn't buying the idea for several reasons, all correlating with Southwest's value system. One was her concerns over operational excellence. Of the major U.S. carriers that have been reporting statistics to the Department of Transportation (DOT) since 1987, Southwest consistently receives the lowest ratio of complaints per passenger boarded.

"I was very concerned about operational excellence. We can't slow down our turns (the time it takes from when a plane arrives at the gate until it departs on the next flight) for anything. If this reality show affected our overall on-time performance, I couldn't do it. I also wanted make sure the actual camera person would be respectful and not disrupt our customers' experiences," she recalled.

The potential for this idea to detract from Southwest's internal culture was another concern. "We are an egalitarian company. My understanding was that, naturally, the camera crews would identify certain employees who tend to fare better on television, gravitating to them. I didn't want the show to pick out favorite employees; that is just not right.

"I wasn't concerned that our employees would be negatively exposed, because if we have people who are underperforming, we would simply approach them and work with them to improve performance. It wasn't that; it was more about a negative effect on our customers that bothered me," she added.

"And last, part of the deal is that there is no first right of refusal—you can't say you don't want something shown. After all, these shows are geared toward creating the most drama possible. " Clearly, Colleen had "issues" with the idea.

Because this was a particularly cumbersome request, the public relations manager proceeded to smartly shape her request to Colleen's overriding filters. After all, the values of egalitarianism and operational excellence aren't considered to be only a rote corporate value statement framed in the company cafeteria; they're *sacred values* held with reverence, commitment, and protection by Southwest employees.

According to researchers, what distinguishes sacred values from others is how people behave when asked to alter them or compromise them. Psychologist Philip

Tetlock referred to it as the "taboo tradeoff." It happens when people become increasingly inflexible and express moral outrage at the request.[90]

But Colleen didn't become inflexible or express outrage. Why? Because to attenuate the concerns wrought by a taboo trade-off requires describing it in terms of costs and benefits. In fact, having a high cost/benefit ratio might be an even bigger Southwest sacred value.

"This PR manager knew what I needed. She came to me with a lot of numbers. She had statistics from Easy Jet, a European airline that did a similar show for eleven years in London. She interviewed three of their executives who testified to the show's positive effect on their brand. She had all the numbers to demonstrate that the repeated exposure of Southwest Airlines would result in hundreds of thousands of dollars of free advertising."

At the time, Southwest wasn't well known in certain markets, and entering the New York market was on Colleen's mind. New in this area, JetBlue was considered to have novel customer service concepts, many gleaned from Southwest. (JetBlue's founder and then CEO David Neeleman is a former short-term Southwest executive.)

"It also mattered that JetBlue was dying to do this reality show—as if JetBlue was the first airline to have a customer service focus. It was certainly the 'fair-haired child' at the time. So despite my own concerns and those of other executives, we all agreed to give it a try. Afterward, I could *not* watch the show. I had someone else watch it for me and report back."

What were the results? "Well, the first season was like I expected. It showed certain types of people—those who had too much to drink and people of size. I told my PR manager I wanted the show cancelled because they were focusing on the same types of people in each show.

"Again, she came prepared. She reminded me that reviews of the show were good and that the viewers already had favorite employees. She knew I had reviewed every viewer letter, email, and phone call transcript. In fact, we received several letters from employees of our competitors who thanked us for showing what a day in the life of an airline employee is really like."

But Colleen, always one for detail, had to do her own cost-benefit analysis. "After the first season, I watched the whole thing in one sitting. I took notes on every episode and wrote down the number of positive interactions versus negative ones, which were much fewer. I already knew the external and internal feedback on the program was ninety-five percent positive." More than that, the TV show featuring Southwest, "Airline," ran for three seasons, giving the airline lots of favorable input and hundreds of thousands of dollars worth of free advertising. (At the time, it cost $100,000 to buy a 30-second spot on the A & E channel, which ran the show.)

"In essence, the reason I said 'yes' was because this manager had the big picture in mind. She knew that one of our values is managing costs. She also knew the show would be a way to get our brand to parts of the country that didn't know about us at the time, and to do it in a cost-effective way. She also had all the facts and figures together. She documented how the exposure translated into the savings of paid advertising dollars. Plus she documented the viewer mail, which convinced me that it had a positive result."

Clearly, the Underdog who changed Colleen's mind had paid attention to her filter, maximizing exposure opportunities while appealing to Colleen's cost management values.

PRESSURE:
LEAVE SOME THINGS UNSAID

I remember reading a column by the late advice columnist Ann Landers who reminded married couples that what often makes for a good marriage is "leaving one thing a day *unsaid*." High performing underdogs do just that. They pay attention. They observe and listen. But it's not always prudent to talk, as Patrice Dell's story demonstrates.

Patrice Dell, a reservations support leader at Southwest Airlines, is also a union negotiator in the Albuquerque Reservations Center. She answers local grievances at the first step, discusses management and union issues on a regular basis with the local stewards, and renders hearing decisions as an officer representing management in employee hearings.

Patrice got involved in an effort led by Southwest to repeal the Wright Amendment, an outdated piece of legislation that prohibited Southwest from flying non-stop into or out of Dallas Love Field. Initially designed to protect American Airlines and Dallas-Ft. Worth International Airport from undue competition, the amendment was named after the former U.S. Speaker of the House, Jim Wright, who shepherded it through the Congress in the '70s. Patrice's goal was to get her member of Congress, Heather Wilson, to co-sponsor the legislation that would repeal the Wright Amendment removing the restrictions on Southwest's ability to fly non-stop into Dallas Love Field airport.

Patrice's insights led her to make a sound persuasion decision—namely, to refrain from nagging her member of Congress and leaving certain things *unsaid*. She called this learning experience her "Grassroots Influence Graduate School."

"Because Heather wasn't supportive initially, I had to learn the importance of 'reading between the lines.' I found out about behind-the-scenes internal politics that had nothing to do with the merits of my argument that were affecting her decision. Then I factored them into my request," Patrice recalled.

Patrice knew that Representative Wilson publicly disagreed with the GOP leadership's attitude toward ethical and legal issues surrounding then-House Majority Leader Tom DeLay. There was debate among the leaders that would allow him to remain in his House leadership post if he were indicted for campaign finance violations. Representative Wilson made no secret of her viewpoint—that if indicted, DeLay should not retain his leadership post.

"Congresswoman Wilson never actually came out and said she couldn't or wouldn't co-sponsor. She did answer my requests by suggesting other 'better and stronger' legislators for co-sponsorship given their Aviation Sub-Committee membership. She repeated that if the bill came to the floor for a vote, she would support it but continued to deflect when I asked her to be a co-sponsor.

"It didn't make sense to me. If she were so certain she would vote for it, why couldn't she co-sponsor it? Then I read a timely headline along these lines: 'House Energy and Commerce Committee Chairman Joe Barton, (R-Texas), is Reportedly Pushing to get Rep. Heather Wilson Ousted from His Committee.'"

According to a local newspaper article, it seems that Congressman Joe Barton was irked following Wilson's vote in favor of forcing the Bush administration to release internal cost estimates for the Medicare prescription drug law. Wilson was the only Republican on the committee to vote for the motion, which Barton said was a partisan effort to disparage the Bush administration. The measure never moved out of the committee. It appeared Barton was sending a message to panel members about loyalty.

To complicate matters, Congressman Joe Barton was a strong ally of American Airlines, the Dallas-Fort Worth airport, and the city of Fort Worth in their efforts to maintain the provisions of the Wright Amendment. "The Wright Amendment battle came down to us against these powerful interests," Patrice explained. She wisely sensed that Representative Wilson was already under pressure from her committee chairman, so for Wilson to take another public stand against him (for the Wright Amendment repeal) would be detrimental to her career. "Definitely, that behind-the-scenes drama impacted our situation. So after our visit, I put two and two together and recognized this as a stumbling block. I never asked her again to co-sponsor the legislation even when I met with her, and I'm sure she appreciated that. During our meeting, we posed for photos and she sent me a cordial Christmas card and personalized note. I sent her one back stating we appreciated the support she had always shown us. Ultimately, she did lose her position on Barton's Committee."

What Patrice did well was listening for what was *not being said* as she observed the environment surrounding Congresswoman Wilson and adjusted her "ask" accordingly. "Later, when I visited with Congresswoman Wilson at a D. C. reception, her aide told me that Congresswoman Wilson wanted me to know we had her support. I told him I 'understood' her position relative to Barton's stand and appreciated his message. I definitely think I could have done damage if I had pushed and pushed for her co-sponsorship," Patrice concluded.

Skilled underdog persuaders are not only aware of the environment surrounding their influence prospects, they adjust with alacrity so their request is more palatable.

In essence, the extreme influence tactics in this chapter revolve around empathy—feeling what your persuasion targets feel and then adjusting your request to make it easy for them to agree that it's the right thing to do. And it works.

THE UNDERDOG'S CHECKLIST
Do You Have Your Eyes Up?

✓ Pack away your passion. When you are trying to persuade an adversary, it only creates more resistance.

✓ Be self-aware. Don't undertake tough persuasion tasks when your willpower muscle is fatigued.

✓ Give the gift of heroics. Will your request make your influence prospect a hero, or will he or she make new enemies? How can your top dog be seen as a hero by agreeing with you?

✓ Will your prospect make new allies by helping you, or will agreeing to your request create new enemies? Who are the allies? How can you prove that they will indeed become an ally?

✓ Keep your eyes up and watch previous behaviors. How can you make your request align with the top dog's past actions?

✓ Listen for value statements. How is your cause consistent with what your big dog believes in and cares about?

✓ What is the mental filter that your request must go through to be approved? How can you make sure your request fits the filter?

✓ Know the difference between values and sacred values. When discussing sacred values, focus on the cost/benefit relationship, not the emotion of the issue.

✓ Listen for what is *not* said regarding your request and adjust accordingly.

✓ Present all sides of the issue and don't ask the top dog for an immediate decision on your first try.

CHAPTER 6

Extreme Influence Tactic #5:
Build Your Pack

"I'm not looking for the best players, Craig. I'm looking for the right ones."

> — *1980 U.S. Men's Olympic Hockey Coach Herb Brooks (in the 2004 movie Miracle)*

"Jim is not a tornado. He's really a quiet storm."

> — *Dr. Eric Chivian*

"They were people I would be hard-pressed to say no to. It was really smart of them to get those people in the room."

> — *California State Assemblyman John Laird*

"I don't want a lead dog that takes me onto thin ice just because I told him to do so three times. A dog is also an independent being and I want to accept that."

> — *Jacco Ulmann*

Because *building your pack* is such an essential component in underdog persuasion of top dogs, I'm gratified to see everyone getting on the bandwagon that underdogs have driven for years.

Business leaders have established the importance of this strategy. For example, David Gergen, director of the Center for Public Leadership at Harvard University, noted in his *U.S. News & World Report* article "The Spirit of Teamwork" that effective leaders are those who can "cross boundaries, forming partnerships worldwide."[91]

He stated that at major management training centers (most notably Stephen Covey's Center for Creative Leadership), leaders are instructed to think of leadership as a personal endeavor. They are to lead themselves first, then their organizations, and then a new circle representing organizations and institutions outside their own group. While I wouldn't quibble with this management advice, it's nothing new to grassroots underdog influencers. As noted throughout this book, our most accomplished underdogs succeeded when they reached beyond their existing borders (both organizational and personal) to get help for their causes and win over their top dogs.

But before you think all you need to do is get a bunch of yaktivists to join your cause, think again. If you read management books, you likely know of Jim Collins's insightful research in his book *Good to Great*. He admonishes companies to "get the right people on the bus." The key—as the 1980 U.S. men's Olympic hockey coach Herb Brooks said—is not necessarily getting the *best* people on your team but the *right* people. When it comes to underdog influence, the "right" people are led by a cohesive lead dog; they are connected; and they are converts.

In this chapter, let's examine these three Cs of a persuasive pack: Cohesion, Connection, and Conversion.

COHESION: STICK WITH THE TASK

As I reviewed the behavioral patterns of persuasive underdog pack leaders, I found that in building their packs, they all exhibit cohesion—specifically, task cohesion, also known as focus.

Let's look first at the benefits of task cohesion in the best example of a merit-based, results-based professional arena: the sporting world. Then we'll review the science.

We usually recognize winners when we see them—the Tim Tebows, Kobe Bryants, Wayne Gretzkys, Mia Hamms, Derek Jeters. They seem to carry their team time after time. Would Tim Tebow have been such a winner if he were playing for, say, Louisiana Tech? What about Kobe suiting up for the hapless Minnesota Timberwolves? Would these individuals make a difference to a losing team?

The sports psychologists say, well, yes.

"One of the most important things the leader does is promote the idea of task cohesion," said Patrick Devine, a professor of psychology at Kennesaw State University and former sports psychiatrist for the Atlanta Braves and Milwaukee Brewers. "He's the guy who can rally a team to work for a common goal instead of individual goals.

"You see some teams with big stars who make it all about *them*. 'How many points can I score? How many home runs did I hit?' But on the basketball court, for example, a true team player—the true winner—gets as much exposure from distributing the ball to a teammate as he does dunking the ball. Involving teammates raises their confidence, includes them in the fun, and motivates them to succeed, improving everyone's performance. The loser measures success in points. The winner measures success in wins."[92]

There are indeed consequences for a team's results when the team leader or "star" doesn't promote team cohesion. Barry Bonds is a prime example.

No Cohesion, No Results

Known as much for his aloofness as his skill, he habitually behaved as if his opponents and teammates weren't worthy of his presence. He hit 762 home runs, yet his team never won a World Series title. "Barry was a cancer," said Brian Johnson, a long-time major league catcher and Bond's teammate on the Giants in '97 and '98. As *Sports Illustrated* columnist Rick Reilly wrote: "If you have a guy who sees himself as better than everyone else, and he feels that he deserves special treatment, he'll never inspire greatness. Just the opposite."[93] Indeed, when the Giants reached the World Series in 2002, many believed it wasn't Bonds but second baseman, Jeff Kent, who was their most valuable player. He never underestimated an opponent and Johnson said, "Jeff was quiet, but had the respect of the clubhouse."[94]

Signs of Bond's lack of team spirit were obvious. When Bonds hit his 500th home run, only one person came out of the dugout to greet him at the plate: the Giants' batgirl. In the 2000 –2001 season, he didn't show up to pose for the team picture. He never boarded the players' bus at the hotel to go to the ballpark but instead rode with the manager, broadcasters, and trainers. Neither did Bonds eat with the team. He had his nutritionist bring in special meals for him. "Someday, they'll be able to hold Bonds' funeral in a fitting room," concluded Reilly.[95]

Cohesive Leaders Do Create Victories

Contrast the Giants with the 1986 New York Mets who had a positive team leader promoting cohesion among a motley group of players. That year, the Mets won 108 of 162 games and easily secured a place in the playoffs. The team had five All-Stars plus a lineup powered by one big-name slugger after another. When the Mets beat the Boston Red Sox to win the World Series, many sportswriters labeled it as a team of winners. But a close examination shows that wasn't true.

Consider the manager, Davey Johnson, who drank a lot and wasn't known for imposing discipline. The two brightest young stars, pitcher Dwight Goodman and right fielder Darryl Strawberry, were beginning to use cocaine. Rookie Kevin Mitchell was a reformed San Diego gang member with a bullet still lodged in his back and a violent temper. Third baseman Ray Knight was a 33-year-old journeyman, and his backup, Howard Johnson, had been dismissed by his former team as a man who would wilt in the face of pressure. A grand total of two Mets had played in a prior World Series. Ed Hearn, the team's backup catcher, said, "There was one thing we had that turned us into winners: one man that wouldn't let us lose, no matter what obstacles we faced. Thank God for Mex."[96]

It was Keith "Mex" Hernandez who created cohesion. "Just something about Mex oozed confidence. It was contagious. It made you need to win." When the Mets seized the championship from the Red Sox against all odds (twice New York was one strike away from losing), nobody in the clubhouse was surprised. Hernandez said at the time, "Hell, we always expect to win. Always."[97] And win they did.

Keith Hernandez provided task cohesion for the Mets, the steadfast center around which everything revolved. And this anecdotal evidence from the sporting world is supported by the science of minority opinion. It indicates how one person can keep a team or a movement together.

How Minority Opinion Thrives with a Cohesive Lead Dog

Classic research on conformity demonstrates that simply knowing or imagining how other people think and feel about an issue is often sufficient to lead one person to the same opinion. You'd think that with the widespread transmission of information via the Internet and mass media (to name just a few vehicles), the tendency toward "group think" would be inevitable. Yet, minority opinion survives and thrives. Social science literature shows us that minority opinions dwell in clusters of like-minded people that are usually formed around strong, cohesive individuals. The cohesion comes primarily from the lead dog—the one who provides group direction and motivation.

Robin R. Vallacher, professor at Florida Atlantic University, has advised the U.S. Department of Homeland Security on the psychology of terrorism. Terrorism is technically minority "influence" albeit in its most *coercive* form. Its practices are held by a few, it's repulsive to virtually all societies, and yet it survives. How can this be when it's clearly a minority view that the majority would like to obliterate?

Vallacher believes that the pressure for uniformity in social groups increases the grit of individuals who hold opinions that differ from the mainstream. Attempts to squelch these minority groups can make them stronger—if they have ardent, gritty leaders.

Scientists have conducted computer automations to provide ways to demonstrate this. Their simulations have revealed that an initial random distribution of opinions among a group of people gives way after several rounds of distribution to a well-defined social structure. As you might expect, the majority opinion *within* the group increases in frequency (from 60 percent to 90 percent) over time as individuals interact with each other.

What I find intriguing is that these minority opinions survive within society in clusters of like-minded people that are *usually formed* around strong individuals. Although these opinions represent a minority within society, they form what Vallacher calls a "local majority." Plus, because weak individuals are more likely to adhere to society's majority opinion than strong individuals, *people in the minority groups are more likely to be stronger on average than society's majority members*. This explains the apathy of the majority. Vallacher's conclusion? "When conditions in a society are destabilized or otherwise changed, minority members are in a position to exert *disproportionately strong influence* in shaping public opinion. Such an effect was observed in Eastern Europe after the collapse of communism in the early 1990s."[98]

So, how does this translate to underdog influence? One application is knowing that the lead dog must be cohesive, strong. As Professor Devine has observed, whether Kobe Bryant played for the Cavaliers or the Minnesota Timberwolves, he would have inspired his teammates to a higher level of performance.

Let's look at two other powerful and cohesive lead dogs, Dr. Jim Muller and Amy Kremer.

To Catch a Falling Knife—Dr. Jim Muller

In 1980, many viewed Dr. Jim Muller, an accomplished Harvard cardiologist, as presumptuous or naïve when he first brought three American and three Russian doctors together to try end the arms race between the United States and the Soviet Union. How could a cardiologist possibly change the Kremlin and the Pentagon with good intentions? But by 1985, the group he cofounded, International Physicians for the Prevention of Nuclear War, had grown to 135,000 members, and Muller won the Nobel Peace Prize. He had garnered not only the practical experience but the stature he needed to lead another "little" grassroots movement—one aimed at the Roman Catholic Church.

In November of 1992, *The Boston Globe* ran a story about 500 priests who had met to discuss the draft of a sexual abuse policy for the Catholic Archdiocese of Boston. That gathering was a result of grassroots pressure. For some time, reports of sexual abuse by American priests had been reported from Boston to California and Minnesota to Louisiana. They noted that many Massachusetts cases were quite egregious. Over the next 10 years, more cases were revealed, and the church failed to respond. In January of 2002, *The Boston Globe* reported that since the mid-1990s, more than 130 people had come forward in Boston alone with stories of horrid childhood sexual abuse. *Globe* reporters questioned how the church had "managed" the revelations.

This led to an underdog movement in 2002 in Wellesley, Massachusetts at St. John the Evangelist Church. It was promoted as a "listening session" for parishioners who were upset about clergy sexual abuse. Each Monday night at 7:30, hundreds of people packed the church—so many that they could no longer fit into the school basement. They named themselves the Voice of the Faithful (VOTF). VOTF's mission statement was this: "Keep the Faith, Change the Church."

Dr. Muller was a committed Catholic from a devoted Catholic family. But after reading about the crimes of Boston-area priests, especially Father John Geoghan's, and the church's non-stop practice of covering up the abuses, he got agitated. Instead of leaving the church, he decided to stay and fight. He joined VOTF and later became its president. Addressing the similarities between the task of uniting physicians across the globe and uniting lay Catholics to assert themselves to the Catholic hierarchy, he said, "It's the same situation. Then, the people were disenfranchised from nuclear policy. Here, the people are denied a voice in the policies of their own church."[99]

One could view Dr. Muller's and VOTF's goals akin to catching a falling knife. It's reported that in a conversation with his wife about the challenges that lie ahead, his wife declared him "crazy" to take on this cause. She had previously told him he needed to join the effort and take on the church, but clarified her advice by saying she'd meant that he should take on St. John's in Wellesley, *not the entire Roman Catholic Church.*

"Jim is not a tornado. He's really a quiet storm," said Dr. Eric Chivian, a cofounder with Muller of the International Physicians for the Prevention of Nuclear War.[100] Chivian, himself a cohesive leader, is also director of the Harvard Center for Health and the Global Environment. In 2008, he was named by *Time Magazine* as one of the 100 Most Influential People in the World for organizing scientists and evangelicals to join in efforts to protect the global environment. Dr. Chivian also said of Muller, "He's extremely articulate and convincing about the things he believes in and he's doggedly persistent about them."[101]

VOTF's convention in the summer of 2002 was attended by about 4,000 supporters from 36 states and 19 countries. With such a highly emotional issue, the convention attracted "hair on fire" activists who viewed this as their opportunity to dramatically change the church's stand on everything from women in the priesthood to homosexuality, abortion, and more. But Dr. Muller promoted task cohesion, which helped maintain the VOTF's credibility. He was passionate about VOTF as a harbinger of change, but he urged members to stay out of issues such as celibacy, women in the priesthood, and sexual morality. He kept the group focused on what mattered most to the Catholic Church—money. He declared, "No more donation without representation. We have to gain financial power in this church. They say the laity is weak, but we are 99 percent of the church and 100 percent of the money, and we now have a structure where we can exert that power."[102]

Muller kept his team cohesive around the theme of representation rather than the cacophony of issues that could prove divisive.

The continual award-winning investigative reporting by *The Boston Globe*—along with the pressure exerted by the Voice of the Faithful (VOTF)—led to the resignation of Boston Archdiocese Cardinal Bernard Law. This effort will also forever changed how the Boston Archdiocese and the American Catholic Church deals with the occurrences of sexual abuse by priests.

Voice of the Faithful now has 200 parish affiliates across the United States and more than 35,000 members worldwide. It continues to play a part in church affairs as a watchdog, particularly but not exclusively, on issues of clerical abuse.

Amy Kremer Provides Tea Party Express Cohesion

When I was talking to a friend about the inspiring people I've interviewed for this book, she referred me to a cohesive leader named Amy Kremer. Amy has started a movement that's changed American politics and given heartburn or help (depending on your side of the political aisle) to candidates and elected officials throughout the nation.

Amy is a former Delta flight attendant and real estate agent who was a single parent most of her adult life. She loved her job as a flight attendant, but due to health issues, she had to step down. This sparked an identity crisis for her.

Amy had always been a news junkie, not a political junkie. She said, "I have the news on in every TV in the house regardless of what's going on. I started blogging and tweeting because I was upset about the government spending going on in the Bush administration. I found some like-minded folks online, and we regularly communicated with each other about our disgust with the government," she recalled.

In February of 2009, CNBC's Rick Santelli delivered his now-famous plea from the floor of the New York Stock Exchange, imploring government leaders to get their act together regarding the mortgage crisis, excessive government spending, and taxes. Santelli revved up Amy and her online friends to another stratosphere.

"He was saying exactly what we thought, but he had a platform none of us had. It inspired us. One week from that day, we came together on Twitter to plan some events. It didn't happen overnight. I think twenty-two of us got together for a conference call to conduct several events. We decided to call them Tea Parties," she said.

The group decided it would define success by conducting 10 Tea Parties with 50 to 100 people at each event. Amy volunteered to be the lead organizer for the Atlanta event, dealing with logistical aspects such as obtaining permits, getting publicity, arranging transportation, buying Tea Party domain names, and fielding media inquiries.

A source close to the Tea Party movement told me that when he learned of the group's ambitious goals… "I thought she [Kremer] was smoking crack for even trying this." Amy admitted that her husband (who, she said, is wildly supportive) thought she was "out of [her] mind" and that… "you can't spend your whole life doing this."

Fifty-three Tea Parties and 30,000 participants (as of April 15, 2010) later, Amy and her Tea Party compatriots across the country have rattled the political status quo and proven the doubters wrong.

Numerous groups are associated with the Tea Party movement, all with different names, governing bodies, and so on. The two primary groups, Tea Party Express (of which Kremer is officially director of Grassroots and Coalitions) and the Tea Party Patriots (the original group that Amy cofounded) have different operating structures and tactics. Those close to the Tea Party movement believe that Amy has kept the Tea Party Express alive in spite of pressure from the Tea Party Patriots because she "is not in this for herself."

Sources reported that when the Tea Party movement started, several experienced political operatives with strong ties to Washington, D.C. got involved and wanted a top-down structure with direction from D.C. They also wanted personal glory. "While Amy was doing the grunt work of standing in line to get permits, and so on," explained one of the sources, "these people wouldn't return her phone calls or emails unless they learned she was calling about an opportunity to appear on TV. Then they quickly called her back. That told us they were in it for the wrong reasons. Amy doesn't care about that. She keeps her head down and barrels through. People follow a person, not a title, and that's what the Tea Party Patriots don't get. It's why Amy and the Tea Party Express have thrived despite their [the Patriots'] attempts to neuter them." (Amy was asked to leave the Tea Party Patriots board of directors late in 2009 because she refused to publicly denigrate a Tea Party Express member.)

Amy Kremer keeps going. "One of our goals is to raise money for candidates who support our goals of fiscal responsibility. Back in January 2010, I told our gang we should endorse Scott Brown for the U.S. Senate seat in Massachusetts. Everyone told me it wasn't looking good; there was no way he could win. I kept pushing. I saw the online chatter, which verified what was already happening on the ground. We raised more than $350,000. We bought up every single ad space we could find and ran national ads. The night he won, not one of us was in Massachusetts, but we were all watching!" she gleefully recalled.

"I don't sense that Amy wants to jump in front of the camera all the time," my source reported. "Sure, she'll go on TV and do media, but it's not about her. She really favors the grassroots volunteers, and some didn't like that." Amy's cohesive leadership is keeping the Tea Party Express together and thriving, despite annoyances from the Tea Party Patriots who want to be seen as the "premier" Tea Party organization.

In addition to promoting cohesion through personal strength, the pack leader has to find the *right* people versus the *best* people. You'll see from the following examples that the *right* people for underdog influence are *the connected and the converted.*

Let's first define what "connected" means in the world of upward influence.

CONNECTED PACK MEMBERS

This book is focused on upward influence—not peer influence, not downward (coercion) influence. For purposes of upward influence, I have a specific definition of "connected." While this may represent heresy to some, when I refer to "connected" here, I don't mean the number of Facebook friends, LinkedIn connections, and Twitter followers you or your pack members may have, although that kind of connection certainly matters. I believe that underdogs must use all the tools in their toolbox to build their pack—and social media provides tools that play a part.

As you'll see, however, the persuasion tasks required for upward influence aren't the same as those pursued by some of the narcissists on Twitter 24/7. I don't mean all Twitter users, mind you—just the narcissists who are trapped like Las Vegas losers at the behavioral slot machines of life.

Rather, upward influence requires varsity team players who have social capital and social networks, two effective avenues of influence. Social capital translates into behavior. When you request a meeting with a top dog, will it be granted? When you try to mobilize friends for your cause, will they join? Will they return your phone calls? Although social capital and social networks rely on each other to a degree, if I were forced to choose, I would select social capital any day. Why? Because it causes behavior change.

But don't take my word for it; read what Malcolm Gladwell said about it in a 2010 speech to the F5 Expo on online technologies. He said that if Fidel Castro had been on Twitter and Facebook, he probably wouldn't have been able to mobilize a revolution to overthrow the Cuban dictator Fulgencio Batista. "What would have happened to Castro?" asked Gladwell. "Would he have gone to the trouble of putting together an extraordinary network that allowed him to defeat Batista?"[103]

Social media advocates point to the power of online networks, citing such examples as U.S. President Barack Obama using them to build support and win the White House. Gladwell, however, has noted that such connections can prove shallow. "Obama's popularity rating plummeted after he was in power. By contrast, the network Castro built launched a revolution."[104]

He also asked, "Do ideas spread through social media? I don't think they are vehicles. People aren't spreading ideas on Twitter; they're spreading observations, perhaps. The point of *The Tipping Point* (his 2002 mega-bestseller) is that I was very interested in face-to-face interpersonal reactions. If social media or online communication is the means to the creation of a personal connection, it's a fabulous thing. But if it's an excuse to not make a connection, it's ultimately a trivial thing."[105]

From my own observations of hundreds of sincere underdog leaders and pack members, social media is frequently used initially as a substitute for personal connections—usually because of its ease and savings in time and money. And that's okay, depending on the goal. People often have a childlike fascination with the possibility of changing the world without leaving their computer or sacrificing their time. Then, after a few years, group members wonder why they're stuck, and they realize they aren't taking those social media tools to the next level—to offline connections. Thankfully, this is changing.

The 2011 revolt in Egypt was organized via social networks. However, the resulting pressure for regime change came about through the vivid presence (see Chapter 3) of Egyptian citizens in the streets. Their presence in large numbers led to extensive attention and resulting support. Do you think Egyptian President Hosni Mubarak would have stepped down if the citizens had only communicated their discontent online?

Clearly, social media tools can be catalysts for change; after all, every persuasion effort needs a medium for its communication. But the medium is not the message. I think because Americans are fascinated with social media, many reporters exaggerated their role in the Egyptian revolution. And the role of Al Jazeera's television coverage, which continually showed vivid images to the Egyptian people, cannot be downplayed.

The *World Factbook*, also known as the *CIA World Factbook*, is a resource produced by the Central Intelligence Agency that includes almanac-style information about the world's countries. It notes that only 25 percent of Egyptians have Internet access! It's hard to believe that all the protesters who pushed Mubarak out of office were a subset of that 25 percent. The thousands of others who filled the streets came because of contacts other than social media. This example leads me to agree with Gladwell who says social media outlets are great for communicating and organizing, but they're not the magic wand that persuades people to take action.

In a media interview, Gladwell said he believes social media fails to deliver trust. "When you look at what the Internet has done, what it has done is brilliantly exploited weak ties." And weak ties are not good for driving revolutions and social transformation, he pointed out. Trust is key to building strong ties, and this has a strong geographic component. "How can you trust the person you're communicating with if you have no clue who they are?"[106]

As I've found, connected people are trusted by the top dogs they want to influence. That's why you need them on your team.

Vince Larsen's (Environmental) Team Connections

Remember the intrepid Vince Larsen who worked to reform clean air regulations and battled Exxon in the process? When I asked him why he was successful, he wouldn't take personal credit but sent me a detailed document describing each person who helped the team succeed. He mentioned each of their contributions in detail, as any good cohesive team leader would do. And as you'll read, they're all connected.

All the people who helped Larsen brought unique skills to the cause and he spelled them out for me. "Ed Zaidlicz was one of YVCC's [Yellowstone Valley Citizen's Council's] most ardent and articulate members. He was a retired former state director of the Bureau of Land Management. A man of unquestionable and uncompromising integrity, he was our unofficial leader. He was an eloquent writer and well respected throughout our community. Sadly, he died shortly after our battles and we all miss him terribly.

"Bob White and Joe Walters were both writers and gave their talent and letters to the EPA, Montana Department of Environmental Quality, and our local papers. Claire Johnson, who's a talented and extremely knowledgeable reporter for the *Billings Gazette*, presented technical information in an easy-to-read form so readers could understand the facts and complexities. Jim Hughes, an air quality and environmental specialist for the Montana Department of Environmental Quality, provided refinery and parkland emissions data. I'd always ask Jim to review our work before submitting it to the EPA or the *Billings Gazette*," wrote Larsen. "Denise Ross-Barber, who was then employed with the Yellowstone Valley Citizen's Council, was an extremely bright and committed worker.

"Surely one of the most courageous people was then-State Representative John Bohlinger, who became a strong advocate for repealing the infamous Hannah Bill. John was a strong, principled, and dedicated legislator who came to our meetings, learned about the issue, and found both the courage and the conviction to do something about it."

Despite having such a well-balanced team, according to Larsen, "A tipping point came when Joe Sample, one of Billings' most prominent and respected businessmen, became involved. I never knew him before, but I was aware of his philanthropy and service to our community.

"Joe had previously owned one of our two TV stations. Because of this, he was aware of the high levels of sulfur dioxide in our air given that it was responsible for corrosion on the equipment at the base of his TV towers. Joe's support came at a critical time because the EPA and state were putting pressure on our polluting industries to reduce their sulfur dioxide emissions.

"Frankly, Joe's support changed the dynamics of our efforts," Larsen explained. As past president of the Billings Chamber of Commerce, he wasn't afraid to write and speak out strongly on the issue. He courageously confronted leaders of the Chamber in an effort to get them to support clean air. However, they did absolutely nothing except continue to cover for our polluting industries," Larsen recalled.

Joe Sample, completely disgusted by the chamber's position, retained a Billings law firm to prepare legal action against the state of Montana and possibly its governor. He based his action on Section 3, Article 2 of the Montana State Constitution, which states that all people have the right to a clean and healthful environment.

"Joe was successful in soliciting the support of five former presidents of the Billings Chamber of Commerce in his action [the connected pulling in others who are connected!]. His efforts scared the hell out of the industry," said Larsen. "We believe it was instrumental in their willingness to start negotiations with the EPA and the state to reduce their high levels of sulfur dioxide."

The entire team was connected, and when a super-connected person like Joe Sample joined it, Exxon came to the table. Sample was uniquely positioned as a business leader who had given back financially to the Billings community and had a history of connecting with key decision-makers. It's hard to ignore someone who gives back.

Dr. Jim Muller's (VOTF) Team Connections

Like the Yellowstone Valley Citizen's Council, the Boston division of Voices of the Faithful led by Dr. Jim Muller didn't have lots of "wallpaper people" on the team. All of its members were prominent in their fields and/or communities.

Mary Jo Bane was a member of the Parish Pastoral Council at St. William's Catholic Parish. She was and is a professor of Public Policy at Harvard's John F. Kennedy School of Government. She's the author of a number of books and articles on poverty, welfare, families, and the role of churches in civic life. Bane placed an opinion piece in the paper that made it clear she would withhold her support from the church until it changed. She wasn't just any concerned citizen. She brought insights as a faithful Catholic and an expert on churches and leadership. She urged lay Catholics who love the church to question its hierarchy. (Bane is now Thornton Bradshaw Professor of Public Policy and Management, academic dean, and chair of Management, Leadership, and Decision Sciences (MLD) and Leadership at Harvard University.)

Peter Pollard, a victim of clerical abuse, was willing to tell his story. While not dismissing the sexual abuse by priests, he eloquently reframed the issue from a victim's perspective as one of not only sexual abuse but abuse of power. Thomas Reilly, the Massachusetts Attorney General, pressured Boston Archdioceses with criminal subpoenas. James Post, a professor of management at Boston University, served as president of VOTF during the 2002 convention and was the public face of Voice of the Faithful. Plus the team had Dr. Muller, an activist with Nobel Prize "street cred."

Would the Pope have pushed one of his favorite Cardinals to resign had not all the people above been marshaled against him? We don't know with 100 percent certainty, but this determined group of lay Catholics upped the ante and thus helped change minds.

John Boyd's (Black Farmers) Team Connections

Remember John Boyd from the National Black Farmers Association? Virginia Governor George Allen had told Boyd he'd ignored him, a black farmer from his state, because he thought John was "a radical and a crazy." But Boyd persevered and benefited from the voice of a connected person who helped gain Governor Allen's support for black farmers. Yes, the butler did it.

Boyd had been trying to talk to Governor Allen about the black farmer settlement issue. Governor Allen casually mentioned the issue to his butler, Tootie. As John recalled, "Governor Allen told me his butler at the governor's mansion overheard him [Allen] talking to his staff about our group picketing on this issue. I guess Tootie spoke up about his own family experiencing lending discrimination, and that they lost their family farm because of their inability to get financing. Well, that got the governor's attention. He changed how he viewed us and the whole issue."

Interesting, isn't it? No matter how much picketing and media attention the National Black Farmers Association received at the state capitol, it was Tootie who made the issue real to Governor Allen. Shortly after, soon-to-be U.S. Senator George Allen cosponsored legislation in the United States Congress to extend the statute of limitations for financial settlements to black farmers.

Judy Darnell's (Uninsured Children) Team Connections

Even the top dogs will admit to the power of the connected and the trust they bring to a negotiation.

John Laird is a member of the California State Assembly representing Santa Cruz. He became the lead champion and sponsor of a bill intended to extend health insurance coverage to all uninsured children in California. But undertaking that initiative had not initially been on his radar screen. In fact, Assemblyman Laird had hesitated to take it on, saying, "Although a lot of people would like the bill, there are always people who think government should not be in the health care business." He was especially concerned about his supporters in the Monterey Peninsula. With its huge tourism industry, hotel and restaurant owners were leery of all health insurance issues. "They believe that if they're burdened with health insurance issues, they will take a financial hit. I really did have to work it through with them."

Assemblyman Laird got behind the issue in part because Judy Darnell secured the right people to "join the pack" in supporting it.

Judy Darnell is director of Public Policy for the United Way of California. As Darnell explained, "John was always a good advocate for social issues, but this one had not been one of his top issues. So five strategically chosen people went with me to see him, including one who ran the county health initiative, one who worked with the hospital, and one who headed the county HMO systems that provided coverage to local children. Not coincidentally, these people also helped Assemblyman Laird get elected."

This Underdog clearly knew better than to recruit just "warm bodies"—as many well-meaning but unprepared underdogs often do—to build her pack. She selected people who had expertise and were also connected. John Laird even acknowledged they were the *right* people, saying, "Every person in the room was an old friend of mine or someone I'd worked with previously on health care issues—people I'd be hard pressed to say no to. That was really smart of them to join forces."

Clearly from Assemblyman Laird's comments, Judy probably would not have been as forceful or impressive if she had approached him alone, even with her "white hat" reputation as a nonprofit organization representative.

She agreed with the mythology of the "one person can make a difference" mantra. "The key is to not go in by yourself. Find allies of your influence targets and constituencies. In this case, each member in our group had different perspectives and areas of expertise. Plus, the United Way volunteer talked about the strong support the organization was getting from business leaders across the state on the children's health insurance issue. That made Assemblyman Laird more comfortable in dealing with the business interests in his district."

Darnell not only recruited the right allies but did her homework so she could understand the person she was dealing with. She knew *who* mattered to Assemblyman Laird. As he said, "The people in this coalition knew what issues I've responded to. It was hard not to respond to *them*, especially when they said, 'We will be here for you all the way through.' And they were asking me for advice, which was a strategically smart way of approaching me."

Human beings may all be created equal, but every person's input is not equal when it comes to persuading those up the food chain. In this endeavor, Judy was particularly proud of a partnership with the California Restaurant Association (CRA), including recruiting one key member—another "right" person—who accelerated the group's progress. She pursued a local restaurant owner, Ted Burke, to join her effort in supporting children's health issues. But Ted Burke wasn't just *any* restaurant owner. He was connected and soon to be converted, he become a *convert communicator*.

Building a pack with a few converts can increase your team's influence IQ. Convert communicators are individuals who previously were averse to your position but have had their Road to Damascus experience and are now on your team. Let's learn why they're persuasive, and then you'll see how Ted Burke helped move Judy's cause to the finish line.

CONVERSION: PUT A CONVERT COMMUNICATOR IN YOUR PACK

Dr. Brad Sagarin is associate professor of psychology at Northern Illinois University. Every year, I hire him to speak about the science of influence at a conference I host.

He said something at the 2011 conference that caught my attention—that "convert communicators can accelerate your influence results." I asked him to expand on why they're especially helpful to have on underdog teams.

"There are two benefits of having convert communicators on your team. First, they can provide insight into the persuasive messages that converted them. We filter persuasive messages through our current attitudes. Because we already believe our own arguments, we're often bad at predicting how our messages will sound to those who disagree. Converts are different. They used to disagree with us, which makes them adept at identifying techniques to sway other opponents.

"Also, they're one of the most persuasive sources of information. One, they are seen by those you're trying to influence as similar to themselves, which we know is a powerful persuasion source as opposed to a message coming directly from you, the opponent. The convert communicator, after all, thinks like they [top dogs] do. There is also the benefit of credibility. Your influence prospect may be thinking, 'This was someone who used to agree with me.' So, the very presence of the convert communicator brings along a possibility of a change in attitude. Your prospect may think, 'That person did it, why can't I?'

"The convert communicator can also walk the target through the process of how he changed his mind by using personal narrative. We know that narrative is exceptionally powerful as a persuasive device because it flies under the radar. We don't throw up defenses when listening to narrative."

Convert communicators are among the many reasons for the life-transforming power of groups such as Alcoholics Anonymous. In the book, *Getting Better: Inside Alcoholics Anonymous*, Nan Robertson profiled former alcoholics who talk to AA audiences about their previous lives and how they stay sober.[107] As perfect examples of "converts," they yield considerable influence because they're alcoholics who've gone straight. They've converted from one lifestyle and ideology to a totally opposite set of beliefs.

In addition, they're not in positions of authority over those they're trying to influence (underdog, anyone?) and yet they're extremely credible communicators. This applies to religious conversions, as well. Notwithstanding the tactics of religious cults, a decision to follow a particular religion is usually made absent of outside pressure, and the true converts behave differently—they're a vivid representation of their new belief system.

Ted Burke as Judy's Convert Communicator

Now let's see how Ted Burke helped Judy Darnell's team get its message across about health insurance for uninsured children.

Burke served on the board of the National Restaurant Association and was the past president of the California Restaurant Association. He'd also chaired the CRA's Political Action Committee, responsible for raising $15 million to fund a 2004 referendum that *repealed* a state law requiring employers to provide health insurance.

Think about that. He had led an effort to do the *opposite* of what Judy's coalition advocated. No, he wasn't a typical health care advocate. He was a convert who could give assurance to legislators that, indeed, some people in the business community supported the initiative.

As Judy said, "Ted was one of many people we talked to early on, and he was at the top of my list because I knew him slightly from over the years. I knew he was a well-respected business person in Santa Cruz County who was thoughtful, influential, and cared about our community. I also knew he was involved with the California Restaurant Association, and he would give us good insight into how best to approach the business community and state associations.

"Ted quickly 'got it' when we presented the problem of uninsured children and how it affects the restaurant industry. After all, he was an employer who did as much as he could for his employees. A good thinker, he got involved in early business meetings when we brainstormed what would and wouldn't work for business. He knew politics and was *well connected*. He seemed to be someone we could trust for honest opinions and thoughtful responses."

During their initial call, Ted said he was impressed by Judy's open mind and understanding of why most restaurant owners couldn't provide health insurance for their employees and families. "Judy had empathy and an understanding of our industry, and she was trying to find ways we could work together. So I felt comfortable telling my CRA colleagues they could work with her," he said.

Burke said many other health care advocates had written off restaurant owners who didn't provide health insurance, labeling them bad employers. "A lot of people are so ideologically bent, they don't care what the facts are. With Judy, I got a whole different attitude when she asked, 'What can we do together?' She had already accepted what we *couldn't* do," he added.

Darnell persuaded Burke that supporting the children's health bill was a way for the restaurant association to play a positive role in the health care debate, to take a stand that would benefit children. (Remember the gift of heroics?)

"Judy helped our restaurant association members see that if we could lend a hand to strengthen those benefits, it would be positive. It fit with the whole philosophy of knowing there are some things we can do, some things we can't do, yet there's a willingness to do what we can," he said.

At key moments, the CRA wrote letters on behalf of its members to the legislators, which had tremendous impact. "The partnership with the CRA proved to be crucial in getting legislators to speak out for this issue," Darnell said.

In 2009, in a remarkable last-minute deal, the California Assembly voted to levy a tax on health plans to save the children's health program through 2010—even after it had been slashed into near-nonexistence as part of cutting the state budget. The Democrats wrote the bill's language and Governor Arnold Schwarzenegger's administration worked with those who sponsored the bill to support the tax. The bill passed with strong bipartisan support. "We counted it as a great victory because of all of our work to get Republicans to support AB 1422. It was such a strong bipartisan vote," Darnell concluded.

Kate Hanni's Convert for Airline Passengers' Rights

Remember Kate Hanni's story in Chapter 4? Her grit enabled her to secure a convert who turbo-charged her campaign for airline passengers' rights.

Hanni's fight against the airline industry got a huge boost in September 2009. That's when three business travel groups, including the influential Business Travel

Coalition, endorsed her passengers' rights bill—one that allows airline passengers the option of returning to the terminal after three hours of sitting on the tarmac. Until then, the three organizations had sided with the airline industry, *not* the passenger advocates.

This happened because Hanni was able to recruit a convert communicator to contribute his talent and supporters to the cause. Specifically, she convinced Kevin Mitchell, chairman of the Business Travel Coalition, to switch to her side of the passengers' rights argument. Here's what happened.

Hanni first met Mitchell when she testified before the Senate Commerce Committee in April 2007. Mitchell sided with the airline industry, *not the passengers*, in his testimony. But Kate watched him and became intrigued. He impressed Hanni with his communication skills. "Of all the people who were against us, he was the smartest," she recalled. "I needed someone of his caliber on our team."

In July 2009, Hanni was feeling stuck and feared the passengers' rights campaign was losing momentum. "I was broke, worried about donations, and in dire need of help" was how she put it. On a whim, she called Mitchell, who told her he'd been on the fence about certain aspects of the issue and had been thinking about her stance. They talked for five hours.

Joking that this five-hour call was "like a long tarmac delay," Mitchell admitted it was pivotal in his decision to join Hanni's fight. "Kate got my attention because she framed the issue in terms of health and safety, unlike other passenger-bill-of-rights advocates who argued that the delays were a nuisance and an inconvenience. She also countered the argument I've always made, that the number of times flights were stranded on the tarmac for hours was statistically insignificant."

Until Hanni pointed it out, Mitchell also didn't know that 20 percent of the passengers on domestic flights each year were elderly, very young, or suffering from an underlying health condition. Because roughly 741 million people were passengers on commercial flights in 2008, Mitchell realized that the number of people who were vulnerable—with their safety potentially threatened—was significant after all.

"Kate changed the issue completely from customer service to health and safety, a shift in thinking that allowed me to reconsider my stance," he admitted.

Mitchell said he greatly admires Hanni, whose story, personality, and communication skills make her an effective grassroots leader. "She has perspicacity and perseverance. She's a good sales person who knows how to read people in different situations and approach them in the right way," Mitchell said. "To be effective, you have to have a passion and knowledge about how to communicate well. Kate has both."

On September 7, 2009, Mitchell issued a press release. It announced that the Business Travel Coalition (representing about 300 corporate travel departments) had changed course and decided to support legislation that allows passengers the option to return to the terminal after three hours of sitting on the tarmac. Since then, Mitchell and his coalition have poured their resources and brainpower into a campaign that supports this safety initiative.

A rule enacted in December of 2009, which took effect in late April of 2010, will let passengers de-plane from stranded domestic flights after three hours. Other provisions in the rule require airlines to provide food and water for passengers delayed for two hours, as well as operating lavatories and medical attention. "We have achieved our near-term goals of a mandatory three-hour rule, and it's akin to a Christmas miracle," said Kate of the December enactment.

Cautionary Words about Converts

The many advantages of a convert communicator might make you think that once you have a convert in your pack, you will automatically win. However, as with all of our techniques, you'll discover nuances. Dr. Sagarin advised that converts be careful not to denigrate their former belief system and believers. Wise converts remember where they came from!

"Converts can hurt your efforts if they destroy their perception of similarity with former compatriots by dismissing their former position. They must validate their old position and explain why they changed. That helps validate the person or people you're trying to persuade. Converts need to remember they felt differently at one time, too, and that it's okay for others to feel that way.

"If a convert communicator wrote an autobiography, he would probably admit that his change was not an overnight thing but rather a slow process," reminded

Sagarin. "Organizations that want to secure the support of converts need to have patience and move them by small steps. Slowly bring them over," he advised.

It's also important that the convert be seen as having *freely made the decision to convert.* A gang member who goes straight may lack credibility if he's seen as making the decision to save his own skin, so he might not be the most effective spokesperson for an anti-crime campaign.

Vince Larsen made his living as a petroleum geologist. He profited from the industry, yet he freely made the decision to convert (at least on one big issue) to the other side of a critical debate and lead that team. Vince became a credible convert.

Examples of convert communicators who lack credibility are ubiquitous in the political world, hence their lack of believability. Think about when members of Congress switch from the Republican to the Democratic Party or from either to become an Independent. They're usually trying to save their seat due to external circumstances. Rarely have they become imbued with a new belief system; they've just become obsessed with a power extension.

The most recent "contrived converts" that come to mind are former Republican-turned-Democrat U.S. Senator from Pennsylvania, Arlen Specter and Republican-turned-Independent U.S. Senate candidate from Florida, former Governor Charlie Crist.

Former U.S. Senator Arlen Specter of Pennsylvania, who "converted" from Republican to Democrat, lost his 2010 Democratic primary election. Exit interviews with Pennsylvania primary voters revealed that they didn't think his conversion was believable and didn't perceive him as a "real" Democrat. In trying to save his Senate seat, not the people of Pennsylvania, the move backfired.

Former Florida Governor Charlie Crist lost the U.S. Senate election to the underdog Marco Rubio. Florida politicos knew that his conversion was hardly authentic, and the voters agreed.

What's the lesson here? While you might gain traction and attention by recruiting *lots* of people (and you should), when you have the *right* people engaged—those who are cohesive, connected, and (truly) converted—you are more likely to change minds.

THE UNDERDOG'S CHECKLIST
How to Build Your Pack

✓ Find the "right" people (cohesive, connected, converted) rather than the "best" people for an effective underdog persuasion pack.

✓ Be (or find) a pack leader who is interested in the team winning, not in personal victory. Your pack leader must promote task cohesion.

✓ Find and engage the connected. Be a human chauvinist connected to people both offline and online.

✓ Do a social capital pre-test with your team members by giving them a small task or favor to ask of someone. Watch what happens. Who has the social capital to get a phone call returned, to make sure their meeting request is granted?

✓ Find connected pack members who have credibility in the community and/or among those you want to influence.

✓ Recruit convert communicators as pack members. Who do you know who was formerly against your cause? What's his or her story?

✓ Make sure your converts have freely made the decision to convert. Converting to save their skin isn't convincing.

✓ Give your converts visibility. Can they serve as spokespersons?

CHAPTER 7

Extreme Influence Tactic #6:

Ask Not What the Top Dog Can Do for You, But What You Can Do for the Top Dog

"You have to have fun. I frankly worry more about the relationship than the outcome. They can see if your approach is not authentic."

— *Brad Neet*

"The moral of the story is that it's all about personal relationships. We get 100 calls a day on different issues. We have to distinguish which ones we get involved in and become active with and that's when a personal relationship stands out."

— *Greg Casey, Chief of Staff for Former Massachusetts State (now U.S.) Senator Scott Brown*

"You don't go to a legislator's office and ask for things."

— *Patti Ann Moskwa*

"You have to become known, and become their friend, because they don't want to make their friends mad. You cannot just come in when you have a problem."

— *Bob Bonifas*

Successful underdogs are methodical. They know that achieving their goals is a long-term process, so their methodology includes building long-term relationships with their influence prospect. They haven't experienced the chimera of "instant influence," and thus many took years to build relationships and reap the reward.

From your own perspective, whose email do you return first? Whose voicemail do you call back immediately? It's typically the people you know and trust, those with whom you already have relationships.

We all do it, and powerful people are no different. In fact, they rely on relationships even more than most people because they're inundated with requests from people they don't know. Listening to those with whom they have relationships accelerates decision making because they don't doubt the credibility and trustworthiness of the underdogs they know.

Not convinced? The research I conducted with state legislators throughout the nation revealed this in no uncertain terms. I asked them this question: "Which types of constituents are the most influential?" The top three responses were all indicative of strong relationships:

1. Family members
2. Personal friends
3. Campaign workers

The following story is an example of how a relationship trumped the input of professional lobbyists and caused a prominent legislator to change her mind.

Getting Reacquainted

As a political science major in college, Matt Plowman worked on many Democratic candidate campaigns, attended rallies, voted in every election, and learned the political process. A college compatriot of Matt's at these political events was Margaret Anderson. After graduation, Matt and Margaret took different paths. She stayed in politics, while Matt went into the insurance business. While they took divergent paths, they later met again over a political issue.

The government relations team at the Westfield Company, Matt's employer, contacted Matt about a "bad faith" bill up for consideration in the Minnesota state legislature. To anyone in the insurance business, "bad faith" legislation cuts to the bone and marrow. It regulates customer service practices by enacting into law specific customer service standards determined by the government. As Matt told me, this was bad news for his profession and for him as an individual claims adjuster.

"Bad faith legislation basically expands legal liability to exceed the negligence standard on the part of an insurance company. It goes into customer service issues. Someone would have a legal cause for action if I, as a claims adjustor, didn't answer the phone after two rings or misspoke on a minor point when discussing a claim. All of my work files would be scrutinized; all my work would be an open book.

"If an insurance company engages in 'reckless disregard of the facts' when settling a claim, then bad faith has occurred," Matt explained. Minnesota's 'bad faith' bill in particular alarmed Plowman. It was the harshest in the nation because it would basically make adjustors like Matt second guess every word they said.

Plowman told the Westfield government affairs staff that he went to college with someone on the "inside" of this debate. Matt's college friend who stayed in politics, Margaret Anderson, is now Margaret Anderson Kelliher, who was elected to the Minnesota House of Representatives in 1998. In 2006, she was elected by her colleagues as Speaker of the House—the highest-ranking and most powerful member of the Minnesota House of Representatives.

About five minutes later, Plowman received a call from the lobbyists at the Minnesota Insurance Federation (MIF), of which Westfield is a member. While Matt was surprised at how quickly the Minnesota Insurance Federation's lobbyist called him, his government affairs staff and the MIF staff knew something that Matt likely didn't know. Because of his knowledge of how the proposal affected the "little guy" and his history with Speaker Kelliher, he would be more persuasive than the full-time professional lobbyists.

The MIF lobbyists and Westfield's team asked Plowman if he would contact Speaker Kelliher. He agreed to do so and set up a meeting with her, thinking that the professional lobbyists would attend the meeting with him. "I thought they'd go into the meeting with me, but after they met me, they suggested I go alone," Matt said. Indeed, the MIF lobbyists knew Matt could show how the legislation impacted not large insurance companies, but claims adjusters like him everywhere.

Plowman didn't know that several of the legislation's co-sponsors were scheduled to participate in the meeting with him and Speaker Kelliher. When Matt showed up alone without the Insurance Federation lobbyists, Kelliher asked the others—including the bill's author and a plaintiff's attorney—to leave. Margaret wanted to hear Matt's information without interruption.

Here's how Matt described the meeting. "We had a great time getting caught up on what's happened since our college political activities. I bet we spent half an hour talking about that. She then cut to the chase and asked me, 'What's the deal with this bill?' I told her I didn't expect anyone to feel bad for the insurance companies because of their concerns about increased litigation and higher fees, although those concerns were valid and would no doubt result if the bill were enacted. I told her the issue was more about the impact on individual claims adjustors. That's what she should be concerned about as a legislator." He reminded Kelliher that this bill wouldn't hurt the insurance companies as much as it would hurt him and everyone like him.

Not only did Speaker Kelliher's party get behind the bill, but she was one of the sponsors, which meant she was the legislation's coauthor. It became her project. She told Matt she understood his concerns and that there might be opportunities to change the bill's language.

The bad faith language that negatively affected claims adjustors was removed from the bill, and the bill passed, in part because Speaker Kelliher wanted to help the "ordinary" people who would have been affected by the bill.

Even though Matt had a relationship with Speaker Kelliher, he didn't rely on remote influence technologies to persuade her. As you read in Chapter 3, vivid communications are vital to changing the mind of a powerful person. Being vivid is integral to building the relationship. And to be vivid, you have to connect in person.

MAKE PERSONAL CONNECTIONS A PRIORITY

Top dogs are human chauvinists who are partial to personal communications over electronic ones. You can't build the kind of relationships they require from behind your computer. In fact, relationships that rely on email may have an uphill battle to succeed at all.

Consider this study by Janice Nadler, Ph.D., a psychologist and law professor at Northwestern University. She paired law students from Northwestern and Duke and asked each pair to negotiate a car purchase. The teams were to bargain entirely through email, but half of them were secretly told to precede the negotiation with a brief getting-to-know-you chat on the good old telephone.[108]

The results were dramatic. The phone negotiators who first connected by phone were 400 percent more likely to achieve agreements than those who used only email. Those who never spoke were not only more likely to stall their negotiations, they also often felt bitter and angry about the exercise.

Of course, online exchanges can be misunderstood, but faceless strangers are especially likely to run into problems. Here are three reasons why.

1. Simply foregoing common pleasantries can come across as rude, especially if the communicators don't know each other. A rushed email can give the impression that the exchange is unimportant. And because first impressions (aka final impressions) set the tone for subsequent interactions, the exchange can easily go downhill.

2. The less we know someone, the more likely we are to engage in what psychologists know as transference—the tendency to project our desires

and fears onto another person. Without social cues, such tendencies can run amuck, causing us to interpret messages in ways that are overly self-affirming and potentially wildly inaccurate.

3. Electronic communications don't give you a chance to develop rapport. As you read in Chapter 3, one of the advantages of vivid, face-to-face interactions is the ability to instantly glean message reception and adjust accordingly. The facial expressions—from raised eyebrows, rolled eyes, and tone of voice—are all cues missing in an email. Those "helpful" emoticons (my system comes complete with an "evil grin" and "money mouth" emoticon) do only so much to replace the real thing. The seeming proximity of the recipient when we email makes us think we can communicate about tough subjects, disagree, and provide criticism, and the tone of our writing will be perceived as we intended it. And let's not forget how, if we feel slighted, we may be more apt to throw a fit by email than by phone or in person.

DC Appeals Bought Time for Bob Bonifas

Bob Bonifas is the owner of an alarm and locksmith company in Aurora, Illinois. Involved in politics for 20 years, Bob has been extremely active for the last 15 years. His accomplishments and grit resulted in the National Federation of Independent Business (NFIB) naming him a "Small Business Champion."

Bonifas became friends with a member of Congress before that person became so powerful. That early friendship paid great dividends. His lesson for all of us is to build friendships and stay in front of people.

"It takes more time than money," said Bob. "To go to these events where you don't know anyone is frankly not fun, but what motivated me is the notion of good government. I think it takes one guy who knows the legislator well because legislators don't want to make their friends mad. You have to stay in front of people so they know who you are when it's time to ask for help," he advised.

In the mid-'90s, Bonifas found himself in an extreme influence situation and needed to ask for help. His goal was to get included in major telecommunications reform legislation a five-year prohibition on phone companies being able to provide alarm service.

"This was a huge bill with lots of different interest groups vying for a piece of the pie, Bob explained. "We had meetings, fights, and discussions over three to four years. The alarm industry was like a gnat on the elephant. No one really cared about our point of view; they were listening to the big guys. But think about what happens when families move into their new homes. They get phone service and then the phone people say, 'Hey, what about alarm service?' The telephone monopoly could easily be used to pre-sell alarm services. That would put us out of business."

Like many underdogs, Bob was not only trying to persuade a powerful person, he had to compete against large entrenched organizations who had more money, power, and resources than he did. Fighting most of the major telecommunications companies at the time, his particular nemesis was Ameritech.

"My colleagues and I attended hearings and heard people whisper in the hallways, saying they were surprised that we alarm guys really thought we could take on Ameritech. At one point, we were told by Congressman John Dingle of Michigan that the committee debating the bill wouldn't include any advantages or favors for any specific industry. We felt we were on the losing end of that situation," Bonifas recalled.

Bob knew Speaker Hastert, but he'd also developed a relationship with the person who managed access to Speaker Hastert. "At that time, Scott Palmer was a prominent Hastert staffer. I saw Scott all the time. In fact, I was the only alarm guy who kept visiting him. I bet I went to D.C. twenty times a year. When I met with Scott, I usually got evasive answers. Sure, he was always very nice, but he repeatedly told us 'there's nothing more we can do.'"

Wisely, like other successful underdogs, Bonifas knew when to state his case and when to keep silent. He met Palmer at local events, strictly social gatherings, and on those occasions did *not* talk about the issue. As he said, "You have to become known and earn a seat at the table. *You can't just come in when you have a problem.*"

So what happened? The legislation included a five-year prohibition on telephone companies being able to enter the alarm market. Naturally, Bob was delighted. "We won. The five years gave us time to adjust and create more of a competitive situation.

"Incidentally, Ameritech lost millions of dollars once they went into the alarm business. Ameritech's people just didn't know what they were doing, so the free market took care of the problem for us."

Bob was vindicated about his belief that success can come down to "one guy knowing the legislator." But here's the rest of the story.

"About two years after the Telecom Act passed, I went to an event in Washington honoring Speaker Hastert. Ameritech's vice president of government affairs walked up to me and said, 'Oh, you're in the alarm business. I know who you are. You're from Aurora. We kept trying to get to Hastert, but they kept telling us they had this guy in the alarm business back home who kept educating them on this issue. *So you are the one.*'" That observation underscored this underdog's victory. "At that point, I felt I was really successful. Our opposition had acknowledged my effectiveness," said Bonifas.

Spending his own money and time to be seen often paid off. Why? Because the more we see people, the more we like them, and likability opens the door to a relationship.

BE SEEN TO BECOME FAMILIAR TO TOP DOGS

Researchers believe that our unconscious plays a part in who we like and why. For example, the more often we see someone, the more we like them. For some time, real estate professionals have plastered their photos not only on their business cards but on benches near bus stops and on billboards. Not many professionals do this, but insurance agents are catching on and doing the same.

In one experiment, researchers flashed faces of people on a screen to research subjects and recorded their reactions. The faces flashed on the screen were people unknown to the research subjects, so they had no familiarity with the faces. The more frequently a person's face was flashed on a screen, the more the research subjects came to like that person in the following staged interaction. Not surprisingly, the research subjects were also more influenced by the opinions of the individuals whose faces appeared the most on the screen. It's not our imagination; the more we see someone, the more we like them.[109]

You've probably noticed how some of our underdog influence tactics complement one another—vivid (face-to-face) communications increases likability, and likability helps build the relationship.

ASK *ABOUT* SOMETHING BEFORE ASKING *FOR* SOMETHING

When smart underdogs want to build a relationship, they don't start with their request, as the following situation shows. They take time to court their top dogs.

In July 2005, the Wisconsin Supreme Court overturned a 10-year cap on non-economic damages in medical liability cases (pain and suffering awards). The Wisconsin Hospital Association (WHA) began an intensive lobbying and grassroots campaign to get the cap restored.

Brad Neet, then Chief Operating Officer of St. Michael's Hospital in Stevens Point, Wisconsin, identified not one but two lawmakers who represented his hospital and were on record against WHA's position.

"A Supreme Court ruling in my state made it easier for medical malpractice claims to succeed despite flimsy evidence," said Neet. "In my job hiring new doctors, I knew this would have a negative impact on recruitment. Doctors consider these things when making career decisions. I came from Illinois where there are no limits on awards in medical malpractice lawsuits, and I saw many doctors leave due to high malpractice premiums," he explained.

Brad described how not talking about the issue directly with his Top Dogs worked for him. "It's important to get to know these individuals as people before you talk issues, before you make any request. We always said hello, asked about their families, and made sure we had a great relationship first.

"I also sought to develop a positive working relationship with the staff in their offices. I'd call just to talk with their staff members from time to time, and I'd show them the same respect I showed the Senator. I didn't try to change their minds as much as listen for their concerns. Then I'd determine an approach that would mitigate those concerns and provide feedback to alleviate them, often using personal stories from our recruitment department and other past experiences," he said.

Neet then ramped up his involvement after the WHA asked members to step up. Even though he held an influential position in the WHA, the legislators he had to persuade weren't predisposed to his point of view. In fact, the political party of Brad's lawmakers decried attempts to limit caps on pain and suffering awards.

Despite their party's opposition to removing the limit on medical damages, the two legislators agreed with Brad and voted to retain the cap—something Brad influenced. "To this day, I have a very positive working relationship with both individuals, and I'm able to meet with them and discuss issues. Legislators can tell if someone's approach is not authentic. We may not always agree on the issues at hand, but I know I can continue to provide input and dialog with them. And it's fun.

"Honestly, I worry more about keeping the relationship positive than the legislative outcome itself," he concluded.

Patti Ann Moskwa agreed with Neet that you have to listen before asking. Patti is the fifth-generation owner of Horn's Gaslight Bar and Restaurant and the Yankee Rebel Tavern on Mackinaw Island, Michigan. When I called her, she was, predictably, driving several hours to the Michigan State House to meet with five state lawmakers. Moskwa makes it a practice to ask her Big Dogs how she can help them.

"I was brought up to give back, to be involved in my community. The standard rule in my family was, 'If you don't vote, you aren't allowed to discuss the issues with the family.' Some of my family members are Republicans, some are Democrats. But mostly I believe in helping legislators do the right thing. When they're elected, how can they act wisely unless they understand how something affects ordinary people? They can't," said Patti.

Moskwa was able to persuade Michigan State Representative Mike Zak to push for increased tourism funding in the Michigan state budget—from $3 million to $60 million dollars. "Mike was not my state representative," said Patti, "so I couldn't vote for him, but he helped us anyway. You don't go to a legislator's office and ask for things. If you want to make a change, you first ask what's needed. I'm lucky, I'm an outgoing person. Doing this doesn't faze me. I know the issues, and I'll walk into anyone's office," she said.

Patti Moskwa's philosophy of *not* asking for things was affirmed through a study by The Policy Council that asked Capitol Hill staffers their "pet peeves" regarding lobbyist communications. One House staffer said, "Sometimes we get contacted because someone wants something. That's not a way to establish a relationship with an office or a staff member. Have some introductory meetings before you ask for something."[110]

FIND WAYS TO COOPERATE

Another relationship-building technique is to find ways to cooperate with the person you want to influence. Joel Ulland did just that with an unlikely ally.

Ulland represented the Minnesota Chapter of the Multiple Sclerosis Society before the Minnesota state legislature. Like Bob Bonifas and Brad Neet, he built a relationship long before he asked for anything.

In the spring of 2005, Minnesota was reeling after three years of budget cuts. A member of several coalitions for Minnesotans with disabilities, Ulland knew this meant tough times for the people he served. He explained the history of his challenge this way: "The state was facing a deficit for the third straight year, and the Republican governor refused to raise taxes. The question became not *if* the state would make cuts in state programs, but *where* the cuts would be made and *when* they would take effect. As advocates for health care programs for people with disabilities, I knew we had a target on our backs. At that time, health care was the biggest part of our state budget."

Ulland wanted to make sure that funding remained intact for people with disabilities. Joel's clients who suffer from multiple sclerosis (MS) have flare-ups of the disease, which makes mobility even more challenging and workplace accessibility an issue. They want to remain independent and support themselves and their families. But without funding that supports transportation and access programs, their ability to do that would be compromised.

Ulland's team prepared the facts and figures to influence decision-makers, but that was only a piece of the persuasion puzzle. They still needed a champion, a lawmaker who would personally promote their position in front of other legislators. "We wrote seventy pages of position papers on sixty or seventy different topics in the state budget," Joel told me. "We basically had a mini-omnibus budget bill of our own. We were telling legislators what needed to be done, but we had to find legislators to sponsor a bill that included our recommendations. We knew that members of the Democratic Party were supportive, and we did indeed get Senator Becky Lourey, who is highly prominent in the party, to be our chief Senate sponsor."

Ulland needed a sponsor in the Minnesota House, so he had to do some reconnaissance work. He regularly watched the cable TV show that featured the Minnesota state legislature in action, complete with committee hearings, floor debates, and roll call votes—the "car-chase scene" of the democratic system. This task didn't happen without suffering. "My colleagues thought I was a dork to keep watching, but it helped me get to know the players better," Joel recalled.

In particular, he watched Representative Tom Wilkin. A controversial legislator who voted against increased taxes and spending, Wilkin wasn't enamored with health care advocacy.

Ulland said, "I listened to his public comments about how government money should and shouldn't be used in the health care system, and I thought, 'We can work with this guy.'" Ulland perceived that the people he served and Wilkin had common ground. Specifically, they had a desire for means to get to work, to have access to workplace assistance, and to help themselves. People suffering from MS value their independence, and Representative Wilkin expressed values related to personal responsibility—a perfect match.

Glued to the screen, Ulland learned that Representative Wilkin had been given more responsibility for the state budget negotiations. He saw an opening to make Wilkin's life easier by helping him decipher the various state health care programs. Joel went to work and became a resource for Wilkin by giving him both sides of all disability issues being debated in the legislature. (In fact, Ulland was so unbiased in his advice that later in the legislative debate, the chairman of the

Health and Human Services Committee asked a colleague, "Is Joel a Republican or Democrat? I can't tell.")

"We started being a resource to Representative Wilkin in 2003," explained Joel, "so when we needed him in 2005, we felt comfortable asking him to be the chief sponsor of our legislation to prevent cuts in disability funding. We also asked for reforms in the county case management system for people with disabilities. We did the usual 'meet and greet' events to become visible and also created opportunities to be seen in the halls of the State House and have those hallway conversations. We kept it light by cracking jokes during our joint elevator rides," Joel recalled.

In addition, Ulland learned from others exactly what *not* to do to build this relationship. "Representative Wilkin saw from our track record and previous interactions that we were willing to work with him and not call him wild and crazy names in the media. Groups who lambasted legislators in the midst of budget negotiations got cut; they got treated worse. By contrast, we weren't 'pains in the butt' to deal with. Being nice allowed us to be a part of the conversation, to be at the table.

"When we approached Wilkin and asked him to be our House sponsor, we feared that he would put the screw to us. But he was quite engaged and read through each of our position papers. He *really* read them. Then he was upfront with what he could and couldn't support in our proposal. He did take a lot of hits from his legislative colleagues and the media because he's frugal by nature, but he saw this as an opportunity to challenge his Democrat colleagues. He told us, 'Don't think I'm as bad as people tell you I am.' He agreed to carry our proposal, and he was constantly in touch with us over the fifteen to twenty changes to the bill to make sure that we had what we needed."

The budget cuts were avoided. Ulland's long-term relationship-building strategy paid off. In addition, his cooperation with Representative Wilkin helped Wilkin to be viewed differently because he supported programs for the disabled, giving him the "gift of heroics" discussed in Chapter 5. And Joel still finds himself inexplicably drawn to the TV broadcasts of the Minnesota state legislature in action.

GIVE FIRST, ASK LATER

Bob Bonifas helped his Top Dog, then Speaker of the House Dennis Hastert, by investing in his career through attending inexpensive events that supported Speaker Hastert. Joel Ulland gave Representative Wilkin exclusive information on the nitty gritty of the state health care budget. Chip Thayer also gave before asking.

Thayer, who died in 2009 of lung cancer, was a retired global technology executive, investor, and executive-in-residence at Babson College. He also served on the American Cancer Society's New England board of directors that he helped establish. In 2003, then Massachusetts Governor Mitt Romney appointed him to the Public Health Council, the policy board of the Massachusetts Department of Health.

Thayer persuaded a legislator to vote for a bill that would ban smoking in the workplace. But that's not the challenging aspect of his story. This legislator had voted *against* the smoking ban when he served in the Massachusetts House of Representatives. Chip had to ask State Senator Scott Brown (now U.S. Senator Scott Brown) to *change* his vote, a request reserved for only the most intrepid underdogs. One way for an elected official to draw unfavorable attention is to change his or her mind (flip-flopping), which was exactly what Chip Thayer was asking Senator Brown to do.

As a town captain working on Mitt Romney's gubernatorial campaign, Thayer met the person who became Senator Brown's chief of staff, Greg Casey. Casey invited Thayer to work on Brown's campaign, and he did, despite not being able to vote for him. As Chip recalled when I interviewed him before he died, "I knew Senator Brown because I had worked on his campaign. I'm a well-known anti-smoking activist who had spoken out publicly about my battle with lung cancer. I had smoked for thirty years. I got a meeting with Senator Brown on my first try. I believe he listened because I worked on his campaign."

Greg Casey reinforced the importance of their relationship in changing Senator Brown's mind. "The senator trusted Chip. He liked him. Chip had worked hard for him in the election. When it came to talking about something Chip felt passionate about, the senator wanted to talk to him. Yes, it's all about personal relationships. We get a hundred calls a day on different issues. We have to distinguish which ones to become active with. That's when a personal relationship stands out."

DO YOUR BIG DOG A FAVOR

As you read this, you might think I'm advising that you grant favors as a manipulative tactic. I'm not. Not only is that "not my cup of tea," it makes me hate tea. I'm just the messenger, reporting what our successful underdogs did and correlating their behavior with the science. And note that none of them used favors in a manipulative way. In fact, when interviewing the underdogs for this chapter, I noted their lack of affectation. They never mentioned that particular "F" word, and I detected no calculation of a "payback."

Favors can open the door to a new relationship and cement existing relationships, but the wise underdog doesn't exaggerate their importance. They know better than to assume that the tired bromide of "you scratch my back and I'll scratch yours" represents reality. They are very different than "blunderdogs" who are neurologically wired to think their "favor" translates into an immediate benefit. And our underdogs' instincts line up with the science of persuasion.

The Difference Between Giving and Receiving

Stanford University researcher Frank Flynn focuses on the psychology of workplace behavior. His findings have implications for underdog persuaders because they remind us that there are nuances to helping others. Helping others by giving favors has a shelf life. And it's not only more blessed to give than to receive; it's vastly different to give than to receive.

To test this idea, Flynn conducted a survey of employees working in the customer service department of a large U.S. airline. The researchers asked half of the employees to consider a time when they had performed a favor for a coworker while the other half of the employees were asked to consider a time when they had received a favor. All the employees in the study were then asked to recall the value of the favor and how long ago it was granted.

Consistent with Flynn's hypothesis, the survey results revealed that recipients of the favor perceived it as more valuable immediately after the favor was performed but less valuable as time passed. Favor-doers, on the other hand, showed just the opposite effect. They placed a lower value on the favor immediately after it was performed but then placed *greater value on it as time went by.*[111]

Although several potential reasons for this discrepancy exist, one likely possibility is that, as time goes by, the <u>memory</u> of the favor-doing event gets distorted. Because people have the desire to see themselves in the best possible light, receivers may think they didn't need all that much help at the time, while givers may think they really went out of their way for the recipient.

These findings have implications when applying the underdog technique of helping others. If you've done a favor, that favor will likely have the most impact on that person's desire to reciprocate in the *short term*. However, if you're the recipient, you need to be aware of the tendency to dismiss the impact of the favor as time goes by. If you fail to recognize the full value of the favor weeks, months, or even years after it has occurred—which Flynn's research showed is a natural inclination—this may ultimately damage your relationship with the favor-doer. To maintain your relationship, *don't forget the favors your top dog does for you.* Take the advice of Dona Wells in Chapter 6 and say thanks—again and again.

On the flip side, because the perceived value of the favor you received is likely to diminish over time, how can you make sure the favors you do will continue to be valued by the recipient?

Altercast to Make Favors Stick

First, *altercast* a positive behavior on your recipient. *Altercasting* is a term for casting someone in a role. It's best used to imbue people with positive qualities so they can also see themselves in a positive light. When they take on that persona, it's difficult for them to disagree with you. They'll see themselves as you see them, and more important, they'll start to act in the way you suggest. When you compliment people on their generosity, they usually don't say, "Oh, no, I'm really not a generous person, I'm really cheap." Rather, they're more likely to tacitly agree with that assessment and take on the behaviors of the altercasted role.

Remind the recipient that you enjoyed helping her because *you know that she would do the same for you* (that's the altercast). It's emotionally obtuse for people not to respond to that type of compliment. You're imbuing them with positive characteristics; you're reminding them of their goodness and light. And, it's true—you'll be glad you had a chance to help them! It never hurts to say it.

Second, don't adopt the "Oh, it was nothing; don't mention it" martyr mantra. *Do* mention it. Gently nudge them about how you helped. Not in the "Hey, remember when I helped you with that project—well, it's payback time!" way. Instead, say, "Did you find that report useful?" When they dutifully reply that, yes, your work was helpful, I'm assuming you do quality work, let them know you are glad you could help. And then *later* (but not too much later) ask for your favor.

While favors are a good way to open the door to a relationship and solidify existing ones, don't be tempted to think that handing out favors willy-nilly will always "win friends and influence people." Like all relationship-building tactics, they must be used judiciously. Not all favors are created equal.

PROVIDE EXCLUSIVE INFORMATION

What types of favors matter most to powerful people? While you need to keep your eyes open, as always, to discern what matters to your targeted top dog, I can tell you one thing social science has discovered. *Exclusive information and contacts are more valued than "common knowledge."*

Exclusive information has tremendous persuasive power. I believe that in today's world of hyper-abundant content, it is more pertinent than ever.

Social psychologists Timothy Brock and Howard Fromkin have developed a "commodity theory" of persuasion that centers on exclusive and/or scarce things, information, etc., as an influence tactic. The more scarce (and often expensive) particular information is, the more valued it is. What else explains the tactics of retailers at Christmas to tout the very latest toy or gadget and their incessant reminders that it's "in limited supply"? And how about those cosmetics and designer handbags that are "limited editions"? We're usually willing to pay more for them because we attribute more value to them than readily available items.

Exclusivity trades on our weakness for mental shortcuts. Aren't things deemed hard to get worth more than those that are easy to obtain?

Scarcity versus Exclusivity

Scarcity and exclusivity largely explain why censorship doesn't work, whether by the state or parental units. When we're told we can't see or do something, we tend to want to see and do it even more.

I was reminded of this at a dinner with one of my best friends, Jo, and her precocious nine-year-old daughter, Mara. I uttered a cuss word to describe someone's treatment of another person. Suddenly remembering I was with a nine year old, I was embarrassed that she heard me. I put my hand over my mouth and apologized for spewing forth ignorant adjectives. Mara replied, "Oh, Aim, it's okay. I know what that means. Now go on, what were you saying?"

I was intrigued that she didn't giggle or express disdain at my expletive as many nine year olds would do. Jo told me she has reviewed the definitions of all curse words with Mara so "she doesn't think she's cool or funny by using them. You have to take the thrill out of it." Indeed, the lack of censorship took away Mara's desire to use them. (And years later, I've never heard her utter any foul language.) I think Jo's technique is smart parenting, at least on language issues. I'm not advocating that you tell your kids about every nefarious activity, but do think about how much exclusivity you ascribe to certain events, activities, and behaviors. Your excessive concern is likely to only increase the allure.

We can conclude from Brock and Fromkin's work that exclusive information equals persuasive information. So what can you share—or what kind of favor can you do for your big dog—that will be valuable or exclusive, and thus enhance your influence? What can you provide that he or she can't access without you? Remember, it has to be *exclusive*. For example, don't be like the dog psychic who, after peering into the eyes of our Siberian Husky, told us with an attitude of profound insight, "He really likes the snow." (She also said he loves to sniff. Duh!)

Let's meet an underdog who put together all these elements: She connected in person, she was seen often, she gave before asking, she provided exclusive information, and she had fun.

CONSIDER THE KARAOKE FACTOR

Southwest Airlines has a culture of engaging employees in legislative issues, an approach so successful that these efforts have saved the company millions of dollars. Kim Delevett is a corporate community affairs manager for Southwest Airlines representing the San Jose, California region. Like Patrice Dell, she was engaged in the grassroots effort to repeal the Wright Amendment, an outdated piece of legislation that prohibited Southwest from flying nonstop into or out of Dallas, Texas.

Kim's goal was to get her Congressman, Mike Honda, to vote in favor of repealing the Wright Amendment. Like others interviewed for this book, she and her Southwest colleagues were underdogs not only to the powerful individuals they were trying to persuade, but to American Airlines, who strongly opposed the repeal of the Wright Amendment. American Airlines was sparing no expense to get its message out. In fact, Southwest estimated that American outspent Southwest eight to one, even spending one million dollars to set up an "organic" grassroots community organization. The organization's mission was to refute Southwest's messages to communities that would benefit from the lower air fares resulting from repealing the outdated law.

Kim recalled the genesis of her relationship with Congressman Honda. "When I initially talked to him about the Wright Amendment, he was neutral on the issue. And American Airlines, who adamantly opposed its repeal, kept knocking on his door. I believe our success in getting his vote was due to my long-term relationship with him about mutual concerns outside of the aviation industry. A series of events helped shape my working relationship with Congressman Honda over the past six years."

Specifically, in June of 2001, Kim met Honda during San Jose State University's Mineta Transportation Institute (MTI) scholarship awards banquet and graduation ceremony. After the event, she asked if she could have a photo taken with him, and she mailed him the photo shortly thereafter. Later in the year, she attended a Southwest Airlines training in Washington, D.C. and met Congressman Honda in his office.

She continued to build a relationship long before she "needed" anything from him, and she didn't limit her contact to discussing issues that affected Southwest. The two of them learned that they shared common values. As Congressman Honda told me, "Kim works in the community promoting Asian-American culture, and I appreciate this. She also works on a lot of Asian children's causes that are very important to me. Little attention gets paid to children with our heritage."

Said Kim, "Because Congressman Honda is the chair of the Asian Pacific American Caucus, we share a passion to help Asian Americans and revitalize San Jose's Japantown. Additionally, we have a mutual friend, former Mountain View Mayor Matt Neely, who used to sing karaoke with Congressman Honda when Matt was a Corro Fellows Program intern in 2001.

"In 2006, when I saw Congressman Honda at a community event, I invited him to join Matt, his wife, my husband, and me to sing at my neighborhood karaoke lounge, Bamboo 7. Unfortunately, with our busy schedules, we couldn't confirm a date," she said, but she was determined to keep working on it.

Consistent in her contact with Honda and his staff, Kim frequently expressed gratitude to him on issues aside from Southwest Airlines. "Because Congressman Honda had given tremendous support to the Vietnamese American fishermen in New Orleans after Hurricane Katrina, I sent him a thank you card and included a poignant and inspirational *Mercury News* article about New Orleans fishermen."

Kim also built relationships with his gatekeepers, meeting with District Director Meri Maben for coffee and sharing highlights of her latest Vietnam trip. She also met with Meri to thank her office for supporting Japantown's preservation. Later that year, she went to the district office and dropped off gifts of Chinese New Year's calendars.

"In addition," said Kim, "I continued to have informal and formal discussions with Congressmen Honda and staff about the Wright Amendment through email and voicemail and at community events. After the Wright Amendment Compromise bill (HR 5830) was introduced by Congressman Don Young, Chairman of the House Transportation and Infrastructure Committee, I left voicemails for Meri and Legislative Assistant Bernadette Arellano to ask for their support.

"That August, I received a voicemail from Meri stating that Congressman Honda would support the Wright Amendment Repeal legislation as long as the cities and airlines were in agreement. She reiterated that Congressman Honda always supports a local solution," Kim said. Once HR 5830 was introduced, she had his vote.

Eventually, Kim did get to sing karaoke with Congressman Honda—when she was nine months pregnant. I asked her which song they sang and she replied, "Hmmm. I think it went something like 'Da de do de dum do be du dum dum.'" She remembered the melody but not the words. As she kept singing it, I recognized the tune—Neil Sedaka's "Breaking Up is Hard to Do"—a perfect choice!

THE UNDERDOG'S CHECKLIST
Are You Building Winning Relationships?

✓ Connect in person.

✓ Be seen often.

✓ Build the relationship before you talk about the issue.

✓ Look for ways to help.

✓ Give before you ask.

✓ Understand the valuation and devaluation of favors. Gently remind your prospect of previous favors without resorting to a "payback" attitude.

✓ Provide exclusive information or contacts.

✓ "Don't go into an office and ask for things." — *Patti Ann Moskwa*

✓ "Don't be a pain in the butt to deal with." — *Joel Ulland*

CHAPTER 8

Extreme Influence Tactic #7:

Don't Bark, Don't Bite, Be Nice

"If you are mean, you'd better hope your argument is so meritorious that it's unassailable. Nice people are given the benefit of the doubt because many decisions are highly subjective."

> — *Executive Vice President Rick Shelby, American Gas Association*

"When you are in extreme influence situations, people can be rude, dismissive and belittling at times, and you have to have a thick skin. You can't take anything personally and you have to remember that it usually isn't about you even if it feels like it is."

> — *Carolyn Dennis*

"Save your passion to motivate your people, rather than spending it on your influence target."

> — *Patrice Dell, Southwest Airlines*

"Greg, in any interaction, you either gain share or lose share. So treat every interaction as kind of a precious moment in time."

— *Mitt Romney, former Governor of Massachusetts*

"We were not offensive; we just exposed what was happening. I think you have to hold your flag high and ride with a smile."

— *Gary Rogers, Levi Strauss & Company*

"Carolyn Dennis was a classy lady. Even though I was adamantly against what she was doing, she always had a smile on her face when she saw me in the hall or stopped by my office to talk to me."

— *Kentucky State Representative Jimmy Higdon*

"Speak when you are angry – and you will make the best speech you'll ever regret."

— *Laurence J. Peter*

"Treating someone rudely, brusquely, or condescendingly says loudly and clearly that you do not regard her as your equal."

— *Richard Boyd, Georgetown University*

Have you ever seen a passionate activist tie himself to a tree to make his point, or camp out at an abortion clinic, or stand in the home driveways of dethroned executives holding signs and screaming at them? How about the teachers protesting in Wisconsin? They yelled names at legislators who disagreed with them in the 2011 fight over collective bargaining.

All of these are well-meaning, committed people whom I refer to as "yaktivists." A yaktivist is someone who uses vivid tactics (that's good) but neglects to use them in a courteous way (that's bad). Yaktivists do get attention, but their behavior, however dramatic, is more likely to alienate decision makers than persuade them.

In the workplace, such behavior may manifest in other bizarre ways. Take the action of Jet Blue flight attendant Steven Slater. In 2010, he infamously communicated his job dissatisfaction by exiting the flight he was serving via the emergency slide. Sure, he got attention, but his exit strategy didn't change the behavior of the offensive passengers who upset him. Last time I flew, I noted there were still relentlessly offensive air travelers on board.

Remember, we're engaged in upward influence, not mob persuasion. Just making noise or creating drama doesn't necessarily mean you've achieved, or will achieve, your desired result—plus doing so takes a lot of energy, which can lead to burnout.

As I researched this book, I gave the top dogs an opportunity to tell stories rather than answer multiple-choice questions to indicate what does or doesn't work when they're being asked for something. In their organic anecdotes, one of the patterns I uncovered was their partiality to nice underdogs. And, as you'll see, nice behavior isn't about saying "please" and "thank you."

Why does being nice even matter to high-powered people? Don't they make decisions based only on facts and evidence?

Actually, no. As the top dogs told me their stories, they described the behaviors of people who caused them to change their minds. This theme emerged: Persuasive underdogs are, quite simply, nice. *And* they're not doormats or pushovers! I like to think of them affectionately as people who have "feet of cashmere and hands of steel." They will get to you, but you'll never feel like you've been had.

Successful underdogs know their persuasion challenge doesn't end after their first request. They keep their eyes up, looking to building relationships with their influence targets (see Chapter 7) and knowing it's a long-term process. They have to exhibit behaviors that create goodwill to accomplish that, which is why this chapter's findings about being "nice" are so valid. Besides being the right thing to do, being "nice" gives you an advantage in a world of thin-skinned people.

OUR PAPER THIN SKIN

We humans are wrapped in a thin skin that harbors negativity. No one likes to hear bad news, receive criticism, and lose status or momentum. We're more likely to remember our annual workplace evaluation feedback of "you need to be more collaborative" more than "you are our top producer"—even if both points are delivered in the same conversation.

We're also more sensitive to loss than gain. The Nobel Prize-winning social psychologists Daniel Kahneman and Amos Tversky called this human sensitivity to loss rather than gain the "universal human propensity." In an experiment that led to this discovery, doctors in two groups were asked to choose between two ways to address an epidemic. For both groups, option A stayed the same, but Option B was described differently for each of the two groups. Specifically, for one group, Option B was described as saving 200 out of 600 lives. For the other, Option B was described as allowing 400 of the 600 to die.

Framed positively as saving 200 lives, 72 percent of doctors favored Option B. However, when the exact same option was framed negatively allowing 400 of the 600 to die, only 22 percent favored it. That's a huge bias distorting supposedly rational behavior. Why does saving 200 sound so much better than losing 400 when it amounts to the same thing? As Kahenman said, "In human decision-making, loss looms larger than gain."[112]

This tells us our minds view negative encounters and feedback as loss. What do we do with loss? We avoid loss itself. We avoid those who make us feel any loss. And we avoid those who make us feel like losers!

Loss aversion explains why long-term partnerships have a five-to-one ratio of positive encounters to negative encounters. One-to-one ratios don't cut it because negative encounters *emotionally* weigh five times more than positive ones.

This aversion to loss occurs in marriage and the workplace, as the science indicates. Dr. John Gottman pioneered the emotional freight of negative interaction in marriage. He is the author or co-author of 190 published academic articles and 40 books, including his breakthrough book, *Why Marriages Succeed or Fail…and How You Can Make Yours Last*.[113] In this book, he unveiled his research findings that enabled him to predict with more than 90 percent accuracy whether a marriage will end in divorce—*just from watching couples interact in 15-minute increments over several years.*

A hallmark finding was Gottman's "magic ratio" of 5-to-1 positive-to-negative interactions. That is, he found that marriages are significantly more likely to succeed when the couple's interactions come close to a 5-to-1 ratio of positive-to-negative encounters. When the ratio approaches 1-to-1, marriages cascade to divorce.

This ratio applies to the workplace as well. A recent study found that workgroups with positive-to-negative interaction ratios of at least 3-to-1 or greater are significantly more productive than teams that don't reach this ratio. Barbara Fredrickson and Marcial Losada's mathematical modeling of positive-to-negative ratios, however, also suggests there's an *upper limit*—things can worsen if the ratio goes higher than 11-to-1. Then it's evidently viewed as "faking it." Co-workers can spot frauds among them, and frauds aren't considered "nice."[114]

Greg Brenneman, chairman of a private equity investment firm CCMP Capital, applies a reality check to workplace relationships. His firm invests in about 50 portfolio companies. As he considers which ones to select, he listens to CEOs tell him how they will build their businesses. In addition to finding out "if they are smart enough to do the job," he also takes into consideration their "nice" IQ, as he said in this interview with the *New York Times*: "The second thing I look for is if I were to get on an airplane with this guy or gal, would I want to fly across the Atlantic with them? Are they nice people to be with? Do you want to be with them? Because I find that people that don't relate well to anybody, from owners or board members to peers to direct reports to folks that actually work for a living in the trenches, they don't succeed very well."[115]

EVEN THE PROFESSIONALS ARE NICE

I wanted to find out if "powerful" and "nice" behaviors can co-exist in the same DNA—that is, can those who are actually paid to influence (e.g., professional lobbyists) be both polite *and* effective? After all, the media and politicians would have us believe that lobbyists are a nefarious presence in our republic, so they must be bad people, right?

In hot pursuit of the truth, I conducted my own research on lobbyists. I considered the findings of popular Capitol Hill publications and my outreach to members of the American League of Lobbyists (ALL), of which more than 900 professional lobbyists are members. Established in 1979 as a nonprofit organization, ALL is dedicated to enhancing the development of professionalism, competence, and high ethical standards for lobbyists. And no, that's not a typo. *The Hill*, a daily Capitol Hill newspaper, periodically publishes a list of the most powerful D.C.-area lobbyists. When one reads this list, it's natural to assume the people on it are tough, ruthless negotiators determined to win at all costs.

I wanted to find out if any of them were considered "nice." So I surveyed the more than 700 members of ALL to find out whom among their peers they deemed to be "nice." (Remember, this organization actively encourages the advancement of ethical lobbying practices; its members must agree to a Code of Ethics.) Would any of the most powerful lobbyists also make the "nice" list? Could there be an intersection between power and kindness?

Indeed, I found an overlap. Four of the top six vote getters in my "nice" survey were also featured on the lists of the most effective lobbyists as published in *The Hill*, as well as similar lists in *CEO Update* and *Association Trends*.

Rick Shelby, executive vice president of the American Gas Association, is one who's appeared on both lists. His experience in two decades of lobbying members of Congress has taught him that many decisions don't relate to the facts and evidence, and that lobbyists can get more time to make their points if they act nicely. "If you are mean, you'd better hope your argument is so meritorious that it's unassailable. Nice people are given the benefit of the doubt because many decisions are highly subjective. If you are nice, you might get thirty minutes to make your point versus fifteen minutes," he commented.

Will Edington, the founder of Edington, Peel & Associates, is another lobbyist whose name appears on both lists. He said, "You have to be aware of the demands on others. Be considerate of the pressures they face. And if you smile, people automatically think you are nice."

Brian Pallasch, managing director of Government Relations and Infrastructure Initiatives with the American Society of Civil Engineers, also was named on both lists. He said that when he asks members of Congress to support legislation favorable to his members, he considers the impact of his request on his persuasion prospects and frames it from their point of view. "It's not *your* bill or *your* legislation; it's about serving others. Persuaders have to ask, 'How does this help the person I'm talking to?'"

Joel Wood, senior vice president of Government Affairs at the Council of Insurance Agents and Brokers, said that being nice aids in the long term. "There is always a debate on how aggressive you should be versus how nice you should be. I read the political needs and personal objectives of the person I'm trying to persuade. Bottom line, the foot you step on today is connected to the ass you will have to kiss tomorrow."

Big Dogs Notice You When You're Nice

Think about it. When you deploy negativity, verbal attacks are least likely to make others change their minds. It's quite irrational to think that, by assaulting another, you'll make that person more sensitive to your position.

Former Speaker of the Ohio House JoAnn Davidson said, "Showing common courtesy doesn't cost you a cotton-picking thing." She reported that many underdog influencers turn their prospects off before they even get to their argument—all because they let their zeal (passion!) take over. "I've had to say to some groups 'this meeting is over' before they even get to their point because they get so emotional. They can even be threatening." So, while it may seem like it's common sense to show common courtesy, it's actually "rare sense." And unfortunately, many underdog influencers don't even *know* they are behaving discourteously.

The following example underscores my point. I was once leading a workshop for a prominent environmental organization well known for its advocacy. Its leaders needed to ramp up their efforts in persuading powerful legislators to support its cause. One woman in the group, obviously well connected socially and politically, knew everyone in her town. More important, they knew *her*. Because she had been advocating for this cause her entire adult life, she also knew her subject cold.

As the workshop continued, I sensed from her questions that she was mystified and frustrated about why she wasn't able to be more influential with her big dog targets. Frankly, so was I. She seemed to have all the necessary ingredients.

Then at one of the breaks, she approached me with another question. Actually, it was a confession. (Many workshop participants share their tales of woe privately with me during the break but never during the session itself. That's why I allocate time for these "grassroots confessionals" during breaks.) She admitted she'd recently been fired from her job for, in her words, "talking too much about how our company could be greener." She told me, "Amy, a light bulb went off while you were speaking. I just realized it wasn't what I was saying, but *how* I was saying it that ticked off my bosses. I wasn't nice about it, and it affected how everyone viewed my work in general."

Now, there may be other reasons why she was terminated, but I bet she was on to something. No matter how sincerely you hold your beliefs, no matter how "right" you are, if your persuasion prospect isn't feeling what you feel, you'd better temper your approach.

Influence and Politeness Go Together

This woman's confession reminded me of research I'd conducted with state legislators in the late 1990s. I asked these legislators to tell me who made up the most influential types of voters and why they were effective. One of the top findings was that the most influential voters were "polite."

Shortly after that, another study with members of Congress by the American Society of Association Executives revealed that having "polite, persuasive communications" was one of the best ways to get a legislator's attention.

Daniel Mica, president and CEO of the Credit Union National Association, believes that influencing up is like a chess match. His article in *The Hill* stated, "The seasoned lobbyist thinks not only of the move he/she is making now, but also the next move and several beyond that. So, as one begins to feel anger building up, calculations should be made: If I make demands now, will those demands be met? If those demands are met, am I preventing myself from a strategic relationship I may need later on? Is this person more important to my long-term strategic advocacy goals? It sounds so simple, and yet many—and on occasion I include myself as well—forget this basic lesson."[116]

Why all the fascination with being nice? Because the higher you go, the more requests you can grant and the more you're looked at as the oracle of all wishes and dreams. You're perceived to have more to give, thus exposing you to more people. And evidently "more" is not "nicer." Therefore, nice behavior takes on greater importance when seeking upward influence.

That brings me to this burning question: What does "being nice" mean in the eyes of the top dogs you want to influence? You have to look nice, pack your passion, respect the path, show humility, avoid nagging, use your public relations skills, and never jump over the gatekeeper.

LOOK NICE TO BE NICE

Top dogs spend more time than the average person listening to and interacting with others, which makes them highly sentient. Remember Carolyn Dennis's success with changing Representative Higdon's mind? Not only did she provide vivid information but according to Higdon, "Carolyn Dennis was a classy lady. Even though I was adamantly against what she was doing, she always had a smile on her face when she saw me in the hall or stopped by my office to talk to me. I had a great deal of respect for her." Note what he said about the "smile on her face." And remember what Will Edington, one of our effective *and* nice lobbyists, said about the smile? ("If you smile, people automatically think you are nice.")

They're exactly right. Science has verified the value of a smile for aspiring influencers. Researchers have found that you can, indeed, judge a book by its cover—and your smile has a lot to do with that verdict.

For example, a large number of experiments conducted in recent years showed that altruistic people versus egoists (a scientific word for self-centered types) actually *appear* different and people can tell them apart simply by looking at them. Specially, a study conducted by Ryo Oda of the Nagoya Institute of Technology and his colleagues demonstrated that you *can* judge a book by its cover.[117]

In this study, a large number of male undergraduate students rated their personal altruism or unselfishness. For the experiment, those who rated themselves in the top 10 percent on the altruism scale were deemed "altruists" while those in the bottom 10 percent were labeled "egoists." These altruists and egoists (also referred to as targets) were then individually videotaped in a normal conversation with a confederate.

The first 30 seconds of the videotaped conversation were then shown to different groups of students at a university more than 800 miles away. This was assurance that the students wouldn't personally know the altruists or egoists. The video clips were shown without sound to prevent those being taped from revealing their level of altruism through their statements.

What were the results? The study showed that the student viewers, when asked to estimate the targets' levels of altruism, accurately guessed who were the altruists and who were the egoists. Men and women were equally good at estimating the altruism level of total strangers. Further, the altruists were judged to be significantly more active, more generous, more responsible, friendlier, kinder, more extroverted, and more capable of leaving a better impression than egoists. However, altruists were not judged to be more discreet, more hurried, or more intelligent than egoists.

Further analysis showed that the key to detecting altruists is *a genuine smile*, which is under involuntary control and is difficult to fake. In this study, altruists genuinely smiled more frequently than egoists during natural conversations. It demonstrated that people can judge other people by looking at them. It also concluded that nice, altruistic, and helpful people *look* nice, altruistic, and helpful while mean, egoistic, and uncooperative people *look* mean, egoistic, and uncooperative. And that people (both altruists and egoists, both men and women) can tell them apart after looking at them *for only 30 seconds without sound!*[18]

THE FALLACY OF "THE PASSION THING"

Chapter 5 noted that "passion isn't the panacea." The degree of passion expressed also affects whether you are perceived as "nice."

I call it "the passion thing" because of the prevalent cliché: If you are passionate, you'll succeed at anything. Oft-repeated advice given to those trying to persuade top dogs include phrases like "be passionate," "let your passion show," "believe passionately in your cause," and so on. Sound familiar?

Let me point out there are lots of passionate but mediocre influencers. And I respectfully disagree that playing the passion card will result in influence success, *especially when pursuing upward influence.*

Among the intriguing findings from my interviews with top dogs was that passion was only effective under certain circumstances and required "modifiers" around its use. Passion does not, I repeat, *does not,* work in every situation. (Refer to Chapter 5 for a quick review.)

In fact, when you use passion incorrectly, you can be viewed as inconsiderate and mean. How many people walking by those rope lines at rallies (pro or con) for abortion rights, gun issues, health care reform, gay marriage, and others have stopped, stroked their chins while observing the screaming hordes, and thoughtfully concluded, "You know, they are so passionate, they must be right. I'm changing my mind!" It rarely works that way. Those behaviors certainly can get attention, so if attention is the goal, then it works. Our underdog influencers, however, are engaged in upward influence.

Bill Novelli is former CEO of AARP and cofounder and former president of Porter Novelli, one of the world's largest public relations agencies. He told me how passion displayed by his opponents on a major piece of legislation insulted him and never endeared him. Here's what happened.

In late 2003, AARP endorsed major legislation (the Medicare Modernization Act/MMA), which required Medicare to cover prescription drugs. Most pundits and insiders say that AARP's endorsement put the bill over the top. As Bill recalled, "The legislation was hugely political and a partisan firestorm. The Republicans, under President George Bush, thought this would win them greater favor with senior voters and lock in their majority status. The Democrats believed they owned Medicare (it was born under President Johnson, a Democrat) and hated the idea of Bush getting credit for something they'd been unable to pass when they were in control.

"As the legislation was debated, passed, and signed into law, all hell broke loose. House Minority Leader Nancy Pelosi stood up at a rally on Capitol Hill and called me (gasp) a Republican. Nearly a hundred thousand people quit their AARP memberships. Over the course of a week, several groups stood outside my office window and burned their AARP cards. Irate callers phoned my wife and me in the middle of the night to give me a piece of their mind. I got hate Christmas cards with messages like 'Happy Holidays, you @*&!#, may you and yours @#&!#.' People interrupted my speeches and stopped me in airports to tell me what a rat I was. Things were rough.

"Personally, I was shaken and knocked off stride. And I was worried that AARP would be badly harmed by this. I decided the best thing was to be visible, to answer back, to keep cool, and to explain logically that no great social legislation is born perfect. 'Perfect' only happens in Hollywood, and this is Washington.

"Time proved us right. Today, millions of people are saving an average of twelve hundred dollars a year on their drugs because of the MMA and over eighty percent report being satisfied with the program. Moreover, it's costing less than had been estimated when it was passed. And I still have the Christmas cards."

Calm, Dispassionate, Yet Influential

When an especially emotional issue involves one's long-held beliefs and values, the influence challenge can induce panic. Yet, goals *can* be achieved. I know of one top dog who changed his mind on abortion rights through the efforts of a calm, almost dispassionate underdog who used unusual tactics to gain his attention and respect.

Remember Dona Wells, who founded EMW, a Louisville abortion clinic, in 1981, from Chapter 5? Given her actions both before and after establishing EMW, it's safe to assume Dona feels passionate about her cause. But she has never behaved like a zealot who turns people off.

In 1986, Dona first met with State Representative Tom Burch, then chairman of the Kentucky House Health and Welfare Committee. As committee chairman, his role involved determining what pieces of legislation do and don't move out of his committee.

On the subject of reproductive rights, Tom recalled, "I had become a poster boy for Kentucky Right to Life and attended its meetings. I didn't know anything about the other side of the coin, but I also knew I didn't like the anti-abortion activists' tactics. Anyway, with the session beginning, Dona Wells visited me several times in my office in the state capitol."

Her timing was good. Dona went to see Representative Burch when he had just been appointed to chair the House's Health and Welfare Committee. At the time, several abortion-related bills had been assigned to it and were being debated. One bill required a 24-hour wait for an abortion; another outlawed abortion altogether.

Now, admittedly this Underdog has lots of experience in upward influence, but Dona's approach is particularly instructive because she successfully influenced decision-makers on a highly emotion-charged topic—a far cry from asking city council members for a new stop light at a busy intersection. She said that being on the board of the National Abortion Federation, she was used to visiting people who were opposed to legalizing abortion. "I had to go see Representative Burch because of his position as committee chairman. I've been thrown out of health departments, so I didn't view this visit as particularly difficult," she recalled.

Tom admitted that if it hadn't been for his conversations with Dona, "I would have left out those bills. She didn't put pressure on me; she was showing me the other side of the coin. Dona knew her facts. She was prepared. She didn't resort to bullying or threats. In a business-like way, she strictly laid the facts on the table."

Dona knew she was making progress because Representative Burch was willing to listen—often an anomaly for lawmakers who hold strong beliefs on the abortion issue. Plus she attended every Health and Welfare Committee meeting. "I didn't know I had changed his mind until the day he refused to call the bills up for a hearing. It was celebration time!" she said.

Not surprisingly, Representative Burch took heat for his stance. "The Right to Life activists went after me. The most ardent opponents painted 'Tom Burch is a baby killer' on the windshields of their own cars. And they plastered cars in church parking lots in my district with flyers that said 'Tom Burch is a baby killer,'" he said. (Their passion didn't change his mind, did it?)

Dona's advice for underdogs who have a tough audience? "Be as respectful of the people who are *opposed to* your issue as those who are *for* your issue. I've had legislators be very discourteous to me, but I've never been discourteous in return. It's not professional.

"When you visit them, compliment them about something they've done. If they don't want to talk to you about your issue, still attempt to continue a relationship with them. Always send them a letter thanking them for seeing you and appreciate what they've done in writing. After they do help you out, write them a letter of thanks," she advised.

Even with the highly charged issue of abortion rights, Dona kept her passion from becoming a pothole. When does letting your passion show work in your favor? When you can make your Top Dog feel like a hero riding the highest white horse, as noted in Chapter 5. In that vein, Dona helped Representative Burch feel like he was helping the women at her clinic by allowing them to think this personal issue through for themselves.

RESPECT THE PATH

All top dogs have a story, one that defines why they chose a particular path. Most feel proud of the path they've selected. Because they cherish their history and legacy, for anyone to belittle their story falls well short of "nice." This example explains the point well.

Leslie Waters, a veteran of the insurance industry, was employed at Allstate Insurance for more than 20 years. In 2000, she got the idea to run for a state legislative seat that was open. She ran and won by slightly fewer than 250 votes. Because she had been a grassroots organizer for many years, she could witness the process from the other side.

During her tenure, Leslie served on the Florida House Leadership team and was also chair of the House Insurance Committee.

Recalling some of the most egregious forms of behavior, she said, "During my first campaign in 2000, I was approached by a representative from the Florida Trial Bar to meet with one of their grassroots volunteers and discuss issues important to trial lawyers. Well, I worked in the insurance industry for years, and we just don't have warm feelings toward the plaintiff's attorneys. But I'd never know if there were things we could work on in the future unless I talked with them.

"Well, my stereotype was unfortunately right on. The first thing out of this guy's mouth was 'Hi Leslie, nice to meet you. I haven't yet had the chance to sue Allstate.' He had disparaged my employer, a place I spent over twenty years of my life." I thought, 'This is the best they've got to meet with me?'

This lack of respect for Leslie's story harmed her perception of his entire organization and reinforced her suspicions about the Trial Bar. By extension, this made it harder for her to work with the Trial Bar in the future. They lost, as Rick Shelby would say, the benefit of the doubt.

Conversely, when talking with Tom Burch about abortion legislation, Dona Wells got it right. She did her homework and found that he, like she, graduated from Bellarmine University in Louisville, Kentucky.

"I learned as much about him as I could. He's Roman Catholic, and I realized we both had attended the same Roman Catholic college, Bellarmine. I remember telling him my senior seminar in the 1970s was about the time of the Roe v. Wade court case on abortion, and that I wrote about why I believed abortion should be legal. I told him if I didn't try to think through issues and allow women the right to think them through either, that wouldn't be consistent with my education at Bellarmine," she recalled.

Beyond being "nice," their Bellarmine connection helped them build a strong relationship that benefited them both.

NAG LESS, HELP MORE

Former Connecticut Congressman Toby Moffett told how a powerful group of "ordinary" people succeeded in changing his mind because they refrained from nagging him for support.

In 1970, he got involved in politics with Ralph Nader's Citizen Action. From 1975 to 1983, he represented Connecticut in the U.S. House of Representatives.

During that time, he chaired the House Sub-Committee on Energy, Environment and Natural Resources.

"The auto workers in northwest Connecticut wielded a lot of power. My perception was that I would not be in elected office if it weren't for the autoworkers' union, the UAW. I won an upset election, so they clearly had a strong influence with me," he remembered.

Dealing with bailout votes proved to be nothing new to Congressman Moffet. "During my tenure in Congress, one of the biggest votes was the Chrysler bailout vote from the federal government to stay afloat. Much was at stake for Chrysler, its employees, and the United States auto industry, as well as the taxpayers. A huge lobbying effort was mounted. Chrysler leaders were doing everything they could; so were its suppliers.

"On the other side, we were also being hit by a budget-conscious conservative group. I'm a liberal with a libertarian streak. Despite that, I was definitely leaning *against* voting for the bailout.

"Naturally, I received lots of communications from my local UAW. The spokespeople were respectful and didn't bludgeon me, even though they were astonished and disappointed at my intention to vote against the bailout. Remember, they made sure that all possible UAW resources were made available to me for my campaign, plus they organized campaign volunteers and did whatever they could do to help me win reelection.

"I didn't generally agonize over my votes in the Congress. Some legislators—they'll never admit this—are known for being undecided because they want the attention, but I wasn't one of them. Anyway, on the day of the bailout vote, I waited until about two minutes before the vote and then headed toward the House floor. "During all this time, I was leaning toward voting 'no' on the bailout. Then I glanced up in the House gallery and saw the UAW workers from my district. I thought, 'These people are the reason you are here, Moffett. What are you *thinking*?'"

Moffett voted in favor of the Chrysler bailout.

BE A PUBLIC RELATIONS AGENT

It's human nature to like people who help us. And it's difficult not to like someone who helps us achieve our goals.

In our surveys, we found that "helpful" behaviors translate into "nice" behaviors. In fact, in our quest to identify the nicest Washington lobbyists, the number-one "nice" behavior was to be "helpful." And digging deeper, that means doing things that aren't easy. If you want to be thought of as a nice (and hence persuasive) underdog, help your big dogs. One way is to be their public relations agent.

Survey respondents stated those lobbyists deemed "nice" are known to bend over backwards to give of their limited time and focus their efforts squarely on activities that made the respondents look good. Favorable comments would be: "They give of themselves to the profession"; "They provide insights and advice"; "They mentor others."

Do you see the pattern here? "Help me, and oh, by they way, sacrifice time and effort to do so, and I'll believe you are a nice, good person." And they are! These lobbyists do what isn't easy or *convenient*.

This turns into a tidy lesson for underdog influencers—that is, to be considered "nice" (and gain the benefit of the doubt from the person you are persuading), you need to help them look good like a PR agent would do.

Rennie Molino is a highly successful insurance agent in Grove City, Ohio. A leading company producer, he's received many sales achievement awards. He said, "In the '90s in Ohio, as in most states across the country and continuing today, there was legislation being considered at the State House to put legal caps on jury awards in liability cases. As an insurance professional and business owner, I saw a need for caps on liability awards.

"Basically, the law said that if my employee was driving a personal vehicle to go to an amusement park and got in a serious accident, my business could be sued and I would essentially go bankrupt. There would be no caps on those awards.

"I was contacted by the lobbyist for my company who asked if I would help influence a particular legislator. She was in a tough re-election battle against the legislator she had beat for the position two years earlier. Her opponent had been a fixture on the State House scene and was coming back to challenge her.

"By profession, she was a plaintiff's attorney, so I knew this issue also affected her. Yet she wasn't convinced there should be caps on these judgments. I remember her looking at me and simply saying 'Tell me why I should support this.'

"I knew she truly wanted to represent her constituents rather than the special interests, so I appealed to that. I explained that, as an attorney, if she has business auto insurance and her employees get in a wreck, she'd be liable for damages—even if her employees were on personal business driving their own vehicles. A claim would probably bankrupt her, and it didn't even matter what car was involved.

"I also told her that if she voted to put caps on the awards, I'd be sure to tell hundreds of my community contacts and clients about her support of small business people during the upcoming election season. I even offered to write a personal endorsement letter to hundreds of them, urging them to vote for her in the next election. Further, I framed this in a way that demonstrated its effect on her personally, not what it would do for my company or my clients."

Notice how Rennie offered help in a highly tangible way? He became his top dog's PR agent by urging his friends to vote for her. As a result, his legislator voted for the legislation that put limits on jury awards in certain liability cases.

HUMILITY IS NICE

Former Florida State Representative Janegayle Boyd expressed her distaste for those who have an exaggerated sense of their own importance. "What I don't like," she said, "are people who come across as too slick. They come in with an attitude of, 'You should just accept me because of who I am.'"

That attitude made it hard for her to help a natural ally, a powerful Florida business interest. "I was voted as the fourth most pro-business legislator by the Florida Chamber of Commerce. There was a proposal before us to vote on funding sources for a new Florida Marlins baseball stadium and the team requested millions of taxpayer dollars. I just said to them, 'How do I give you millions of dollars and not help other deserving business people who are not as big as you?' I think they believed that because of their fame and size, they didn't need to sell their issue to me.

"You've always got to sell your story—and you need to be humble doing it," she advised.

Not including key people in the decision-making chain also reflects humility. "What really irritated me were the high-level executives who would talk to the 'treetops'—the Speaker of the House and other legislators in leadership positions. While I understand the need for this, they have to recognize those legislators in their own backyard representing the district where their business is domiciled. They shouldn't be ignored," she said.

Former Florida state representative Leslie Waters endorsed Janegayle Boyd's comments with this example: "A coupon company wanted some economic incentives. My office is one mile down the road from its headquarters, so I represented its business in the Florida state legislature. The company's leaders set up a meeting with the chairman of the Economic Development Committee as well as the chairman of the Appropriations Committee, but didn't meet with me first, even though their business was in my district! They later had their lobbyist set up an appointment with me at my state capitol office. Not only was that a waste of time since my district office was so close, but they had ignored me in the beginning."

DON'T BE A GATE-JUMPER

One thing political professionals can teach those in the private sector—because they do it better than any other profession, is how they show respect to the gatekeepers—and all staff members, for that matter. In the world of politics, this is rule number one.

So remember this: Staff people working for your top dog should never be overlooked. Recently, I asked a member of Congress what happens when someone treats a staff person poorly. The question caused him to roll his eyes and put a look of disgust on his face, then he said, "It would be a non-starter. Once you are disrespectful of the staff, that's it. I just can't work with someone who doesn't understand that." Think about that. If you're disrespectful to the person who *can't* grant your request, you may lose the opportunity to even make your request.

I'm painstakingly amused by "smart "professionals *outside* of politics who exclaim (as if they just invented cold fusion) that they were able to make inroads with a powerful person by befriending that person's staff members. It's unfortunate that they view it as a novel technique to be used only when they need something.

Why aren't people savvier about how they treat these access-givers? Maybe they simply forget that even though they don't make the final decision, they certainly influence your prospects' point of view.

Former Florida State Representative Janegale Boyd provided an earlier example of an underdog influencer she helped by passing legislation to reform state pension law. She said, "Not only was this woman credible to me, but my staffer was convinced that I needed to pursue this issue. Staff members are my eyes and ears. Sometimes they know my potential interests better than I do, so I credit them with helping me help others in this situation."

Remember in Chapter 7 learning about Chip Thayer changing then-State Senator Scott Brown's mind on a workplace smoking ban? Chip passed away in 2009. Russet Morrow Breslau, executive director of Smokefree Massachusetts, remembered Chip's persistency and politeness with Senator Brown and his staff. "He plugged into things like knowing Brown's chief of staff's father was ill. He took time to ask about his father's health in a concerned and caring way." To Chip, all gatekeepers were important.

THE MEANER THEY ARE, THE NICER YOU MUST BE

A great example of "nice" in the face of rudeness from those you want to influence comes this classic (and notorious) email exchange between a Top Dog's assistant and a company representative who had to show aplomb, courtesy, and lots of patience.[119] Read and learn.

No Name-calling

If you want to score a meeting with Rep. Jim McDermott (D-Wash.), know this: His scheduler/office manager at the time, Elizabeth Becton, is to be addressed by her full name—not Liz or any other variant. An executive assistant at McBee Strategic recently learned this the hard way.

A few weeks before, the assistant emailed Becton to set up a meeting with Congressman McDermott and a client, JPMorgan Chase. Days later, the assistant checked back and unfortunately began the email with "Hi Liz."

Becton curtly replied, "Who is Liz?"

The assistant wrote back, "Hi Elizabeth, I thought you went by Liz - apologies if that is incorrect." Becton turned up the heat. "I do not go by Liz. Where did you get your information?" she emailed back.

In his next two emails, the assistant over-apologized for the mistake. Liz's response was to lecture him about the name-calling, writing that if someone said using "Liz" was acceptable, then that person is "not your friend." She wrote, "If I wanted you to call me by any other name, I would have offered that to you." Plus she said, "It's rude when people don't even ask permission and take all sorts of liberties with your name."

The back and forth went on for 19 emails. Her final, searing missive stated, "In the future, you should be VERY careful about such things. People like to brag about their connections in D.C. It's a pastime for some. It's also dangerous to eavesdrop, as you have just found out. Quit apologizing and never call me anything but Elizabeth again. Also, make sure you correct anyone who attempts to call me by any other name but Elizabeth. Are we clear on this? Like I said, it's a hot button for me. And please don't call the office and not leave a message. My colleague told me you called while I was away…I do sometimes leave my desk."

After the exchange was made public, McDermott spokesman Mike DeCesare responded to the situation saying, "An apology is being issued as we speak," adding, "This isn't reflective of the way we do business in this office."

Bravo to the long-suffering assistant at McBee Strategic for this world-class demonstration of self-control with a mean gatekeeper!

THE UNDERDOG'S CHECKLIST
How to Not Bark or Bite but Be Nice

- ✓ Look nice. Smile (genuinely). Nice people look nice, and nasty people look, well, nasty.

- ✓ Modify your passion! It's not wrong to be passionate about your cause, but you have to be judicious in how you deploy it. It does not add to your persuasiveness unless you help your prospect become a hero.

- ✓ Respect the path. Your persuasion prospect has a story that led him or her to where they are, and they're proud of it. Don't disrespect the path.

- ✓ Avoid nagging. Instead, analyze your ratio of "nagging" versus "helpful" communications. What is it? How can you improve it?

- ✓ Be your top dogs' PR agent. What do they do well? How have they helped you? Who can you tell about their accomplishments?

- ✓ Don't be a gate jumper. Instead, befriend the top dog's staff. How can you show sincere interest in them?

- ✓ Disarm the meanies. The meaner they behave, the nicer you need to be.

- ✓ Be as respectful of the people who are against your issue as those who are for it.

- ✓ When you visit your prospects, compliment them on something they've accomplished.

CONCLUSION:
The Dogs Unleashed

At the end of each interview with the top dogs and underdogs, I asked, "What's your bottom-line advice for aspiring underdog influencers?" This chapter includes the don'ts and do's I gleaned from those interviews—first from the top dogs, then from successful underdogs. Remember, this advice is for people who are 1) influencing *up* the food chain; and 2) trying to *change the mind of someone* who is up the food chain.

TOP DOG DON'TS

Let's start with the dark side—the top dogs' recommendations of what you should *never* do. Following this list is a recap of how top dogs interviewed for this book respond to each point.

DON'T...

1. Think it's all about you.
2. Neglect to prep.
3. Ignore the gatekeepers.
4. Be foul.
5. Be a time vampire.

6. Ignore me.

7. Fake it.

8. Be rigid.

9. Surprise me.

10. Lecture me.

TOP DOGS SAY...

1. DON'T think it's all about you.

- "One thing I don't like are people who come across as too slick. They come in with an attitude of, 'You should just accept me because of who I am.'"

- "You've got to sell your story and you need to be humble."

- "If someone is too slick, I'm probably going to pass. By 'slick,' I mean they are going for the close before bringing me along and finding out what my issues are. I'll pass on that, even if it's something I'm interested in."

- "I think on any issue, how to present it is how it would affect the masses—not just your personal interest."

2. DON'T neglect to prep.

- "My advice for those who want to successfully influence is to understand how people make decisions. The problem is that citizens can't articulate what they want. Citizens aren't sure where they fit into the process."

- "Some people are well intentioned but ill-informed. Those who were confused just didn't understand the 'governmentese' used by the folks in D.C."

- "I found out quickly that I didn't know anything about a lot of issues… constituents who are prepared help educate us; we don't always know the details and we have some screwy ideas."

- "Repetition, awareness, and optimism are the ticket."

When you aren't prepared, three things happen and none of them is good. First, you have less confidence, which affects your delivery and, in turn, your credibility. Second, you waste your top dogs' time, and they hate that. (See #5, DON'T Be a Time Vampire.) People don't say "yes" to things they hate. Third, you've heard the "one person can ruin it for everyone" cliché. It's true, especially when you're trying to persuade someone who's averse to or uninformed on your issue. That person may assume that, because you don't know your stuff, *everyone* from your group lacks knowledge of the facts.

3. DON'T ignore the gatekeepers.

Support staff members are gatekeepers because *they* will determine whether you get in to see your top dog.

- "Do your best to know the gatekeepers. If you have a relationship with them, you can advance your cause."

- "The challenge is how do you get by the gatekeeper? To get by the gatekeepers, you've got to tell them your story and tell it well. They have a quick route to the boss, and the staff can sometimes fix things. While not the ultimate decision maker, they're very influential. They do the work and we take the credit."

- "What people have to remember is that on some issues, their staff members are huge lobbyists in and of their own right. Staff is usually lobbying members, urging them to vote one way or another."

- "My staff members are my eyes and ears. They know me better than I know myself."

I not only think this rule is right on, but I don't think it's smart to ignore *any* human beings.

For reasons unknown to me, this rule prevails more in the political world than any other. I've seen successful, smart lobbyists publicly crushed and humiliated after treating legislative staff with disrespect. In fact, I was once the cause of a crushing myself. While interning for an Ohio state senator who went on to be a member of Congress, I was called a "hack" by a prominent Common Pleas judge in his district because we couldn't grant his weekly wish. Ten minutes after I told on the judge to the senator (successfully continuing my kindergarten practice as a "tattle tale"), the senator was on the phone to the judge berating him for calling me names and telling him to never try that again. Not many powerful people would take the side of a 22-year-old intern versus a powerful Common Pleas court judge. These people are loyal!

Treating the gatekeepers with respect opens doors and creates goodwill.

4. DON'T be foul.

- "Just have normal manners and show good breeding. Don't be foul."

- "I am watching how people handle themselves."

- "Show (un)common courtesy."

- "Be respectful."

- "Be sensitive to others and show some etiquette."

- "Stand up when I come in; I still do this for others."

I've had audience members exclaim, "Showalter, that goes without saying! Of *course* we need to be polite. We know that. Why do we have to cover this topic?" We might like to think, "it goes without saying" to be polite, but I'm afraid it needs to go *with* saying.

I've found that otherwise articulate, even-tempered people lose their composure when they're fighting for a cause and run into opposition. They don't keep their eyes up (see "Eyes Up" in Chapter 5), so they get riled when they don't hear the response they expect. That, in turn, can elicit nastiness. Not only top dogs but underdogs offer this kind of advice, which tells me it's not my imagination. (See "Cool It" advice from both the top dogs and the underdogs.)

5. DON'T be a time vampire.

- "It's really like in that book *All I Ever Needed to Know I Learned in Kindergarten*. Be on time."

- "Always be conscious of the time."

- "Understand that we are always rushed."

- "Be respectful of my time."

Powerful people are "wanted" men and women. They don't have the luxury of dissecting each request in detail. Everyone wants a chunk of their time, and that can drive many powerful people crazy.

Why do powerful people tend to be so time-conscious, and how can you work within their reality? Kay Cannon, Master Certified Coach and former president of the International Coach Federation, is hired by individuals and organizations to keep their "Type A" performers engaged without causing damage throughout the organization. She said, "Type A's are high-achievers. They're highly driven by accomplishment, so virtually all politicians and executives fall into this category. Quite simply, time is their most valuable commodity because its wise use determines what gets done. And, fair or unfair, they have a low tolerance for anyone or anything that wastes their time. Wasted time is an impediment toward their goals. Plus, they're very impatient with inefficiencies. Inefficient communications, processes, and systems keep them from moving forward."

How can influential underdogs get their messages across while respecting their top dogs' time? Kay recommends starting at the end. "Before you go in, list your most important points. But what you think you're going to say last, say first, because your Type A will check out if you don't get to the most important point. Start at the end," she advised.

6. DON'T ignore me.

- "Establish a relationship with me."

- "It's irritating when some interest groups ask for your help throughout the year, but ignore you three months before the election so they don't appear 'partisan.'"

- "Take the extra nickel and come to meet with me on my turf. That gets my attention."

When we think about people who ask us for favors, who are we more likely to help? You'll probably first help those you know or those with whom you're acquainted. Top dogs deal with a plethora of requests and have to filter those requests. Remember, the relationship that's in place is the consummate filter. (See Chapter 7.)

7. DON'T fake it.

- "Some people are cavalier. They have a job to do, my name is on their list, so they come to see me. They assume they know my position and they're just playing a numbers game. They really don't believe in the cause. Those who do believe in their cause have a tremendous impact."

- "Some people come in just because their association ginned them up to do so, but they really don't care about the issue. And they aren't really effective."

Are you checking a box, or do you really care? Remember that powerful people do a lot of listening and watching. They can tell if you sincerely believe in your cause, or if you're crossing your request off someone else's "to do" list. Attention goes to the sincere.

8. DON'T be rigid.

- "People who are so inflexible they have no objectivity don't make an impact. Then they try to threaten us—not a winning combination."

- "Be aware that the person you're meeting with has lots of conflicting pressures."

How your top dog meets your request will rarely be perfect; you can't be looking for Jesus. Do these admonitions infer compromise? Probably. But would you rather have something or nothing? A slogan in the Restoration Movement, commonly attributed to St. Augustine (but actually penned by Lutheran theologian and pastor Petet Meiderlin) reads: "In essentials, unity, in non-essentials, liberty, in all things, charity." That's not bad advice!

9. **DON'T surprise me.**

    *   "Some groups have a subversive approach. One construction organization sends out campaign mailers in the middle of the legislative session. To do it in the middle of a legislative session seems inappropriate. It certainly doesn't build goodwill. It has a very threatening quality to it that makes you believe they will not be easy to work with."

    *   "Try not to give me any surprises."

    *   "I have to know who you are, who you are affiliated with. Don't surprise me with attacks in the public domain."

This behavior is a variation of the infuriating technique of "going behind the other guy's back," commonly practiced in junior high days. Adults still do it, thinking it provides an influence advantage. Although it might accomplish short-term coercion, it doesn't achieve long-term influence.

10. **DON'T lecture me.**

    *   "I remember being told by a lobbyist once that 'I had to be a statesman' on that person's particular issue. I found that kind of insulting because I do not feel that one vote makes a career. It is my constituent communications, my track record of votes over the years, and so on, that counts."

Unless you've "been there and done that," it's not wise to give your top dogs career advancement tips.

After all, there's a reason *you* are asking *them* for help.

TOP DOG DO'S

That's a long list of DON'Ts, but let not your heart be troubled. Top dogs also conveyed the positive behaviors that get their attention. Next, let's look at tactics you'd be wise to employ.

DO…

1. Show you know.
2. Cool it.
3. Keep your eyes up.
4. Help me.
5. Bark less, listen more.
6. Help me help you.
7. Tell the truth.
8. Make us feel the heat.
9. Say thanks.

TOP DOGS SAY DO…

1. Show you know.

- "When you contact me, don't make up something to support your view."

- "Be smart enough to recognize the cons, reveal the cons, and work with us on them."

- "Articulate what you want. What's the solution?"

- "Know what you're talking about! Read the bill."

- "People who tow the line from headquarters and don't know the specifics of legislation, who haven't even read the bills, are ineffective."

- "The 'cause' people can be tough to deal with. For those people who come in with a cause, the best thing they can do is organize their thoughts. Give me four to five reasons why I should support you and what you want to happen. It's all about being prepared."

A meeting with your top dog should not be an episode of CSI. At that point, neither of you has time to figure out fact from fiction, so you'd better have the facts down pat. It's even more vital if you're an amateur influencer to "show you know." You're not a professional lobbyist and likely not a topic expert, so you want to avoid "choking" when the time comes to make "the ask."

Our underdogs didn't experience much fear in their influence attempts; that's probably why they made the cut for this book. However, you may be reading it because you've been challenged to succeed in an upward influence environment. The scientific literature shows that novice performers (in sports, entertainment, business presentations, speeches, etc.) are more likely to choke and make mistakes when they're *being observed* in an activity that's outside their area of expertise.[120] That's why you can sing so well in the shower, but when you perform karaoke at the birthday bash, you freeze up. Or why you can do well in a difficult conversation with your boss, but talking to an elected official with a group of your colleagues makes you break out in hives.

So if you can, schedule a private meeting with your top dog. With or without observers, knowing your content cold mitigates the chance that you'll choke.

2. Cool it.

- "Don't threaten, don't bully. I tried to disarm my opponents with humor. To those who threatened me, many times I had to just say, 'You do what you need to do and I will do what I need to do, and I will be elected so you will have to deal with me in the future.'"

- "Don't get completely bent out of shape when adjustments to your idea are proposed."

- "Be objective when listening to my concerns and questions."

- "Sometimes you can surprise us by not fighting so hard."

- "When the fist pounding on the desk starts, I just inform them that the meeting is over."

There's danger in not cooling it, as author and humorist Dave Barry once wrote. "I argue very well. Ask any of my remaining friends. I can win an argument on any topic, against any opponent. People know this and steer clear of me at parties. Often, as a sign of their great respect, they don't even invite me."[121]

Barry's comment summed up quite well the reason to "cool it" with your top dog. If you lose your cool, you'll lose your invitation to the table.

When are we ever persuaded by someone who turns a disagreement into a Dr. Seuss scene on acid? Do you really process that person's request? Are you thinking, "You know, he's right. I'm ignorant and thoughtless. I'm lucky to be in the position I am, and I deserve to be yelled at like this, so I'm going to change my mind."

3. Keep your eyes up.

Both the top dogs and our underdogs stressed the importance of underdog influencers to "keep their eyes up," as discussed in Chapter 5. Here's how they described it:

- "You have to be aware of the environment in which you're making your request."

- "You have to understand how people make decisions."

- "You have to know the big picture. There are many 'nice to do' things that are not necessities."

- "Find the other person's value system and play off it."

You'll soon read that our underdogs have much more to say about this.

4. **Help me.**

- "She had worked on my campaign and that, of course, got my attention."

- "Those guys did everything legally possible to help me get elected, so of course I listened to them."

- "There are people who help you win elections either financially or with their time. I may not always do what they want, but if they call me, I'm absolutely obliged to take their call."

- "There's a group of people in the community who, ever since I was elected, have formed an entourage around me. I don't know why, and I didn't know them prior to running for office. They come to my town hall meetings, to other events, and they always pack the house for me. Will I be able to vote with them on every issue? I don't know, but I do know that if they wanted a meeting with me, I wouldn't say no."

The comments above show the top dog's unabashed response to reciprocity, one of the persuasion principles that have guided (and will, no doubt, continue to guide) human behavior throughout infinity. It represents the essence of many top dogs, and frankly, all of us. *Help them by investing in their career, and you will see the doors open.*

Before you start thinking that this behavior is only typical of those in power, think again. When you're deciding which emails and voicemails to return first, which ones do you give priority? Admit it, you pay more attention to those who've helped you in some way, whether it was the small favor at work the other day or—as with our top dogs—a boost to help you achieve your goals. Naturally, you appreciate those who have invested in you.

And if you don't prioritize your communications, you should. Virtually every civilization and tribe views those who don't reciprocate as ingrates. We have other names for them: energy vampires, moochers, takers, and more.

Who looks favorably on those who take without giving?

5. Bark less, listen more.

- "Listen to my side of the story."

- "With one underdog, I knew that on some issues we wouldn't even be on the same planet. But she always listened to me, and I, in turn, gave her my undivided attention."

We tend to forget that influential people do a lot of listening. The underdog who reverses that dynamic by sincerely asking clarifying questions will stand apart from those who are talking *at* their top dog.

6. Help me help you.

- "I got the feeling that I was doing the right thing."

- "They made me feel like I was the only person who could help them."

Top dogs aren't engaged solely in the pursuit of power. They want to help people, and to feel good about it. (See Chapter 5 and its discussion about the gift of heroics.) Let's not forget they ascended to their position in part by helping others and by using terrific interpersonal communications skills on their journey. They're the proverbial "people persons." They like helping others, so find ways they can help you and *feel good about it.*

7. Tell the truth.

- "Tell me your story without prejudice."

- "Be totally honest."

The fact that this basic admonition made the list tells me lying is going on.

8. Make us feel the heat.

- "You have to convince us (legislators) that we will lose the next election if we don't take up your cause. That's not easy to do because so many legislators are primarily concerned with keeping their seats long enough to get a state pension."

Admittedly, this blatantly honest tip only works with elected officials who have to periodically renew their job contracts. How can you, without threatening your prospect, let him or her know that your organization is able to mobilize enough people to influence an election outcome? This technique should be practiced only by confident groups who can back up their words with action. If you aim for the top dog and miss, you'll certainly be remembered—but not the way you want!

9. Say thanks.

- "Always, when you're done, express thanks for listening and thanks for the work we do."

Apparently, some underdogs still fail this basic test of courtesy. If you say thanks, you'll be remembered favorably.

AND NOW, ADVICE FROM THE UNDERDOGS

A few of the DO's from the underdogs mesh with the top dogs' counsel. Here, however, we have only one prevalent DON'T.

UNDERDOGS SAY...

1. DON'T show fear.

- "Don't be afraid; your legislators will listen to you, even if you have opposing political leanings; if you show up, they listen."

- "I didn't have a lot of fear going into it because I had written all my comments out and practiced beforehand. It was a little intimidating, though, because the legislators sit on a raised platform and you're looking up at them."

- "I'm an extrovert, and I think that helped me."

- "Stand your ground. Don't bluff and be afraid."

- "I meet them in person in their district offices. It's a less stressful environment."

Never, ever, show or talk about your fear. It can't help your cause. Here's a story about what can happen when fear combines with lack of answers to defend one's case.

Scene: The Senate Appropriations transportation subcommittee hearing on Capitol Hill, Wednesday, Sept. 6, 2000.

Players: Masatoshi Ono, then Bridgestone/Firestone Chief Executive, appeared before House and Senate committees investigating tire blowouts that led to the recall of millions of tires made by his Bridgestone/Firestone company. It was a rare public appearance for Ono, a Japanese national, who admitted he was nervous and had practiced his opening speech so he could deliver it in English.

Action: Ono began his testimony. "I'm sixty-three years old, and I have never made a public appearance like this before, so I am more than a little bit nervous." Well, his "trial" was far from over at that point. Ono apologized for deaths linked to the blowouts but could not explain why they happened. Lawmakers spent nearly 13 hours excoriating Ono and his company, the U.S. division of the Japanese Bridgestone rubber conglomerate. Senator Barbara Mikulski, D-MD, even asked where his "sense of concern as a human being was."

Consequence: A month later, Ono resigned.

We've heard the common refrain that people can "smell fear." Although probably more realistic in the animal realm than with humans, our fellow homo sapiens can certainly ascertain fear in us. As an influencer, showing fear represents a distinct disadvantage because it does three things. Again, none of them good.

First, it makes your top dog nervous for you. People pick up the emotional signals of others, and they tend to reflect those emotions. This doesn't mean top dogs will become fearful, but they'll become nervous *for you*. They'll see your fear (usually expressed in nonverbal behaviors) and get uncomfortable. So, they're not paying attention *to* your request; they're hoping you make it *through* your request. Your message gets lost in your trepidation and their reactions to it.

Second, showing inordinate fear, while sometimes received as obsequious respect, communicates that you're not a peer of your top dog. I know, you're thinking, "Isn't the point of this book how to make a request of someone who's *not* your equal?" Not exactly. Let me explain. While you may not be a peer in terms of position power, you *do* have power in terms of expertise, information, fairness, dependency, and values (see Chapter 1).

However, you won't get to that part if your first impression conveys you're not a peer in terms of the power *you* wield. A subtle signal that lessens the impact of everything you say and do is exchanged.

Third, your fear can make your prospect doubt your sincerity. Think of the times you hit home runs in your efforts to communicate, whether it was a formal presentation, asking your spouse to marry you, or offering advice in making a customer service encounter. You may have been nervous, but you believed in your message so much, you weren't self-conscious or second-guessing every word. You *believed,* so you didn't show your fear. In fact, when you strongly believe in what you're saying, fear tends to disappear.

So when you show fear, your top dog may be thinking, "If it's so nerve-wracking to make your case, how much do you really believe in it?"

UNDERDOG DO'S

Here are the tactics recommended by our Underdogs:
DO…

1.   Show you know.

2. Keep your eyes up.

3. Show gratitude.

4. Relate.

5. Cool it.

6. Give to get.

7. Watch the time.

8. Laugh.

9. Look for similarities and connections.

10. Do what you promise to do.

UNDERDOGS SAY DO...

1. Show you know.

- "I had an immediate advantage—the advantage that I knew more about the legislation than the legislator did."

- "I had to learn how to talk in narrative. People make decisions without being fully informed. But, facts and figures do not totally make the case. They're helpful to set the stage, but more people with more facts and figures are not always the answer."

- "Be honest and make sure your information is correct. Make sure it's not going to come back and bite you."

- "I learned from my mistakes and talked to successful influencers who had been doing this for a while. I had to learn to give accurate testimony."

- "Get the basics down. Know your issue. I'm an extensive note taker."

- "Know your facts! If you don't, keep your mouth shut. Intentionally or not, you will lose credibility."

- "Prepare. I had all of my comments written out with key bullet points."

- "Do as much research on your subject as possible."

- "Learn as much as you can."

- "Have objective data not necessarily produced by your organization."

- "Know your stuff—their attention span is extremely short."

- "Be aware of your opponent's issues. Bring them up in the conversation."

- "Provide prompt and honest information."

- "Bring out not just the facts, but the consequences of the facts."

- "You have to immerse yourself in the issue and be knowledgeable in these meetings. You cannot stumble around."

In today's world of hyper-abundant content, there's no excuse for not knowing your subject. As discussed in Chapter 1, your content represents a source of information power. Plus, as you can read in the comments above, showing you know will boost your confidence. So do your best to bring new insights to the discussion. As one member of Congress told me, "Many of these groups have been promoting their issue so long, for God's sake, I know their talking points. I can recite them."

2. Keep your eyes up.

As noted in Chapter 5, "eyes up" is standard operating procedure for professional race car drivers (look to the road ahead, not at the hood of the car) as well as downhill skiers (look down the hill, not at the tip of your skis), quarterbacks (look downfield, not at the monstrous guys barreling toward you)—and underdogs (look at the environment around you and be aware of all relevant factors).

Our underdogs pay attention. They keep their eyes up and suggest you do the same.

- "Know who you're dealing with; the legislators and their positions and why they have voted in that way."

- "Some audiences expect a big gesture. You just have to watch for what they respond to."

- "You have to see the world from their point of view while retaining your own objectivity."

- "We very quickly learned that we had to really listen and ask—up front—how they feel about an issue."

- "I had to learn to address their objections and concerns—to be aware of those before even making the ask."

- "Sometimes advocates can be their own worst enemies by giving too much data or by being too formal at first. Find out what those legislators care about and how your issue helps them meet their goals."

- "I watch who is in trouble and who needs help."

- "I observed their body language as well. If they were disinterested, I went to the next point, and I tried to always keep to three points."

- "I try to understand the person I'm approaching—their issues and the politics surrounding them."

- "Find out what their interests are."

3. **Show gratitude.**

- "When you go in to see them, compliment them about something they've done. Appreciate them."

- "Show gratitude for previous ways they have helped you."

- "I think you have to be 'politely persistent'; offer information, do not wait for them to get back to you because they probably will not."

- "Be polite and thank them for their time."

- "It's vital to circle back and thank people. Tell them how their action benefited you or your company, and share appreciation for the effort they put forth on your behalf."

- "Be businesslike and say thank you."

- "I like to follow up with letters, and if they've indicated their support during the meeting, to reiterate and to reinforce their support."

- "When they do help you out (and especially when they don't), send them a letter thanking them for seeing you."

- "Before I ask for anything, I always start the conversation by thanking them for previous actions on our behalf."

The top dogs mentioned gratitude, but not nearly to the extent our underdogs did. Not surprising. Grateful underdogs are persuasive underdogs. Gratitude can help you achieve goals, not to mention improve your health, energy, and emotional state, according to an ongoing study. Robert Emmons of the University of California, Davis, and Michael McCullough, University of Miami, are creating and disseminating a large body of scientific data on the nature of gratitude, its causes, and its potential consequences for human health and well-being.[122]

Their initial findings include the following:

- Those who kept gratitude journals on a weekly basis reported fewer physical symptoms and were more optimistic about the upcoming week versus those who recorded hassles or neutral life events.[123]

- Participants who kept gratitude lists were more likely to have made progress toward important personal (academic, interpersonal, and health-based) goals.

- A daily gratitude intervention with young adults resulted in higher reported levels of positive states of alertness, enthusiasm, determination, attentiveness, and energy compared to a focus on downward social comparisons.

- Those who regularly attend religious services and engage in religious activities such as prayer and reading religious material are more likely to be grateful than those who don't. Gratitude does not require religious faith, but faith enhances the ability to be grateful.

4. **Relate.**

- "Get to know them as people before you talk about your issues."

- "Relationships matter. I have to invest time to make it work and cannot expect people to listen to me just because I'm wearing a white coat and have M.D. after my name."

- "Build relationships. I have never wanted an 'easy button' relationship with my legislators."

- "Establish a relationship with local legislators first."

- "You have to stay in front of people."

- "It sometimes just takes one guy who knows the top dog to get that person's attention."

Relationships create long-term influence opportunities. You'll probably need your top dog's help in the future, so build a mutually beneficial relationship.

5. **Cool it.**

- "You have to keep it at another level. I just don't take things personally. It's absolutely necessary not to when you're talking to someone who's opposed to you. When personalities get involved, you become less open to a consensus approach and you can end up with a different outcome."

- "You have to be gracious; go the extra mile in being polite, watch your tone of voice, and don't expect people to jump through hoops."

- "Don't get offended and show you're ticked off."

- "Try to calm down and listen to why they're opposed to your idea."

- "Pick your fights. The odds of doing it again are remote."

- "Don't just attack people. Talk things through."

As you influence up, at times you'll be told things you don't want to hear. You won't get what you want. If you demonstrate impulse control, you'll live to persuade another day.

6. **Give to get.**

- "The only reason I didn't get the bum's rush from him is I had worked on his campaign."

- "I told her if she voted with us, I would let all my clients know and ask them to vote for her in the next election, which was just months away. She took me up on the offer."

- "I had worked on her campaigns over the last ten years, so of course she met with me and gave me inside tips on the best ways to put pressure on those who disagreed with us."

- "If you want to make a change, ask how you can help them. Ask what they need."

- "Losers don't legislate. Get involved in campaigns."

- "Volunteer for local campaigns."

Our top dogs revealed that helping them reach their goals can open doors. Winning underdogs do this instinctively.

7. **Watch the time.**

- "Be prepared for them to be short with you. After they learn who you are, they will give you a few minutes."

- "Have a plan. Be prepared to discuss your issue in twenty minutes, five minutes, or one minute."

Remember Kay Cannon's advice? Individuals who waste time and don't get to the point are seen by Type A's as standing in the way of the top dog's goal. Be an accelerator, not a brake!

8. Laugh!

- "Try to use humor."

- "Have fun."

Remember to keep your sense of humor. Consider keeping an "influence humor journal" and record three funny things that have happened during each influence campaign or encounter. When you start looking for the humor, you'll find it. You'll also start "thinking funny" and become less tense in your interactions.

9. Look for similarities and connections.

- "I always try to look for a thread of personal connection. One of my employees dated one of the Congressman's nephews, so I would bring that up in conversation. You just look for whatever you can."

10. Do what you promise to do.

- "Do what you say you're going to do."

This explains itself!!

WHERE WE AGREE TO AGREE

These DON'Ts and DO's represent a lot to remember, so let me make it easier for you. The top dogs and underdogs agree on these four major themes:

1. Show you know.

2. Cool it.
3. Keep your eyes up.
4. Show gratitude.

(Although considerably more underdogs than top dogs advised "showing gratitude," both believe in its power to create a favorable influence milieu. Perhaps many top dogs thought it was too obvious to mention.)

So if you can't remember every tactic mentioned, simply remember the four key items both the underdogs and top dogs agree on: *know your content, maintain your cool, keep your eyes up,* and *say thanks!*

These, combined with the Extreme Influence Tactics you've studied in the chapters of this book, will make all the difference. You'll see!

ABOUT THE AUTHOR

More than 150 organizations, including Southwest Airlines, the American Heart Association, International Paper, Pfizer and the National Restaurant Association have hired Amy Showalter to elevate their grassroots influence and PAC programs. Over 85% of her long-term consulting clients have experienced an increase in budget, staff, and senior management recognition after collaborating with Amy. She has spoken in 35 states to more than 25,000 corporate executives, management teams, boards of directors, and nonprofit volunteer leaders about how to get powerful people on their side.

Amy has authored or co-authored more than five national research projects that explore the influence strategies of the nation's most powerful interest groups, as well as the tactics that persuade high-powered elected officials. In addition, she has surveyed thousands of "everyday" grassroots advocates who have shared their secrets for influencing up the food chain.

Her insights have been featured in *The Washington Times, Roll Call, Politico.com, The Baltimore Sun, The Dallas Morning News,* and *The Christian Science Journal*, over 100 Creators Syndicate newspapers, and 15 Tribune Media Services publications, to name a few. Amy has been a regular columnist for three magazines and has published more than 100 articles on grassroots influence. She is the author of *105 Ways to Build Relationships with your Elected Officials.*

Amy has served as a faculty member at the U.S. Chamber's Institute for Organization Management, and has been a guest lecturer at George Washington University's Graduate School of Political Management. She is a Past Chairman of the American Society of Association Executives Government Relations Section Council, and is the Cofounder and Producer of Innovate to Motivate, an annual national conference for veteran political involvement professionals.

Amy has a BA in Political Science from Wright State University and an MSA from Central Michigan University.

Amy and her husband, Randy Boyer, reside in the greater Cincinnati area with their two Siberian Huskies, Houdini and Jackson, and Finnegan the Pomeranian.

As their one violation of the underdog philosophy, Randy and Amy are fervent Ohio State Buckeye fans.

END NOTES

1   Maureen Dowd, "The Naked and the Dead" January 24, 2010, *New York Times.*

2   Steven Kotler, "Why We Love Losers" www.psychologytoday.com, April 28, 2008.

3   H. Tajfel & J.C. Turner, "The Social Identity Theory of Intergroup Behavior." S. Worchel & W. G. Austin (Eds.), *The Social Psychology of Intergroup Relations.* Chicago: Nelson Hall, 1986, pp. 7-24.

4   Ridgeway, 2003; Sachdev & Bourhis, 1987; Sande, Ellard, & Ross, 1986; Sherif, White, & Harvey, 1955.

5   Vandello, Goldschmied, & Richards, *Personal Social Psychology Bulletin* 2007; 33; 1604.

6   P. C. Bernhardt, J. M. Dabbs, J. A. Fielden, & C. D. Lutter, "Testosterone Changes During Vicarious Experiences of Winning and Losing Among Fans of Sporting Events." *Physiology and Behavior*, 65, 1998, pp. 59-62.

7   Cited in Vandello, Goldschmied, & Richards, *Personal Social Psychology Bulletin* 2007; 33; 1603.

8   Cited in Vandello, Goldschmied, & Richards, *Personal Social Psychology Bulletin* 2007; p. 1610.

9   www.ScientificAmerican.com "Powerful and Bad in 2009,"Christie Nicholson podcast http://www.scientificamerican.com/podcast/episode. cfm?id=powerful-and-bad-in-2009-09-12-31.

10   Robert Frank, "Do High Incomes Make CEOs Mean?" *The Wall Street Journal,* July 15, 2010.

11   "Capitalizing on the Underdog Effect." Harvard Business Review, November, 2010, p.32.

12   Center for Responsive Politics, www.opensecrets.org.

13   "How Business Trounced the Trial Lawyers." *Business Week* January 8, 2007.

14   Michael Luo, Jo Becker, and Patrick Healy, "Donors Worried by Clinton Campaign Spending." *The New York Times,* February 22, 2008.

15   Ibid.

16   Leslie Wayne, "Companies Used to Getting Their Way." *The New York Times,* December 4, 1998. http://www.nytimes.com/1998/12/04/business/companies-used-to-getting-their-way.html?pagewanted=all.

17   "Obama: It's not all in the name." Associated Press, 1/24/07.

18   "Quick Guide & Transcript: Candidates consider presidential bids." CNN.com, 1/17/07.

19   CBSnews.com, 6/8/2008.

20   MSNBC, *Meet the Press,* 8/29/04.

21   Malcolm Gladwell, "How David Beats Goliath: When Underdogs Break the Rules" *The New Yorker,* May 11, 2009, p. 40-49.

22   Lee Jenkins, "For You, New Orleans." *Sports Illustrated,* February 15, 2010.

23   Kevin and Jackie Freiberg, *Nuts! Southwest Airlines' Crazy Recipe for Business and Personal Success.* Bard Press, 1996.

24   "Southwest Thrives on free-bags policy." USA Today, December 13, 2009.

25   Carlin Flora, "The First Impression," *Psychology Today,* May 14, 2004. www.psychologytoday.com/articles/200405/the-first-impression?page=2.

26   Jenni Laidman, "Making an Impression" *Toledo Blade,* Monday, June 25, 2001.

27   Ibid.

28   Marina Krakovsky, "Mixed Impressions," Scientific American Mind, January/February 2010.

29   Moore, D. A., & Healy, P. J. (2008). The trouble with overconfidence. Psychological Review, 115(2), 502-517.

30   "We Can Measure the Power of Charisma," Harvard Business Review, January-February 2010.

31 Carlin Flora, "The First Impression," Psychology Today, May 14, 2004. www.psychologytoday.com/articles/200405/the-first-impression?page=2.

32 Jenni Laidman, "Making an Impression," *Toledo Blade*, Monday,June 25, 2001.

33 Gerald Seib and Jim Vandehei, "A Lobbying Machine Springs Up to Revive Issue of Internet Taxes," *The Wall Street Journal*, June 29, 2000.

34 Ibid.

35 Joe Keohane, "How Facts Backfire: Researchers Discover a Surprising Threat to Democracy: Our Brains," *The Boston Globe,* July 11, 2010.

36 Linda L. Golden and Mark I. Alpert, "Comparative Analysis of the Relative Effectiveness of One- and Two-Sided Communication for Contrasting Products," *Journal of Advertising,* Vol. 16, No. 1, M.E. Sharpe, Inc., 1987, pp. 18-25+68. www.jstor.org/stable/4188610.

37 David G. Meyer, Malcolm A. Jeeves, & Nicholas Wolterstorff. *Psychology Through the Eyes of Faith.* HarperSanFrancisco, 2002, p. 88.

38 R. Nisbett & L. Ross. *Human Inference: Strategies and Shortcomings of Social Judgment.* Englewood Cliffs, N.J.: Prentice Hall, 1980.

39 Martha T. Moore, "Haiti relief less than Katrina, 9/11." *USA Today,* May 14, 2010.

40 R. Nisbett & L. Ross. *Human Inference: Strategies and Shortcomings of Social Judgment.* Englewood Cliffs, N.J.: Prentice Hall, 1980.

41 R. Guadagno, K. Rhoads, & B. Sagarin, "Figural Vividness and Persuasion: Capturing the Elusive Vividness Effect." Submitted to *Journal of Personality and Social Psychology,* November, 2009.

42 Milgram, S., *Obedience to Authority: An Experimental View,* Harper Perennial Modern Classics; Reprint edition (June 30, 2009).

43 B. Latane, "The Psychology of Social Impact." *American Psychologist*, 36, 1981, pp. 343-356.

44 J. Y. Moon & L. Sproull, "Essence of Distributed Work: The Case of the Linux Kernel." Chapter in *Distributed Work,* P. Hinds & S. Kiesler. Cambridge, Mass.: MIT Press, 2001.

45 D. Sally, "Conversation and Cooperation in Social Dilemmas: A Meta-Analysis of Experiments from 1958 to 1992." *Rationality and Society*, 7, 1995, pp. 58-92.

46　M. Deutsch, "Trust and suspicion." *Journal of Conflict Resolution*, 2, 1958, pp. 265-279.

47　N. L. Kerr & C. M. Kaufman-Gilliland, "Communication, Commitment, and Cooperation in Social Dilemmas." *Journal of Personality and Social Psychology*, 66, 1994, pp. 513-529.

48　Alan Gerber & Donald Green. *Get Out the Vote.* Washington, D.C.: Brookings Institution Press, 2004.

49　Daniel Vance interview with Tim Pawlenty, "Executive Privilege." *Connect Business*, September 2004.

50　Lefkowitz, Blake, & Mouton, "The Dynamics of Influence and Coercion." *International Journal of Social Psychiatry*, Vol. 2, No. 4, 1957, pp. 263-274.

51　Stanford W. Gregory, Jr. & Stephen Webster, "A Nonverbal Signal in Voices of Interview Partners Effectively Predicts Communication Accommodation and Social Status Perceptions." *Journal of Personality and Social Psychology*, 70: 1231-40, 1996.

52　Kathleen McGowan, "Second Nature: Your Personality Isn't Necessarily Set in Stone." *Psychology Today*, March / April 2008, pp. 78-79.

53　Ibid, pp. 78-79.

54　Ibid, pp. 78-79.

55　Ibid, p. 77.

56　Ibid, p. 77.

57　Angela Duckworth, interview with Scott Barry Kaufman, "Confessions of a Late Bloomer." *Psychology Today*, November/December 2008, p. 76.

58　A. Duckworth, C. Peterson, M. Matthews, & D. Kelly, "Grit: Perseverance and Passion for Long-Term Goals." *Journal of Personality and Social Psychology*, 2007, Vol. 92, No. 6, pp. 1087-1101.

59　Ibid.

60　Ibid.

61　Peter Doskoch, "The Winning Edge." www.psychologytoday.com, October 16, 2005.

62　Jonah Lehrer, "The Truth About Grit." *The Boston Globe*, August 2, 2009. www.boston.com/bostonglobe/ideas/articles/2009/08/02/the_truth_about_grit/

63 Ibid.

64 http://74.125.113.132/search?q=cache:-UnakvcZm5YJ:www.politico.com/ news/stories/0209/18915.html+Will+Obama's+grassroots+stand+tall%3F&c d=1&hl=en&ct=clnk&gl=us

65 Notes/transcript from Mara Liasson on NPR: "Can Obama's Grass Roots Sway Midterm Elections?" March 16, 2010. http://www.npr.org/templates/ story/story.php?storyId=124613714.

66 David Schaper on NPR: "'Camp Obama' Trains Campaign Volunteers," June 13, 2007.

67 Bob Stone. *Confessions of a Civil Servant: Lessons in Changing America's Government and Military.* Rowman & Littlefield Publishers, Inc., 2003. Excerpts used with permission.

68 David Packard, et al. *A Quest for Excellence, Final Report to the President.* The President's Blue Ribbon Commission on Defense Management, June 1986.

69 Carlin Flora, "Profiles in Perseverance." November 1, 2005. www. psychologytoday.com.

70 www.portfolio.com/business-travel/features/2007/09/18/Kate-Hanni-Profile/index1. html#ixzz0lx2mE1Dm.

71 www.portfolio.com/business-travel/features/2007/09/18/Kate-Hanni-Profile/index1. html#ixzz0lx4xbvng.

72 Krissah Thompson, "A Quest to Be Heard." *The Washington Post,* June 21, 2009.

73 Ibid.

74 Marvin Eisenstadt, André Haynal, Pierre Rentchnick, & Pierre de Senarclens. *Parental Loss and Achievement.* Madison, CT: International Universities Press, Inc., 1989.

75 Bruce Grierson, "Weathering the Storm." *Psychology Today*, May 2009.

76 Martin Seligman, Ph.D. *Learned Optimism: How to Change Your Mind and Your Life.* New York: Pocket Books, 1998, pp. 85-87.

77 *Journal of Personality and Social Psychology*, 1994, Vol. 67, No. 1, pp. 92-104.

78 "Probing the depression-rumination cycle." *Journal of Personality and Social Psychology*, Vol. 77, No. 4, pp. 801-814.

79 Scott Barry Kaufman, "Confessions of a Late Bloomer." *Psychology Today*. November/December 2008.

80 Chuck Salter, "Fight to Survive." *Fast Company*, April 2003, p. 96.

81 Adapted from Lawrence Block, *Telling Lies for Fun and Profit*. HarperCollins, 1994.

82 Timothy A. Pychyl, Ph.D. "Self-regulation failure (Part 2): Willpower is like a muscle." www.psychologytoday.com, accessed February 23, 2009.

83 Ibid.

84 Amen, Daniel G., M.D., *Change Your Brain, Change Your Body*. Harmony Books, 2010.

85 Timothy A. Pychyl, Ph.D., "Self-Regulation Failure: Eight Tips to Strengthen Willpower." www.psychologytoday.com/node/3627 accessed March 3, 2009.

86 Greg Jaffe, "To Understand Sheiks in Iraq, Marines 'Ask Mac,'" *Wall Street Journal*, September 10, 2007.

87 Tim Craig and Michael D. Shear, "Allen Quip Provokes Outrage, Apology," *Washington Post*. August 15, 2006. p.A01.

88 Michael Barbaro, "Rosy Words for Clinton by 90's Nemesis," *New York Times*, March 31, 2008.

89 Ibid.

90 Philip Tetlock, "Thinking the unthinkable: sacred values and taboo cognitions." *Trends in Cognitive Science*, Vol. 7 No. 7 July 2003. p. 320.

91 David Gergen, "The Spirit of Teamwork." U.S. News & World Report, November 12, 2007. http://politics.usnews.com/news/best-leaders/articles/2007/11/12/united-they-stand.html.

92 Jeff Pearlman, "Success: Winners and Losers." *Psychology Today*, March 1, 2009. http://www.psychologytoday.com/articles/200903/success-winners-and-losers.

93 Rick Reilly, "He Loves Himself Barry Much," *Sports Illustrated*, August 21, 2001.

94 Ibid.

95 Ibid.

96 Pearlman. http://www.psychologytoday.com/articles/200903/success-winners-and-losers.

97 Ibid.

98   Robin Vallacher, "Dynamics of Minority Influence: The Federation of Behavioral and Psychological Cognitive Sciences." www.thefederationonline. org/events/Briefings/2006_SPSP_DHS/index.php#anchor.

99   Eileen McNamara, "Reclaiming Their Church." *The Boston Globe*, April 14, 2002, p. B1.

100   Ibid.

101   Shari Rudavasky, "Celebrated Cardiologist, Also a Planter of Grassroots Groups." *The Boston Globe,* January 6, 2004.

102   Michael Paulson, "Lay Catholics Issue Call to Transform Their Church." *The Boston Globe*, July 21, 2002, p. A1.

103   Malcolm Gladwell, 2010 speech to F5 Expo, http://www.vancouversun.com/business/ Social+media+promote+significant+social+change+author+says/2776878/story.html.

104   Gillian Shaw, "Social media don't promote significant social change, author says. Rather, they have become an 'instrument of the status quo'." http://www. vancouversun.com/business/Social+media+promote+significant+social+change+auth or+says/2776878/story.html#ixzz18Q4lSPHb.

105   Patrick Brethour (writer and interviewer of Malcolm Gladwell), "Malcolm Gladwell: The Quiet Canadian." *The Globe and Mail*, CTVglobemedia Publishing, Inc., April, 2010. Excerpted with permission.

106   Op. cit. Shaw.

107   Nan Robertson, *Getting Better: Inside Alcoholics Anonymous.* IUniverse, 2000.

108   Janice Nadler, "Rapport in Legal Negotiation: How small Talk Can Facilitate E-mail Dealmaking." Vol. 9, *Harvard Negotiation Law Review*, 2004, pp. 223–253. www.law.northwestern.edu/faculty/fulltime/nadler/number10.pdf.

109   R. F. Bornstein, D. R. Leone, & D. J. Galley, "The Generalizability of Subliminal Mere Exposure Effects." *Journal of Personality and Social Psychology,* 53, 1987, pp. 1070-1079.

110   2007 Advocacy Effectiveness Survey, The Policy Council, 2007.

111   Flynn F.J., Brockner, J. (2003), "It's different to give than to receive: Asymmetric reactions of givers and receivers to favor exchange.*" Journal of Applied Psychology*, 88(6): 1-13

112 Jeremy Sherman, Ph.D., "Why be nice? Because with us chickens, a little negativity goes a long way." www.psychologytoday.com/node/314536.

113 Dr. John Gottman, *Why Marriages Succeed or Fail ... and How You Can Make Yours Last.* Simon and Schuster, 1994.

114 Tom Rath, Donald O. Clifton, *How Full Is Your Bucket?* Gallup Press, 2004.

115 Adam Bryant, "Can You Pass a C.E.O. Test?" Corner Office, *New York Times*, March 13, 2009.

116 Daniel A. Mica, "A lobbyist's worst enemy: Temper unchecked." The Hill, 7-14-09.

117 Ryo Oda, Noriko Yamagata, Yuki Yabiku, Akiko Matsumoto-Oda. "Altruism Can Be Assessed Correctly Based on Impression." *Human Nature*. Volume: 20, Issue 3, 2009. pp. 331-341.

118 *Satoshi Kanazawa, "You really, truly CAN judge a book by its cover: Nice people look nice, nasty people look nasty," August 30, 2009, www.psychologytoday.com/node/32436.*

119 http://www.politico.com/blogs/anneschroeder/0609/No_namecalling. html?showal.

120 Sian L. Beilock, Ph.D., student, Departments of Psychology and Kinesiology, and Thomas H. Carr, Ph.D., Department of Psychology, Michigan State University, East Lansing, Mich., Year. "On the fragility of skilled performance: What governs choking under pressure?" *Journal of Experimental Psychology.* General, Vol. 130, No. 4.

121 Dave Barry, www.quoteland.com/author.asp?AUTHOR_ID=142.

122 http://psychology.ucdavis.edu/labs/emmons.

123 R.A. Emmons and M.E. McCullough. 2003, "Counting blessings vs. burdens: Experimental studies of gratitude and subjective well-being." Journal of Personality and Social Psychology, 84: 377-389.

BUY A SHARE OF THE FUTURE IN YOUR COMMUNITY

These certificates make great holiday, graduation and birthday gifts that can be personalized with the recipient's name. The cost of one S.H.A.R.E. or one square foot is $54.17. The personalized certificate is suitable for framing and

will state the number of shares purchased and the amount of each share, as well as the recipient's name. The home that you participate in "building" will last for many years and will continue to grow in value.

Here is a sample SHARE certificate:

YES, I WOULD LIKE TO HELP!

I support the work that Habitat for Humanity does and I want to be part of the excitement! As a donor, I will receive periodic updates on your construction activities but, more importantly, I know my gift will help a family in our community realize the dream of homeownership. **I would like to SHARE in your efforts against substandard housing in my community!** *(Please print below)*

PLEASE SEND ME _____ SHARES at $54.17 EACH = $ $_____

In Honor Of: _____

Occasion: (Circle One)   *HOLIDAY*   *BIRTHDAY*   *ANNIVERSARY*

     OTHER: _____

Address of Recipient: _____

Gift From: _____ *Donor Address:* _____

Donor Email: _____

I AM ENCLOSING A CHECK FOR $ $_____ PAYABLE TO HABITAT FOR HUMANITY <u>OR</u> PLEASE CHARGE MY VISA OR MASTERCARD *(CIRCLE ONE)*

Card Number _____ Expiration Date: _____

Name as it appears on Credit Card _____ Charge Amount $ _____

Signature _____

Billing Address _____

Telephone # Day _____ Eve _____

PLEASE NOTE: Your contribution is tax-deductible to the fullest extent allowed by law.
Habitat for Humanity • P.O. Box 1443 • Newport News, VA 23601 • 757-596-5553
www.HelpHabitatforHumanity.org

CPSIA information can be obtained at www.ICGtesting.com
Printed in the USA
LVOW10s0702290913

354574LV00003B/6/P